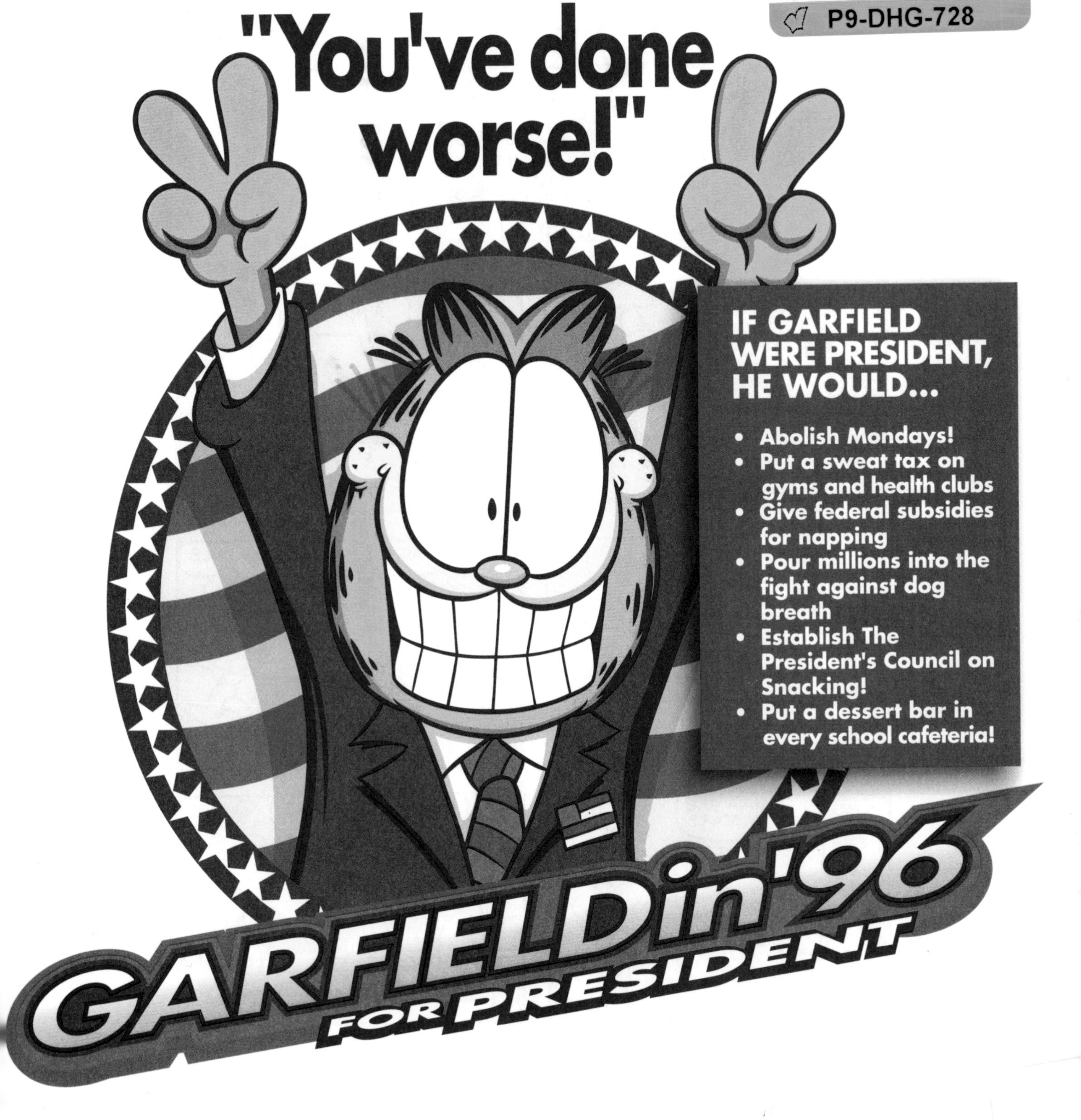

"You've done worse!"
IF GARFIELD WERE PRESIDENT, HE WOULD...
• Abolish Mondays!
• Put a sweat tax on gyms and health clubs
• Give federal subsidies for napping
• Pour millions into the fight against dog breath
• Establish The President's Council on Snacking!
• Put a dessert bar in every school cafeteria!
GARFIELD in '96
FOR PRESIDENT

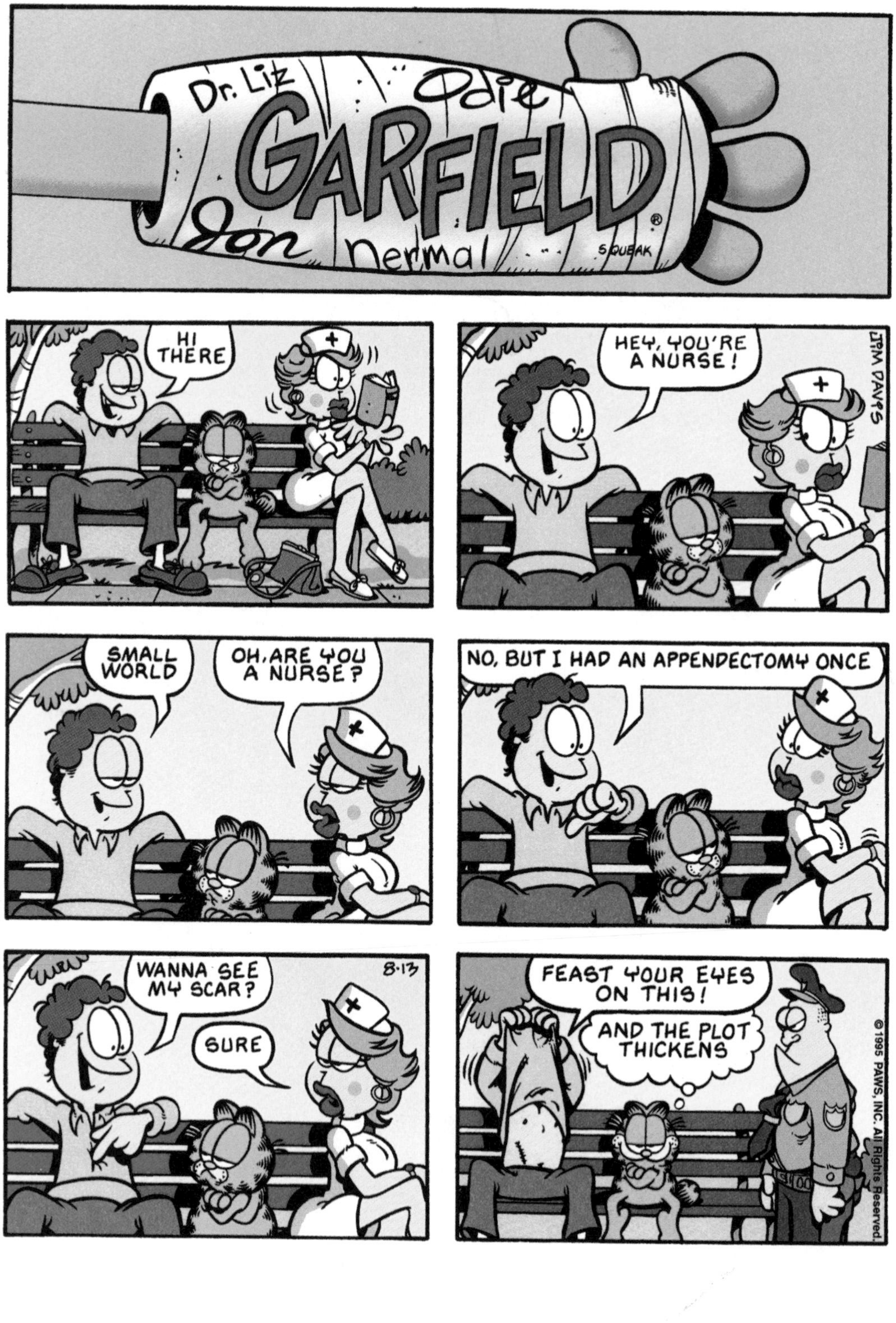
Dr. Liz
Odie
GARFIELD®
Jon
Nermal
SQUBAK
HI THERE
JIM DAVIS
HEY, YOU'RE A NURSE!
SMALL WORLD
OH, ARE YOU A NURSE?
NO, BUT I HAD AN APPENDECTOMY ONCE
WANNA SEE MY SCAR?
8-13
SURE
FEAST YOUR EYES ON THIS!
AND THE PLOT THICKENS
© 1995 PAWS, INC. All Rights Reserved.

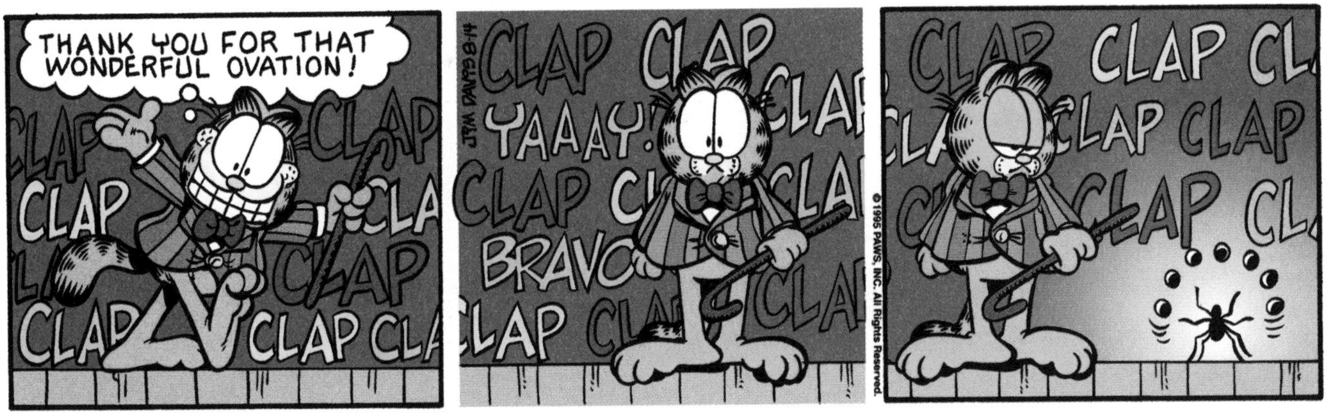
THANK YOU FOR THAT WONDERFUL OVATION!
CLAP CLAP
YAAAY!
BRAVO
CLAP CLAP
JIM DAVIS 8-14
© 1995 PAWS, INC. All Rights Reserved.

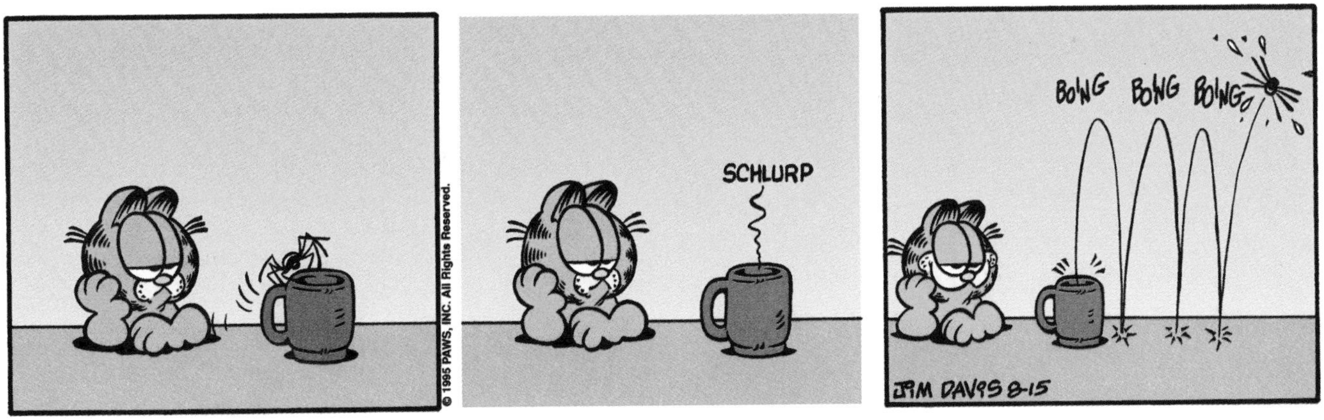
© 1995 PAWS, INC. All Rights Reserved.
SCHLURP
BOING BOING BOING
JIM DAVIS 8-15

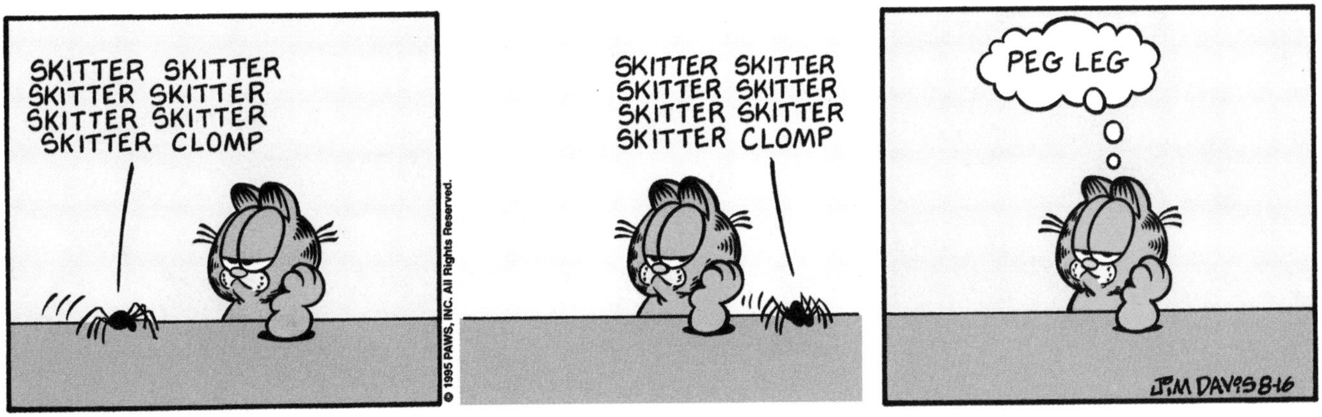
SKITTER SKITTER
SKITTER SKITTER
SKITTER SKITTER
SKITTER CLOMP
© 1995 PAWS, INC. All Rights Reserved.
SKITTER SKITTER
SKITTER SKITTER
SKITTER SKITTER
SKITTER CLOMP
PEG LEG
JIM DAVIS 8-16

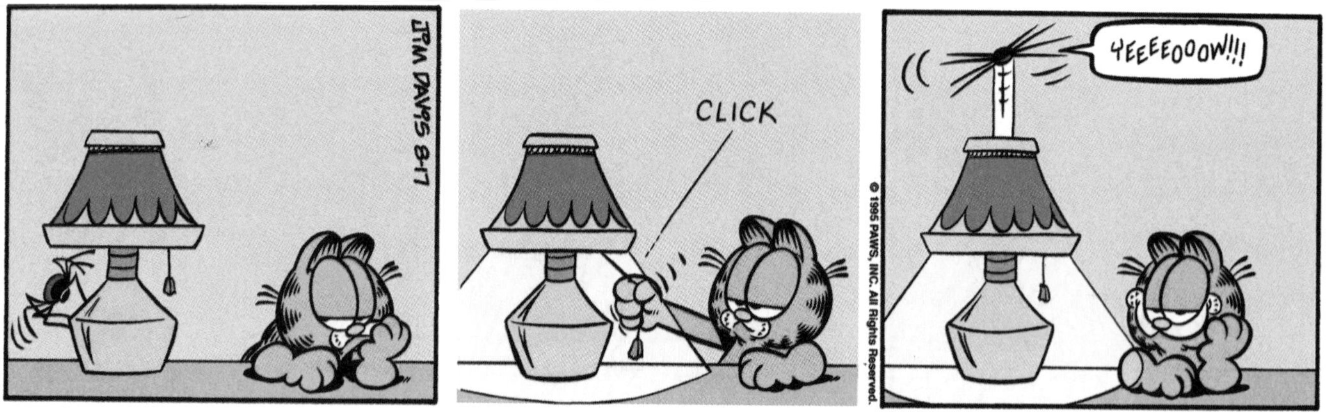
JIM DAVIS 8-17
CLICK
© 1995 PAWS, INC. All Rights Reserved.
YEEEEOOOW!!!

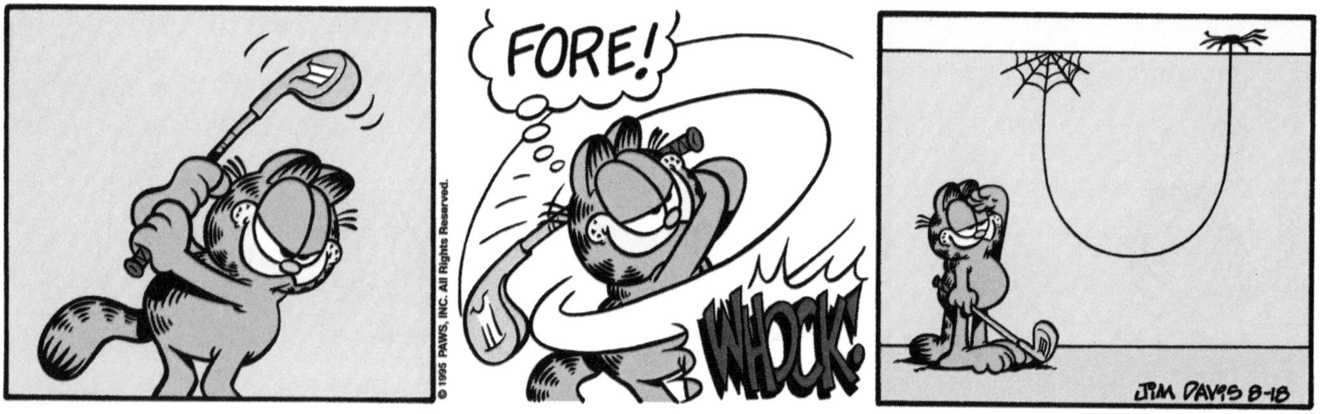
© 1995 PAWS, INC. All Rights Reserved.
FORE!
WHOCK!
JIM DAVIS 8-18

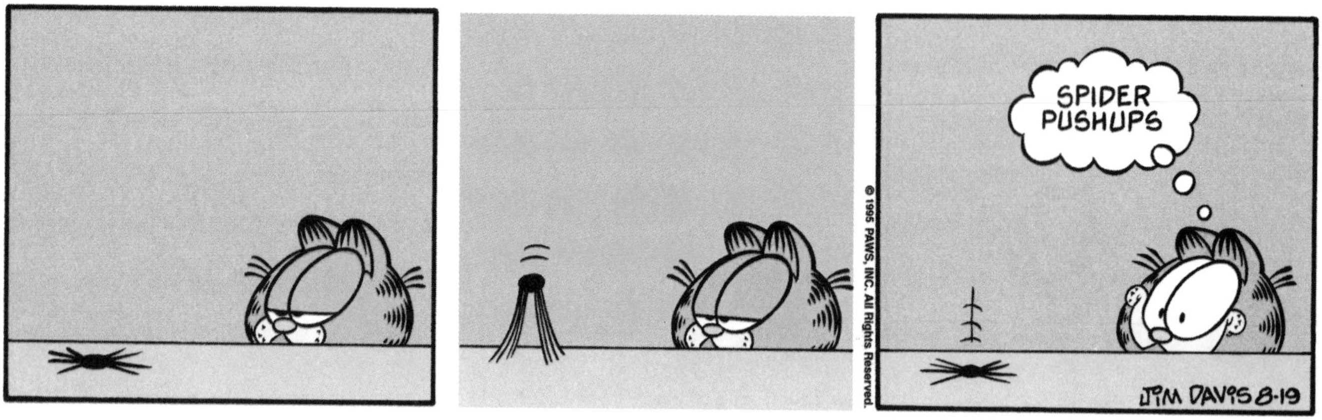
© 1995 PAWS, INC. All Rights Reserved.
SPIDER PUSHUPS
JIM DAVIS 8-19

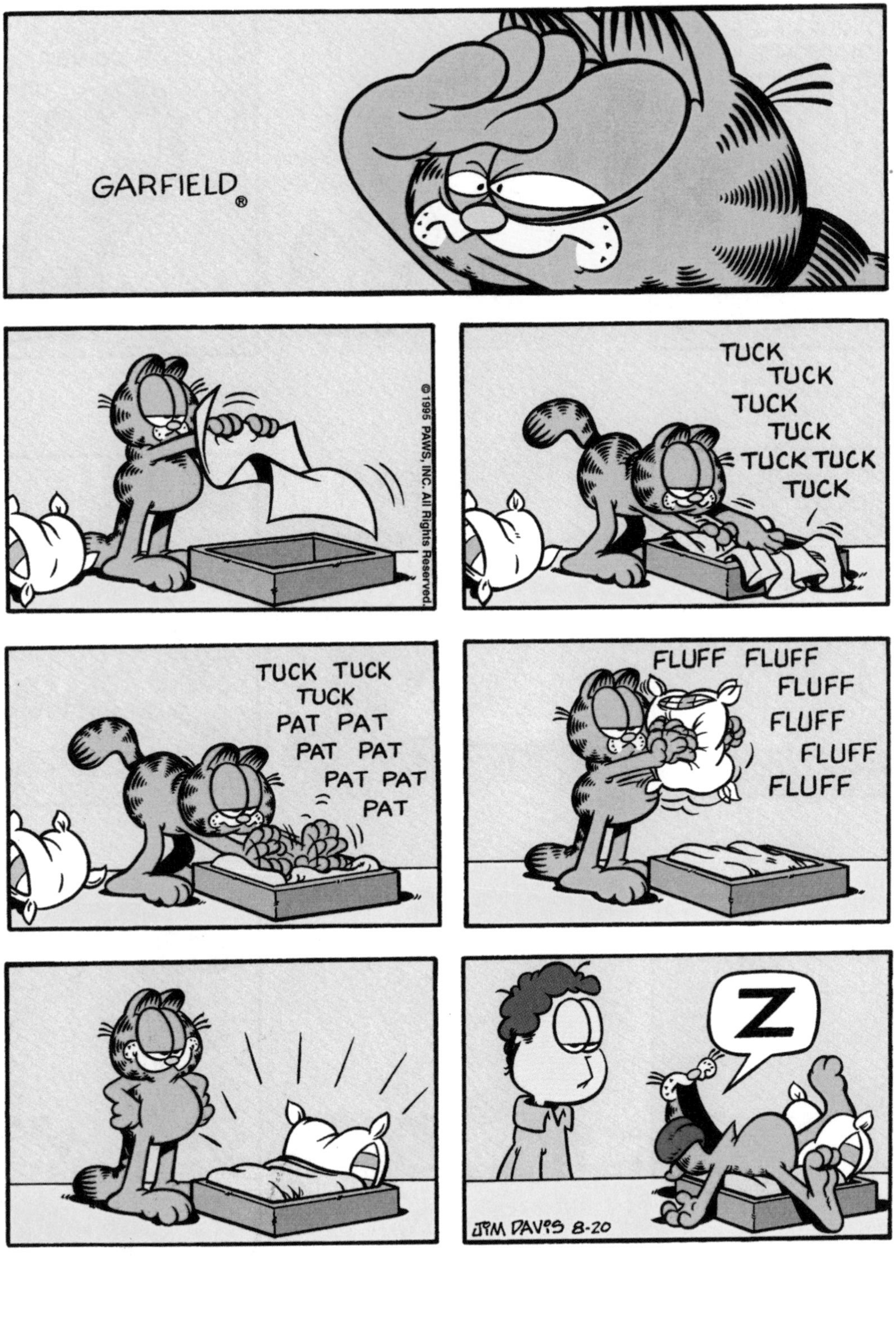
GARFIELD®
© 1995 PAWS, INC. All Rights Reserved.
TUCK TUCK TUCK TUCK TUCK TUCK TUCK
TUCK TUCK TUCK PAT PAT PAT PAT PAT PAT PAT
FLUFF FLUFF FLUFF FLUFF FLUFF FLUFF
Z
JIM DAVIS 8-20

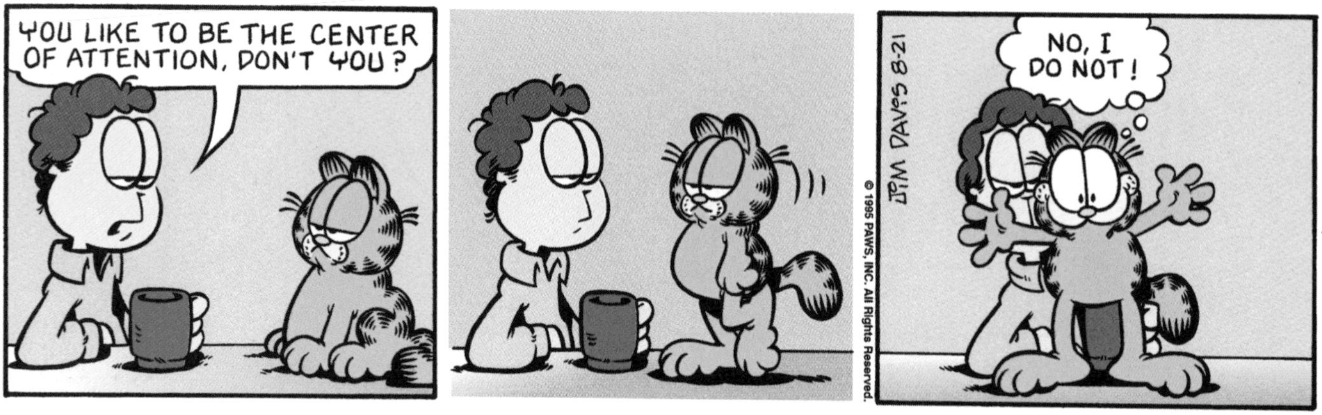
YOU LIKE TO BE THE CENTER OF ATTENTION, DON'T YOU?
© 1995 PAWS, INC. All Rights Reserved.
JIM DAVIS 8-21
NO, I DO NOT!

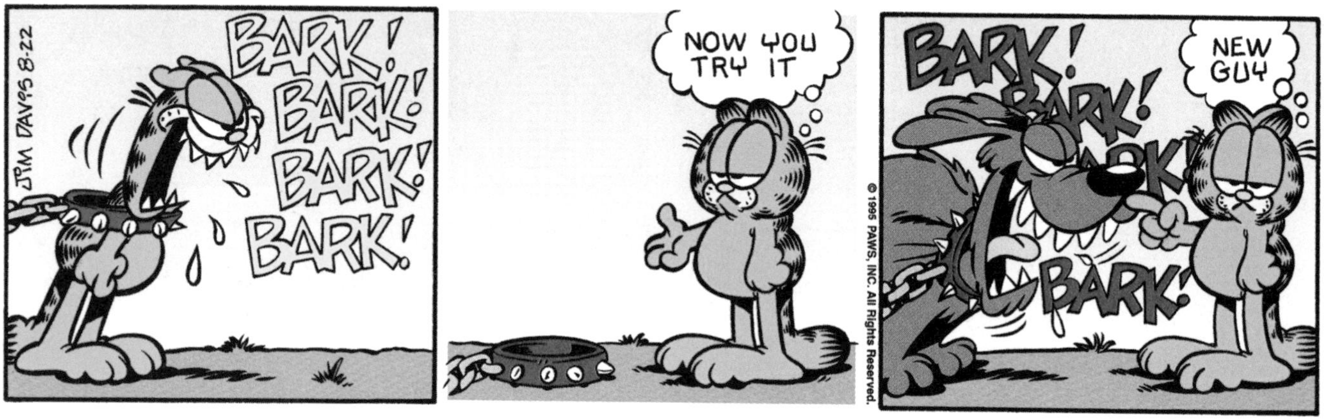
JIM DAVIS 8-22
BARK! BARK! BARK! BARK!
NOW YOU TRY IT
© 1995 PAWS, INC. All Rights Reserved.
BARK! BARK! BARK! BARK!
NEW GUY

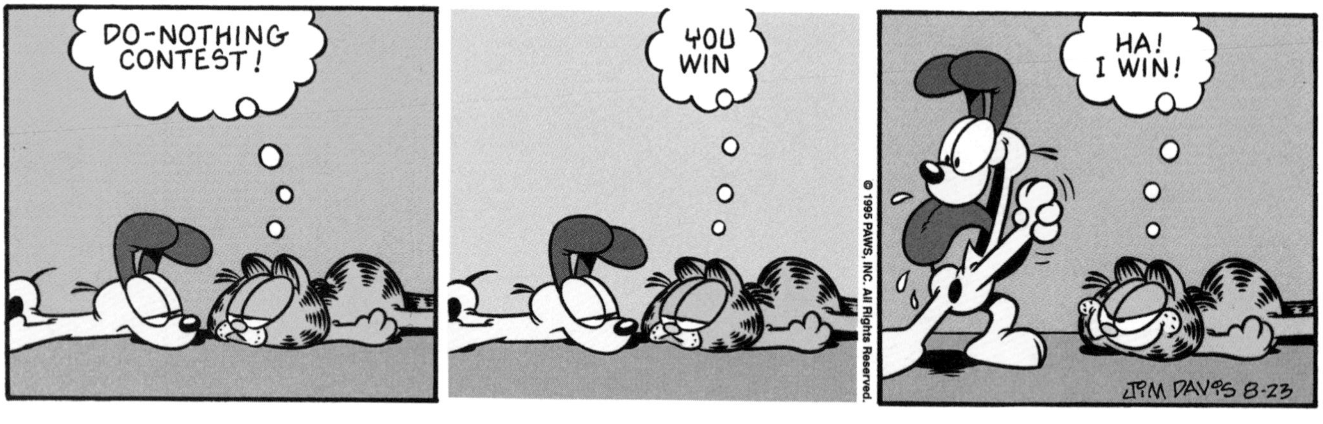
DO-NOTHING CONTEST!
YOU WIN
© 1995 PAWS, INC. All Rights Reserved.
HA! I WIN!
JIM DAVIS 8-23

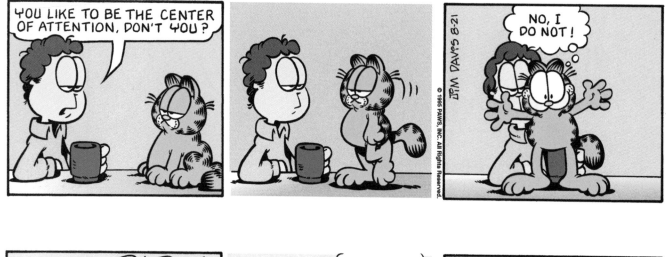

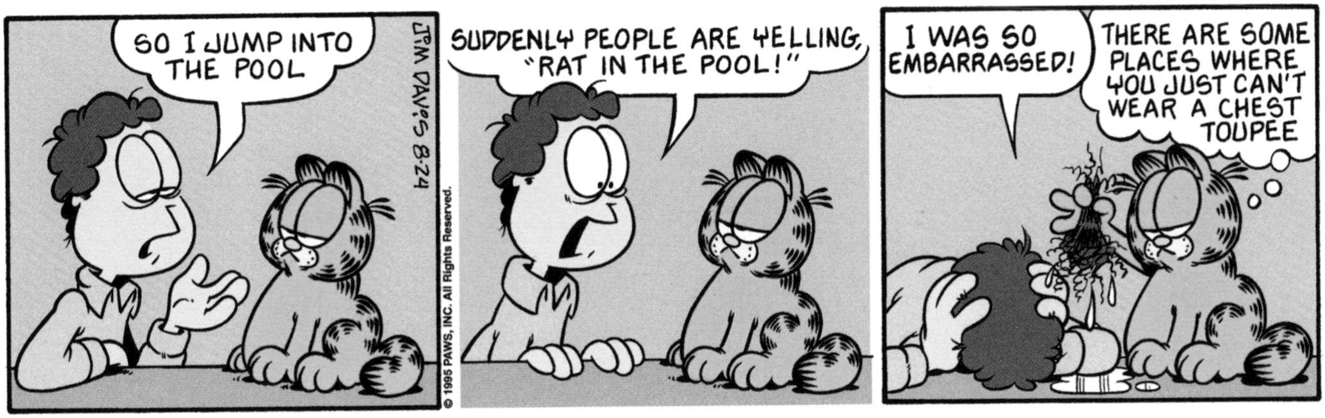
SO I JUMP INTO THE POOL
JIM DAVIS 8-24
© 1995 PAWS, INC. All Rights Reserved.
SUDDENLY PEOPLE ARE YELLING, "RAT IN THE POOL!"
I WAS SO EMBARRASSED!
THERE ARE SOME PLACES WHERE YOU JUST CAN'T WEAR A CHEST TOUPEE

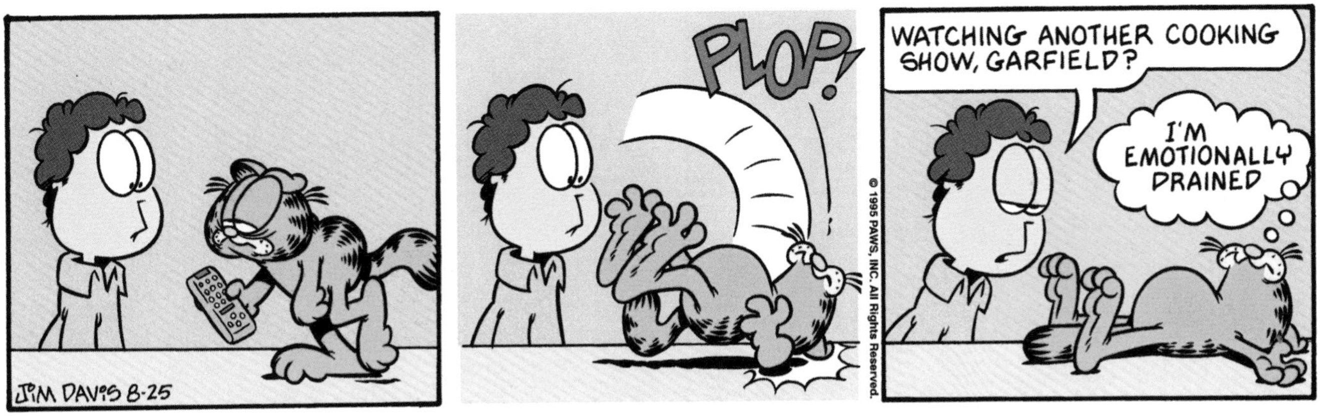
JIM DAVIS 8-25
PLOP!
© 1995 PAWS, INC. All Rights Reserved.
WATCHING ANOTHER COOKING SHOW, GARFIELD?
I'M EMOTIONALLY DRAINED

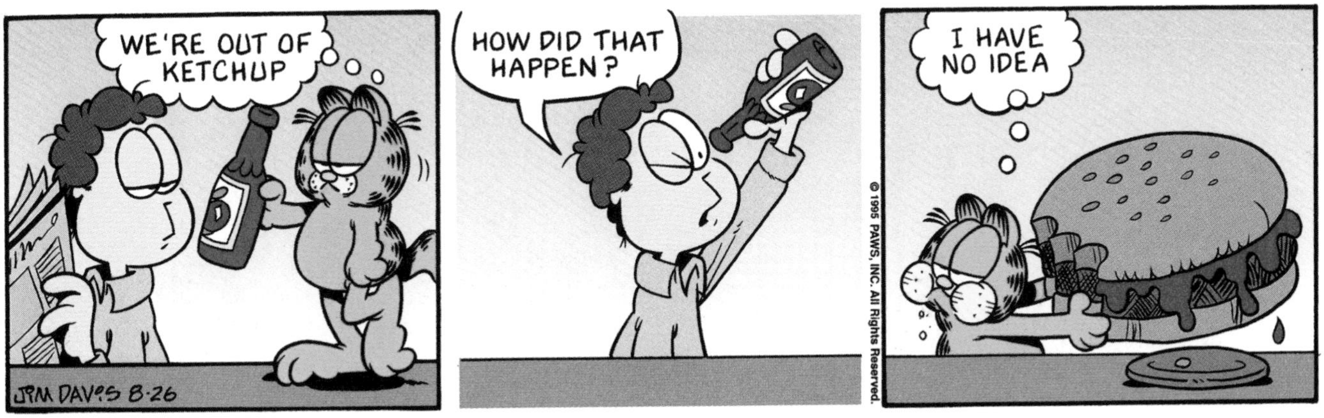
WE'RE OUT OF KETCHUP
JIM DAVIS 8-26
HOW DID THAT HAPPEN?
© 1995 PAWS, INC. All Rights Reserved.
I HAVE NO IDEA

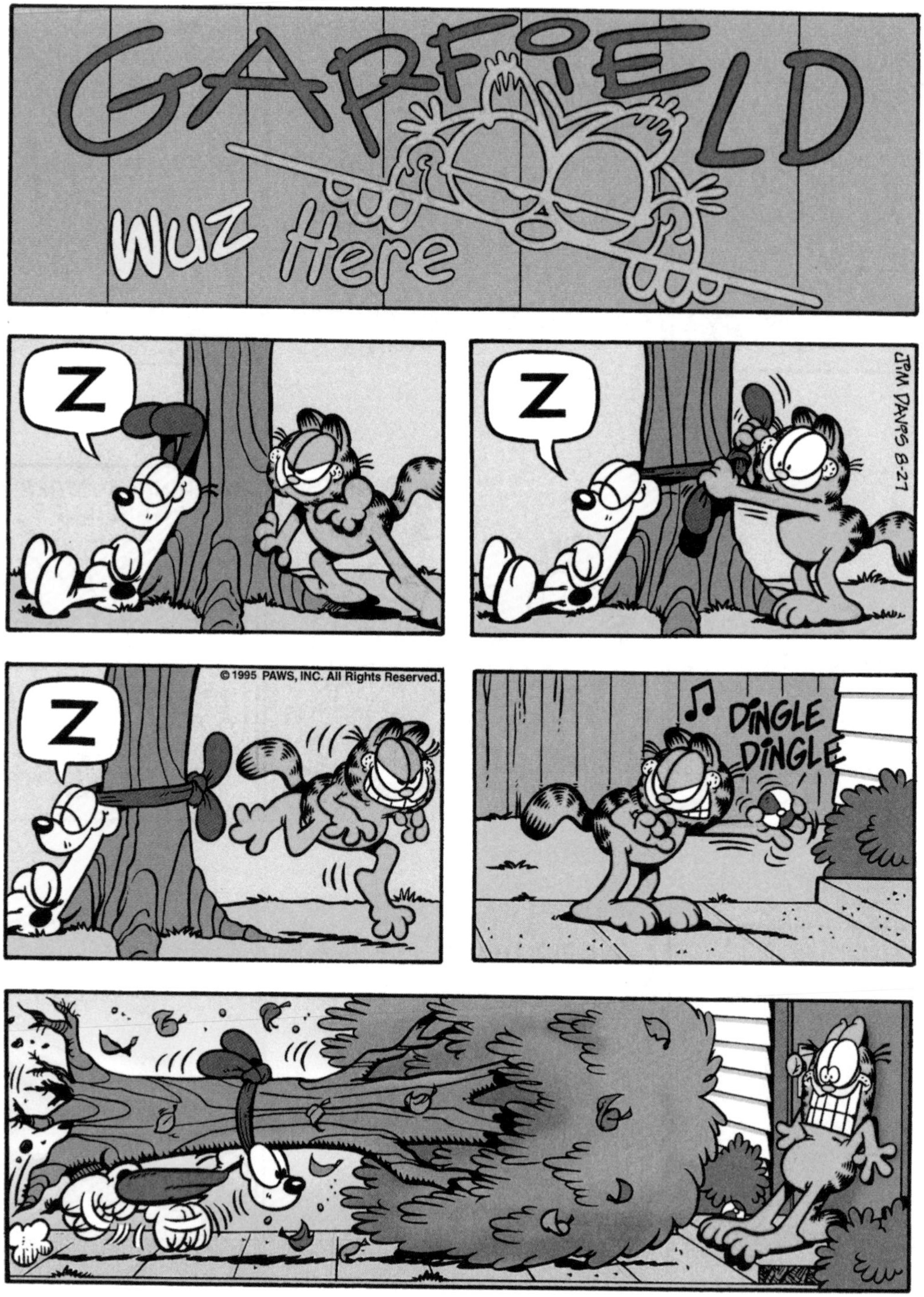
GARFIELD
Wuz Here
Z
JIM DAVIS 8-27
Z
Z
© 1995 PAWS, INC. All Rights Reserved.
DINGLE DINGLE

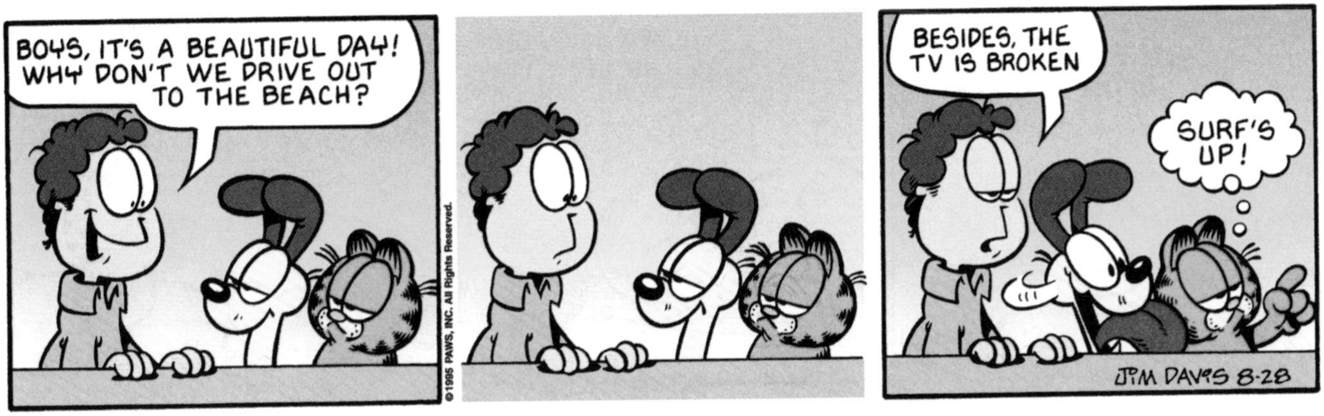
BOYS, IT'S A BEAUTIFUL DAY! WHY DON'T WE DRIVE OUT TO THE BEACH?
© 1995 PAWS, INC. All Rights Reserved.
BESIDES, THE TV IS BROKEN
SURF'S UP!
JIM DAVIS 8-28

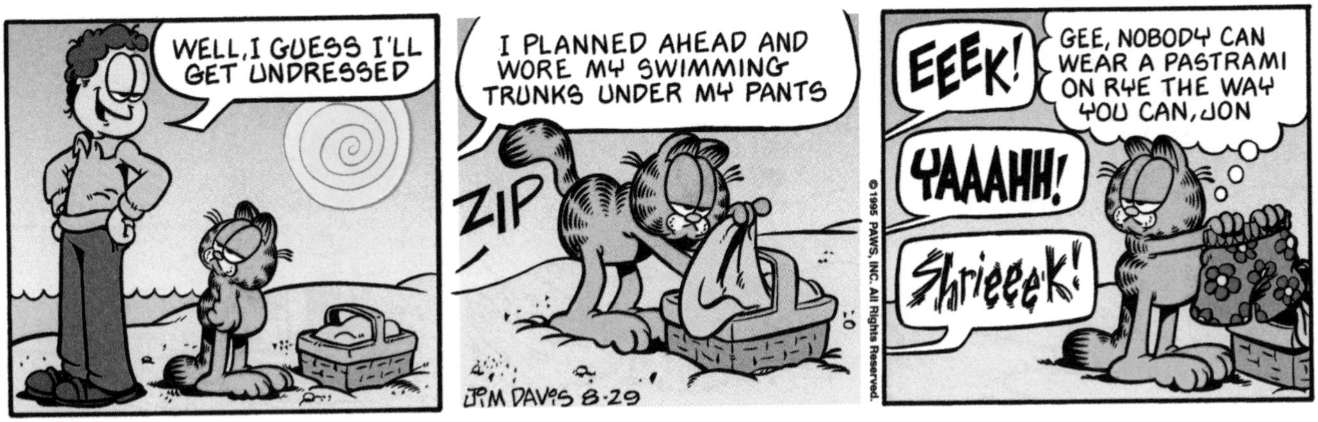
WELL, I GUESS I'LL GET UNDRESSED
I PLANNED AHEAD AND WORE MY SWIMMING TRUNKS UNDER MY PANTS
ZIP
JIM DAVIS 8-29
© 1995 PAWS, INC. All Rights Reserved.
EEEK!
YAAAHH!
Shrieeek!
GEE, NOBODY CAN WEAR A PASTRAMI ON RYE THE WAY YOU CAN, JON

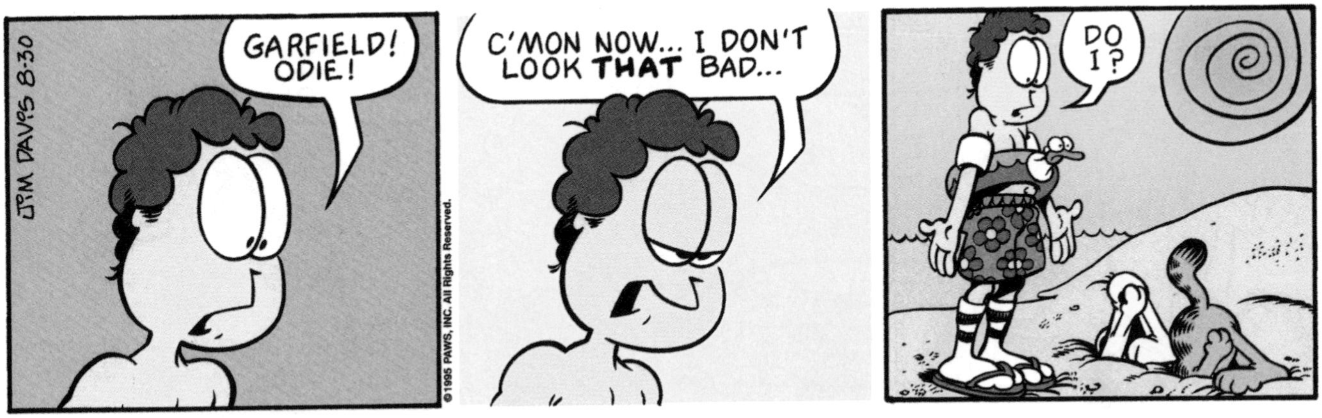
JIM DAVIS 8-30
GARFIELD! ODIE!
© 1995 PAWS, INC. All Rights Reserved.
C'MON NOW... I DON'T LOOK **THAT** BAD...
DO I?

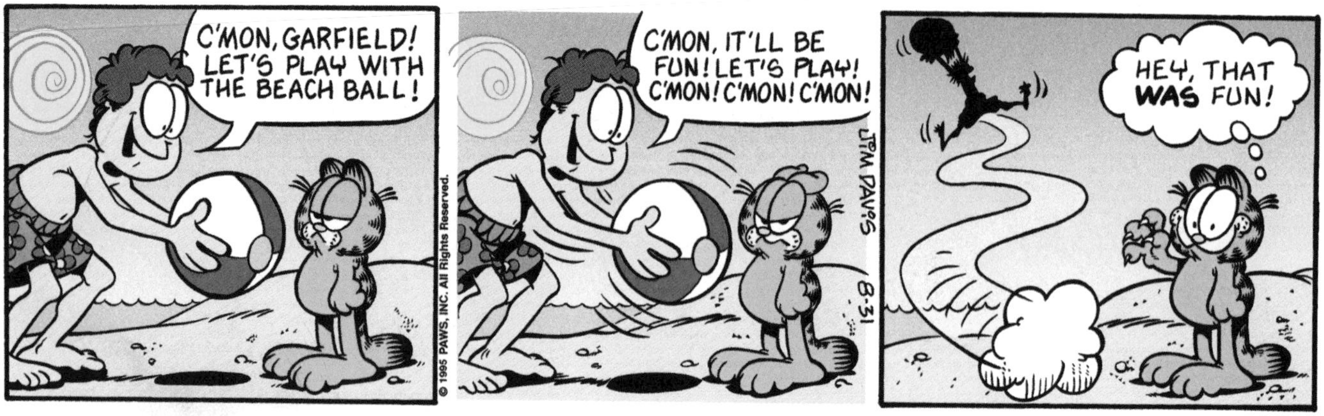
C'MON, GARFIELD! LET'S PLAY WITH THE BEACH BALL!
© 1995 PAWS, INC. All Rights Reserved.
C'MON, IT'LL BE FUN! LET'S PLAY! C'MON! C'MON! C'MON!
JIM DAVIS 8-31
HEY, THAT **WAS** FUN!

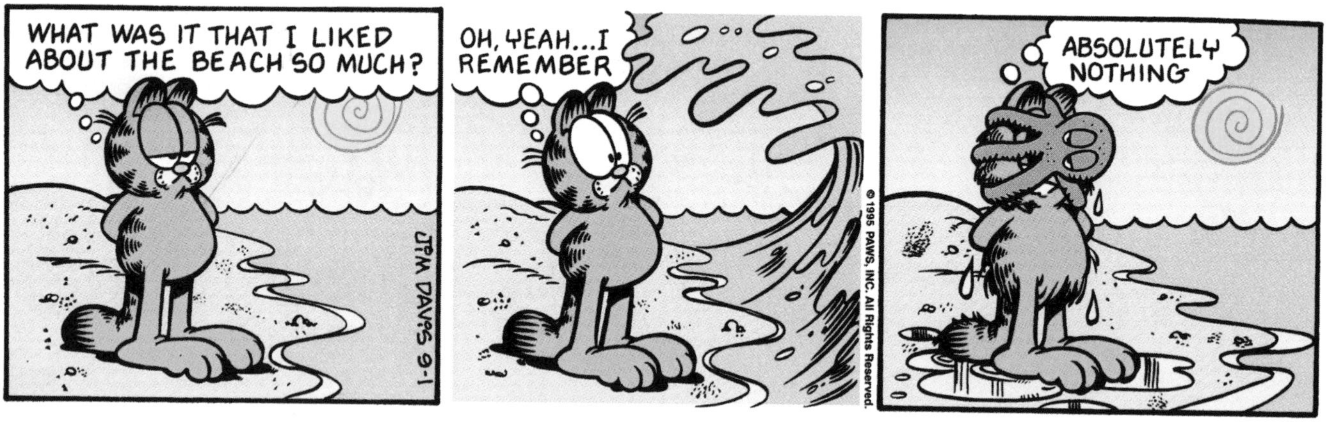
WHAT WAS IT THAT I LIKED ABOUT THE BEACH SO MUCH?
JIM DAVIS 9-1
OH, YEAH... I REMEMBER
© 1995 PAWS, INC. All Rights Reserved.
ABSOLUTELY NOTHING

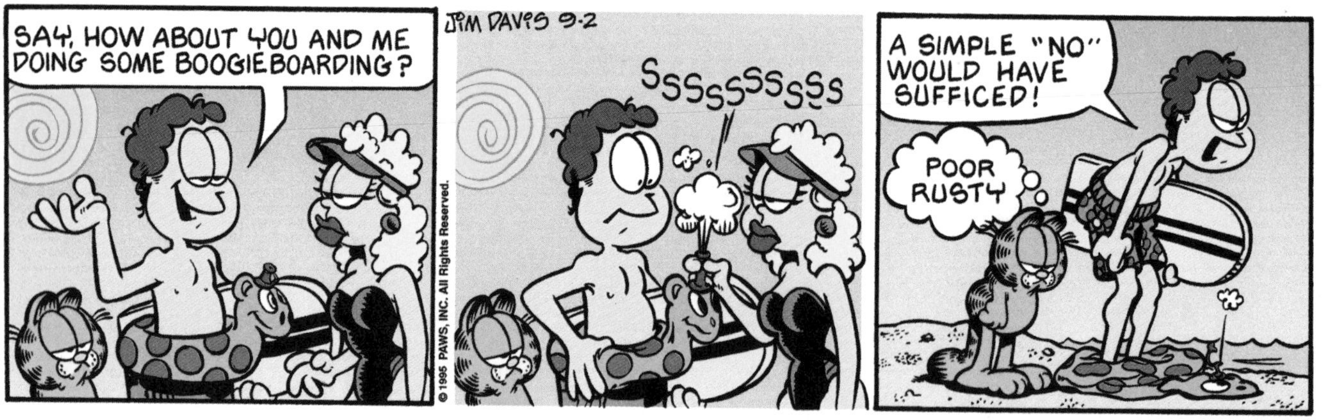
SAY, HOW ABOUT YOU AND ME DOING SOME BOOGIEBOARDING?
© 1995 PAWS, INC. All Rights Reserved.
JIM DAVIS 9-2
SSSSSSSSSS
A SIMPLE "NO" WOULD HAVE SUFFICED!
POOR RUSTY

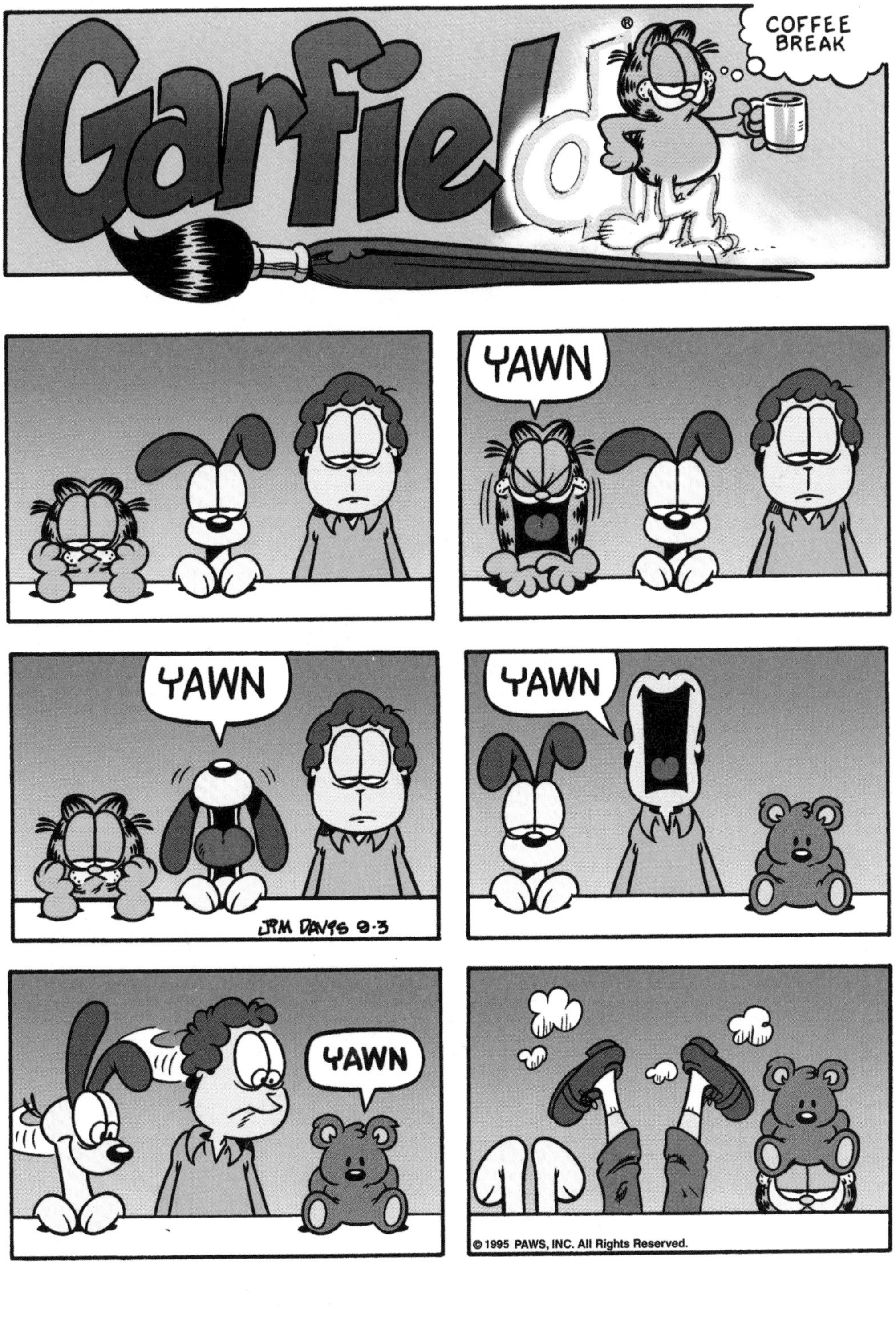
Garfield®
COFFEE BREAK
YAWN
YAWN
JIM DAVIS 9-3
YAWN
YAWN
© 1995 PAWS, INC. All Rights Reserved.

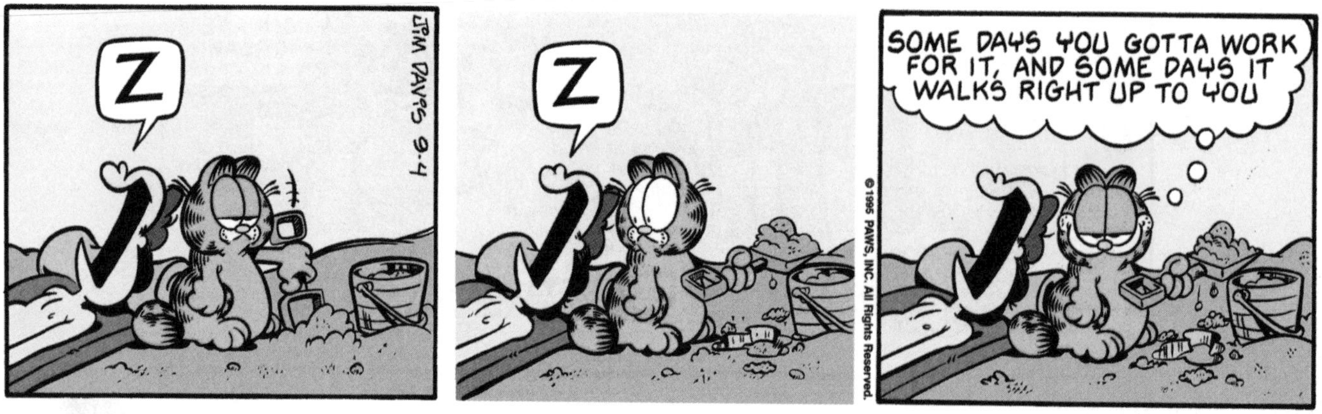
JIM DAVIS 9-4
Z
Z
SOME DAYS YOU GOTTA WORK FOR IT, AND SOME DAYS IT WALKS RIGHT UP TO YOU
© 1995 PAWS, INC. All Rights Reserved.

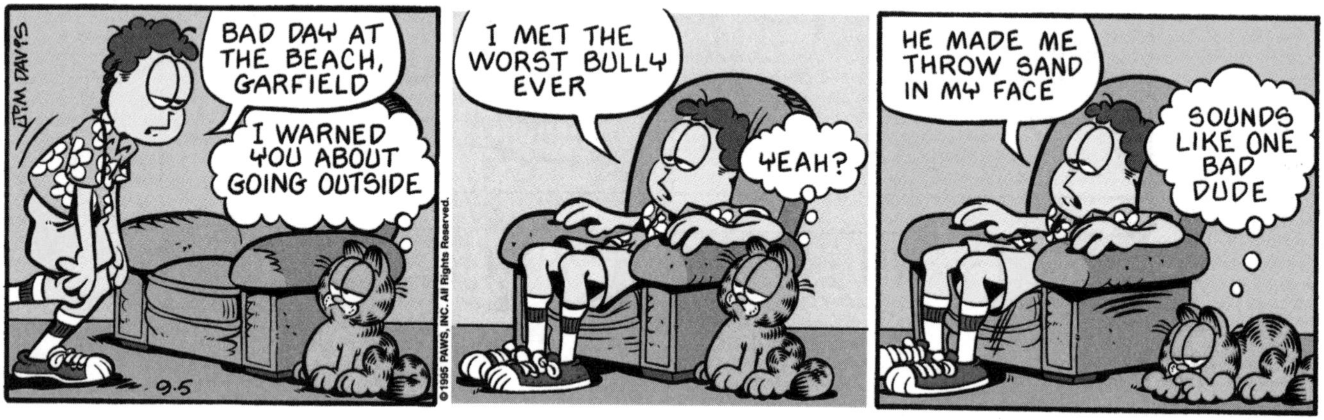
JIM DAVIS 9-5
BAD DAY AT THE BEACH, GARFIELD
I WARNED YOU ABOUT GOING OUTSIDE
© 1995 PAWS, INC. All Rights Reserved.
I MET THE WORST BULLY EVER
YEAH?
HE MADE ME THROW SAND IN MY FACE
SOUNDS LIKE ONE BAD DUDE

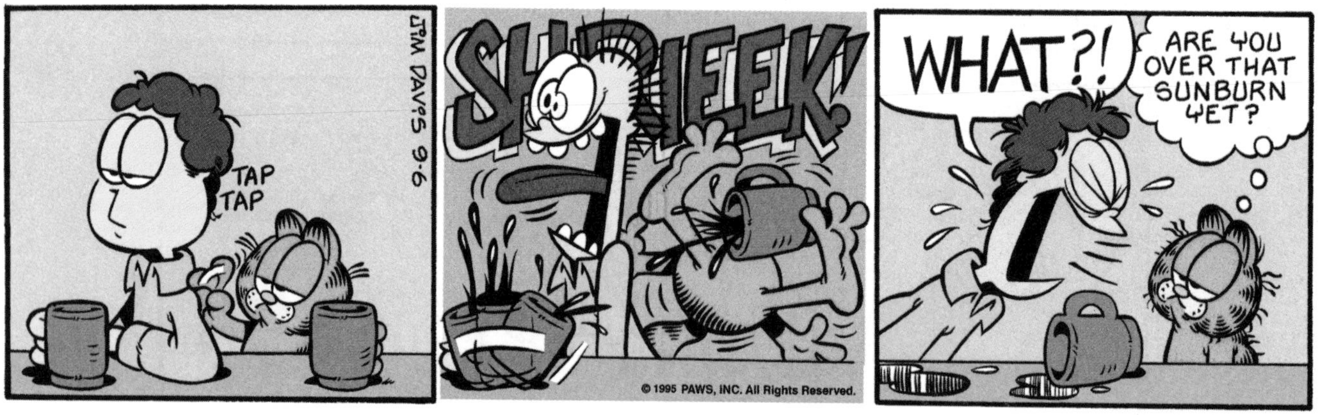
JIM DAVIS 9-6
TAP TAP
SHRIEEK!
© 1995 PAWS, INC. All Rights Reserved.
WHAT?!
ARE YOU OVER THAT SUNBURN YET?

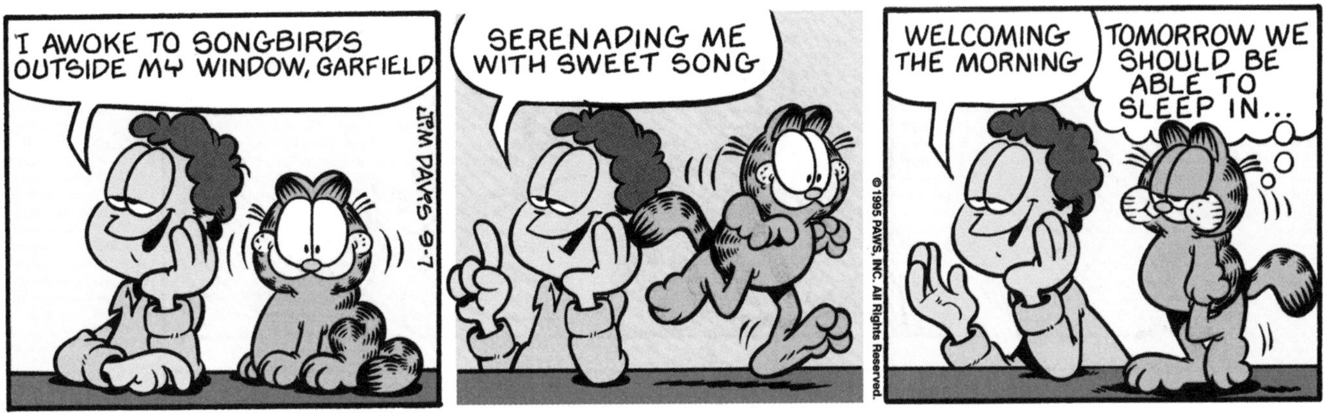
I AWOKE TO SONGBIRDS OUTSIDE MY WINDOW, GARFIELD
JIM DAVIS 9-7
SERENADING ME WITH SWEET SONG
© 1995 PAWS, INC. All Rights Reserved.
WELCOMING THE MORNING
TOMORROW WE SHOULD BE ABLE TO SLEEP IN...

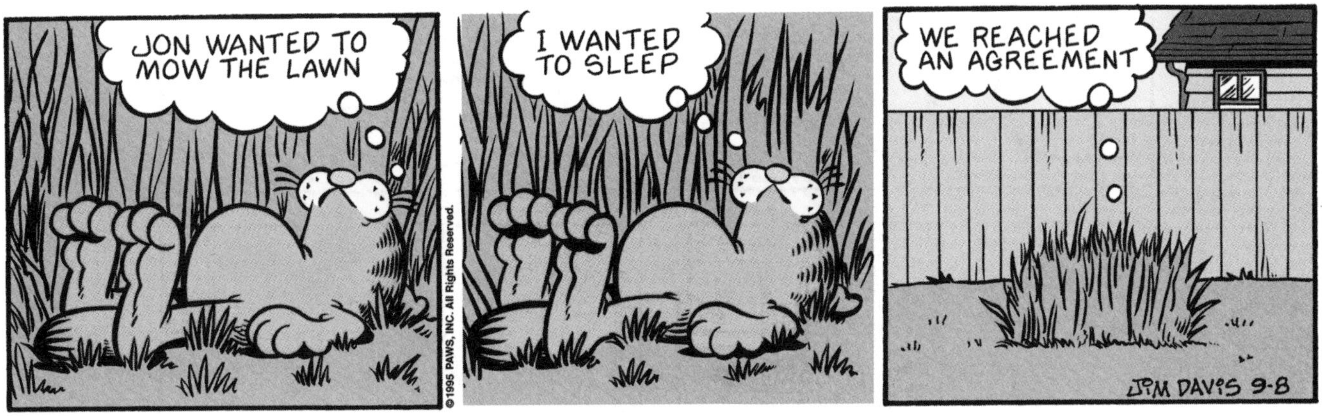
JON WANTED TO MOW THE LAWN
© 1995 PAWS, INC. All Rights Reserved.
I WANTED TO SLEEP
WE REACHED AN AGREEMENT
JIM DAVIS 9-8

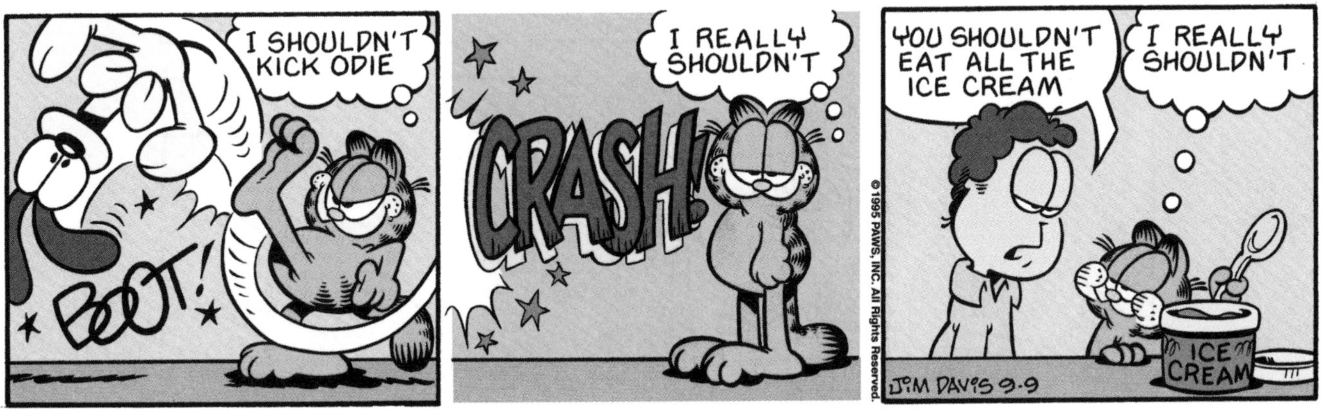
I SHOULDN'T KICK ODIE
BOOT!
CRASH!
I REALLY SHOULDN'T
© 1995 PAWS, INC. All Rights Reserved.
YOU SHOULDN'T EAT ALL THE ICE CREAM
I REALLY SHOULDN'T
ICE CREAM
JIM DAVIS 9-9

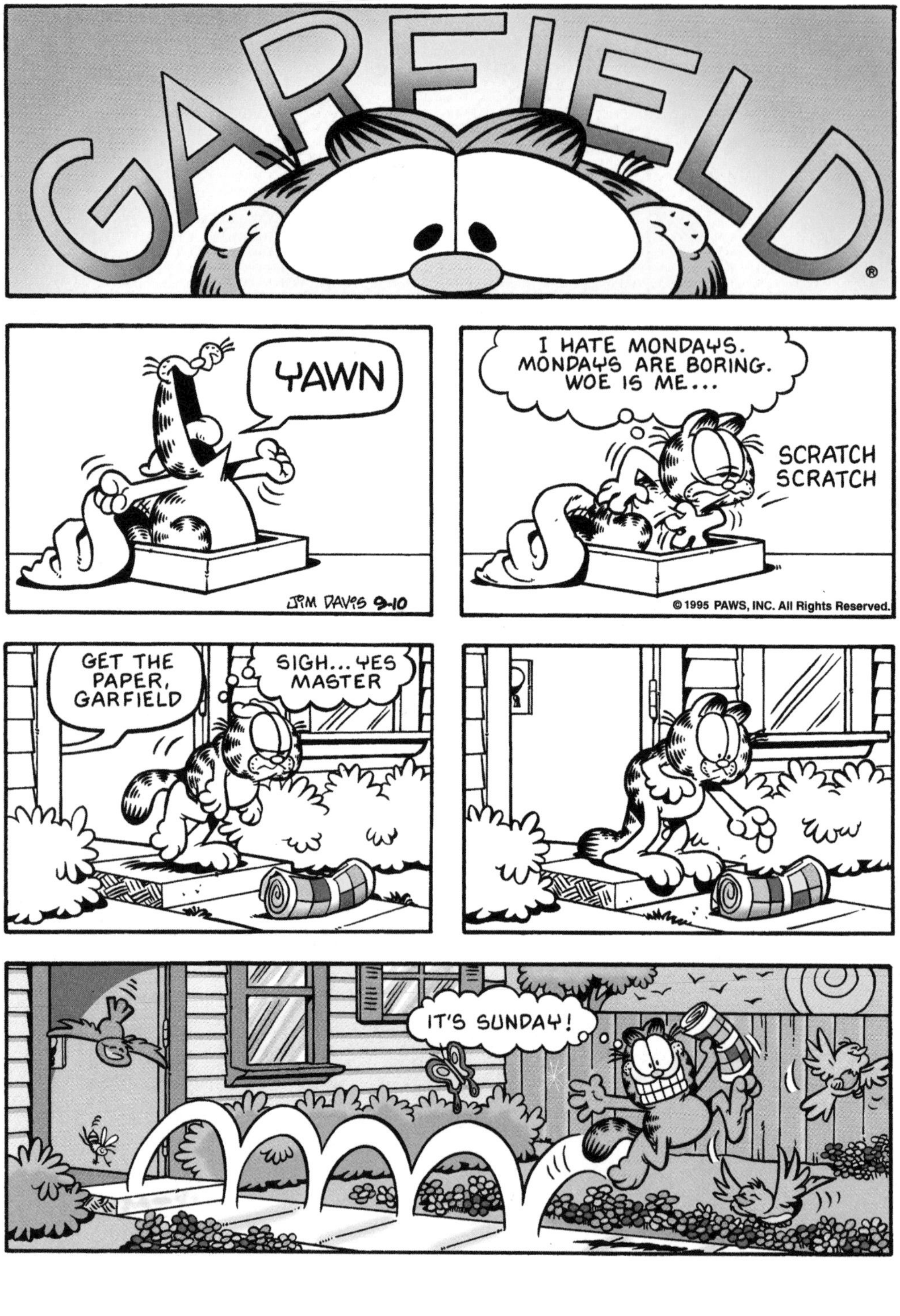
GARFIELD®
YAWN
JIM DAVIS 9-10
I HATE MONDAYS. MONDAYS ARE BORING. WOE IS ME...
SCRATCH SCRATCH
© 1995 PAWS, INC. All Rights Reserved.
GET THE PAPER, GARFIELD
SIGH... YES MASTER
IT'S SUNDAY!

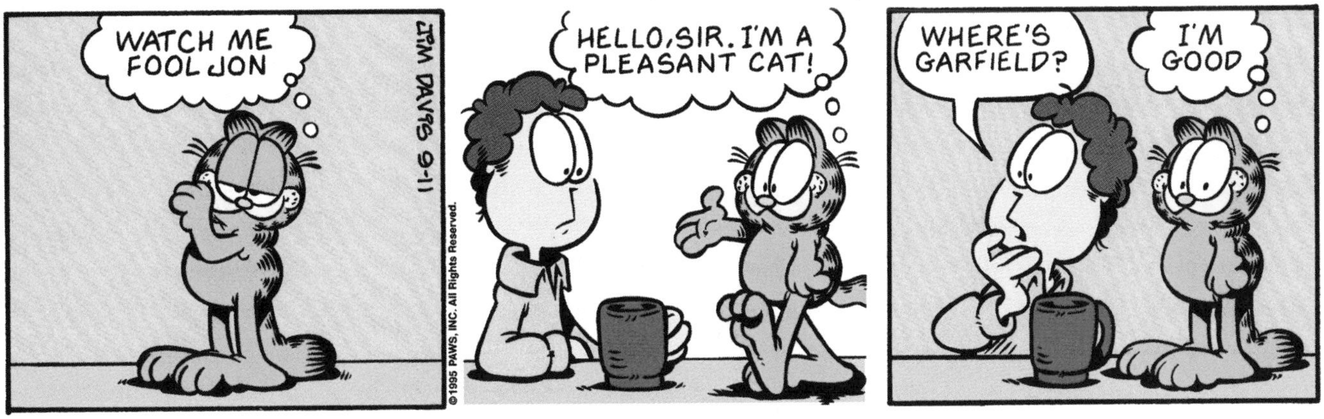
WATCH ME FOOL JON
JIM DAVIS 9-11
© 1995 PAWS, INC. All Rights Reserved.
HELLO, SIR. I'M A PLEASANT CAT!
WHERE'S GARFIELD?
I'M GOOD

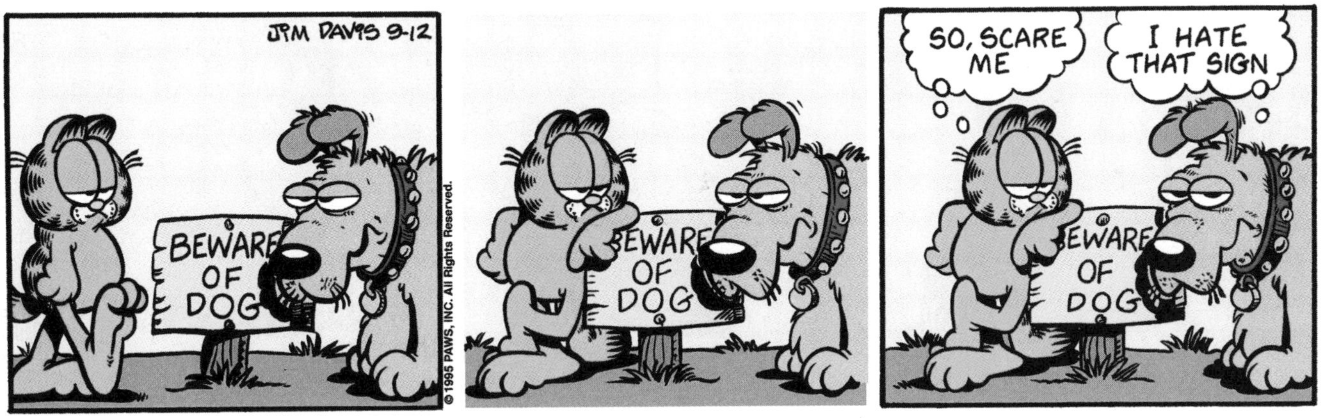
JIM DAVIS 9-12
BEWARE OF DOG
© 1995 PAWS, INC. All Rights Reserved.
SO, SCARE ME
I HATE THAT SIGN

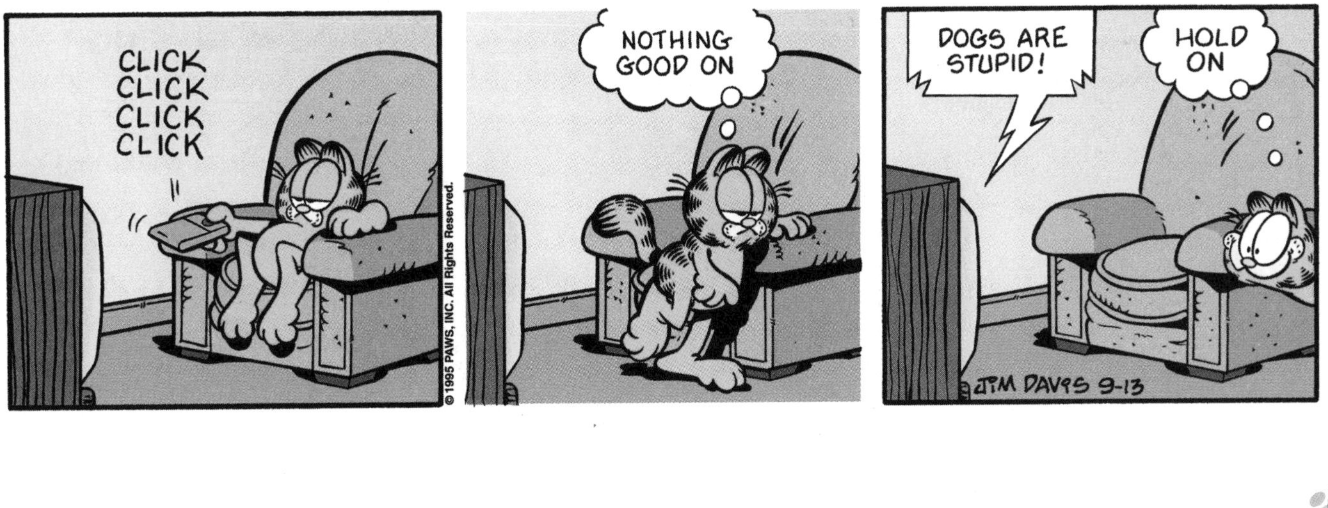
CLICK
CLICK
CLICK
CLICK
© 1995 PAWS, INC. All Rights Reserved.
NOTHING GOOD ON
DOGS ARE STUPID!
HOLD ON
JIM DAVIS 9-13

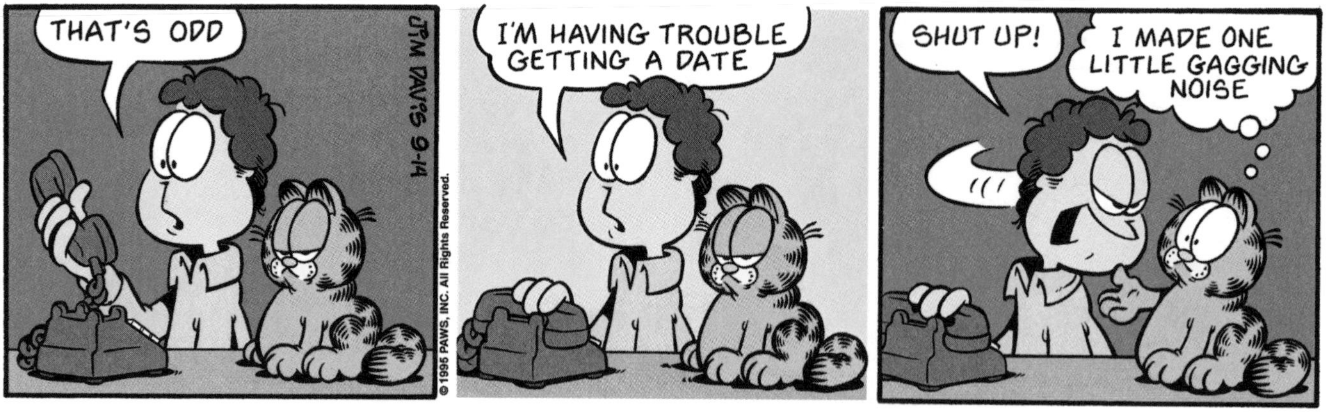
THAT'S ODD
JIM DAVIS 9-14
© 1995 PAWS, INC. All Rights Reserved.
I'M HAVING TROUBLE GETTING A DATE
SHUT UP!
I MADE ONE LITTLE GAGGING NOISE

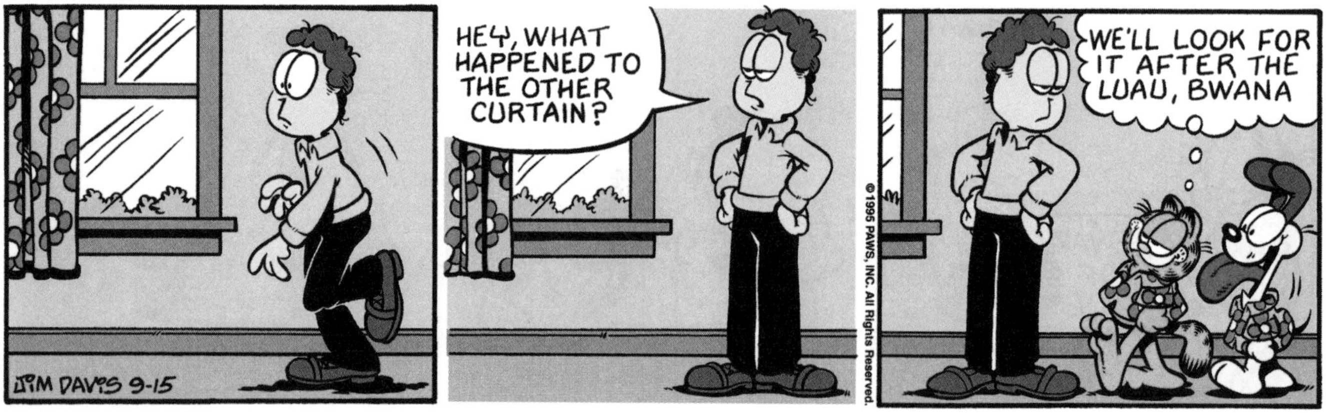
JIM DAVIS 9-15
HEY, WHAT HAPPENED TO THE OTHER CURTAIN?
© 1995 PAWS, INC. All Rights Reserved.
WE'LL LOOK FOR IT AFTER THE LUAU, BWANA

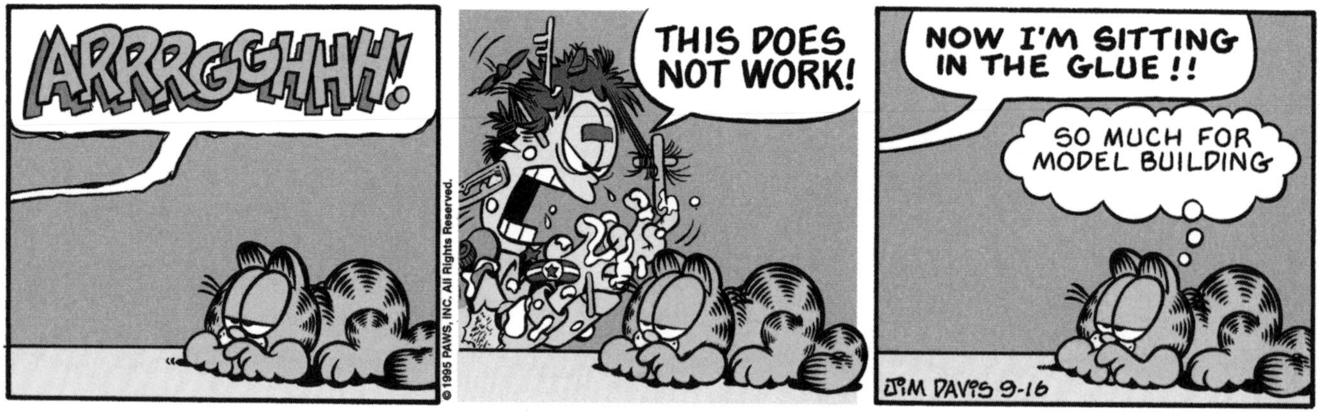
ARRRGGHHH!
© 1995 PAWS, INC. All Rights Reserved.
THIS DOES NOT WORK!
NOW I'M SITTING IN THE GLUE!!
SO MUCH FOR MODEL BUILDING
JIM DAVIS 9-16

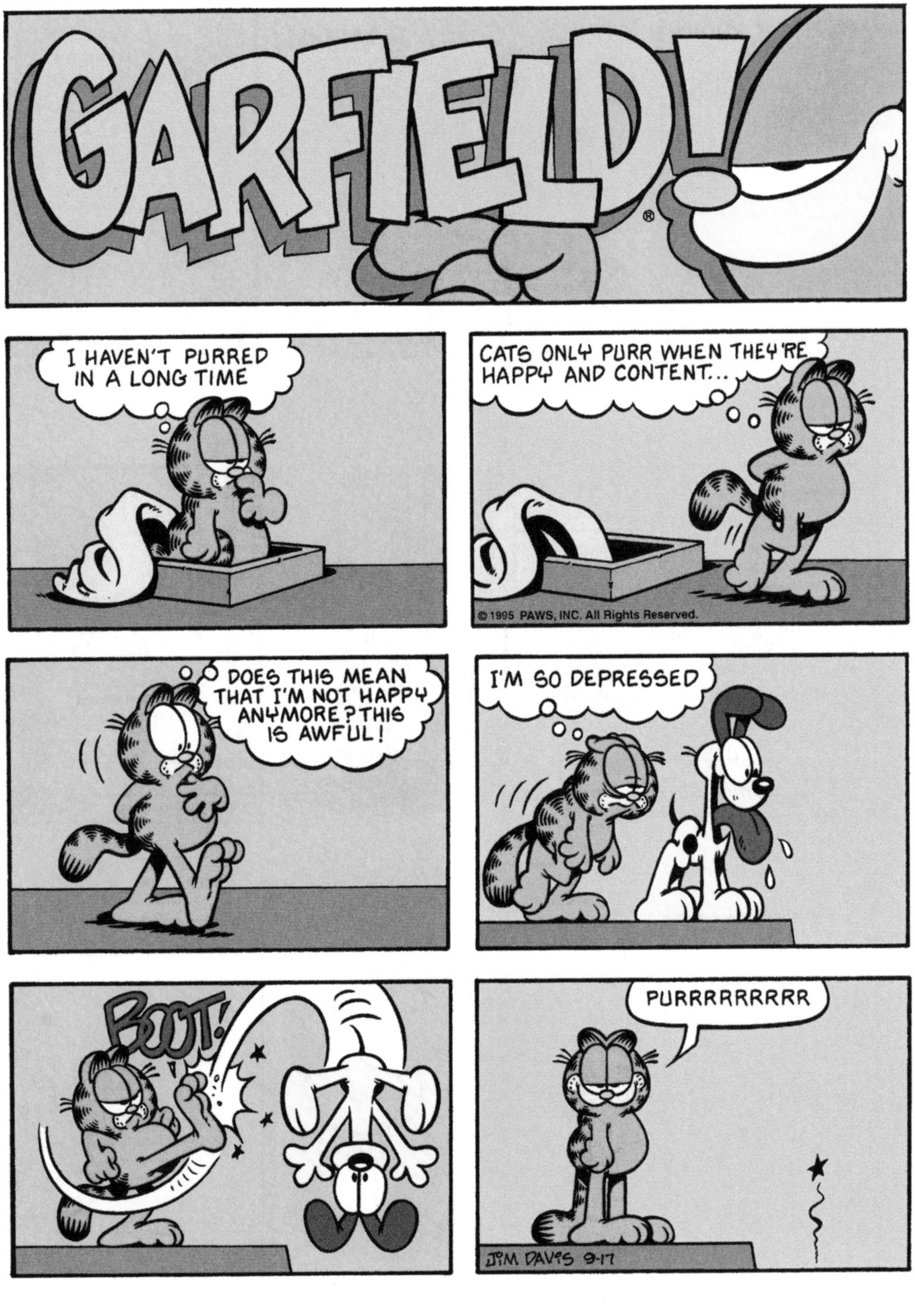
GARFIELD!®
I HAVEN'T PURRED IN A LONG TIME
CATS ONLY PURR WHEN THEY'RE HAPPY AND CONTENT...
© 1995 PAWS, INC. All Rights Reserved.
DOES THIS MEAN THAT I'M NOT HAPPY ANYMORE? THIS IS AWFUL!
I'M SO DEPRESSED
BOOT!
PURRRRRRRRR
JIM DAVIS 9-17

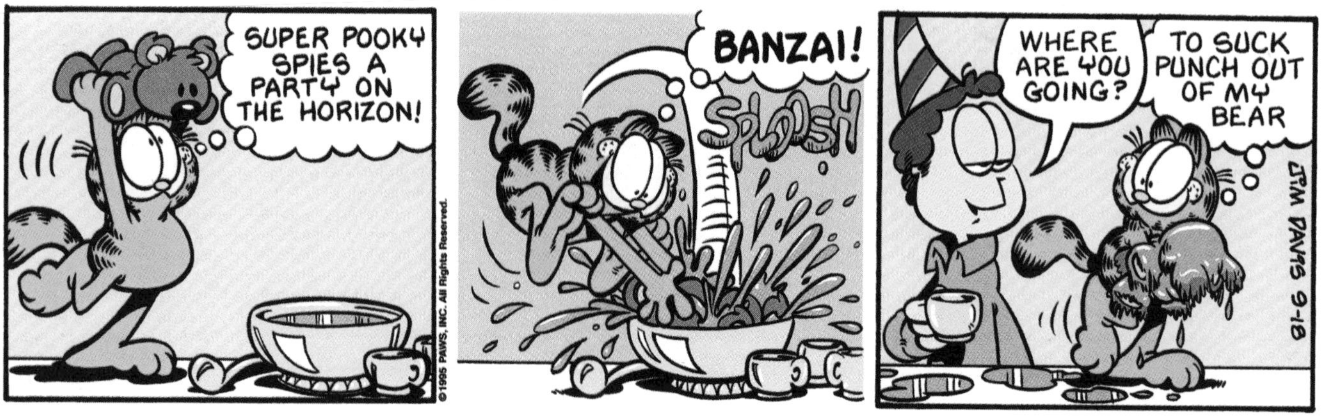
SUPER POOKY SPIES A PARTY ON THE HORIZON!
© 1995 PAWS, INC. All Rights Reserved.
BANZAI!
SPLOOSH
WHERE ARE YOU GOING?
TO SUCK PUNCH OUT OF MY BEAR
JIM DAVIS 9-18

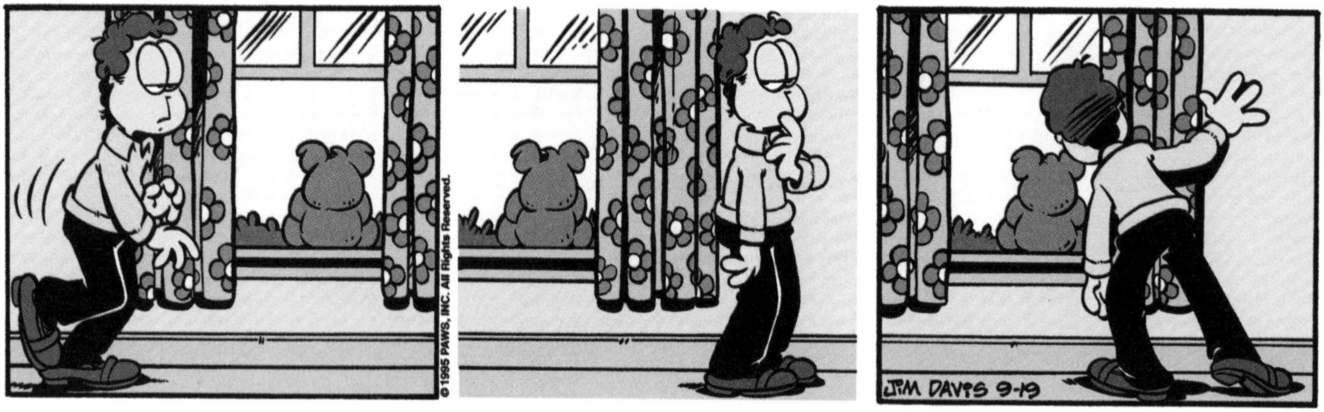
© 1995 PAWS, INC. All Rights Reserved.
JIM DAVIS 9-19

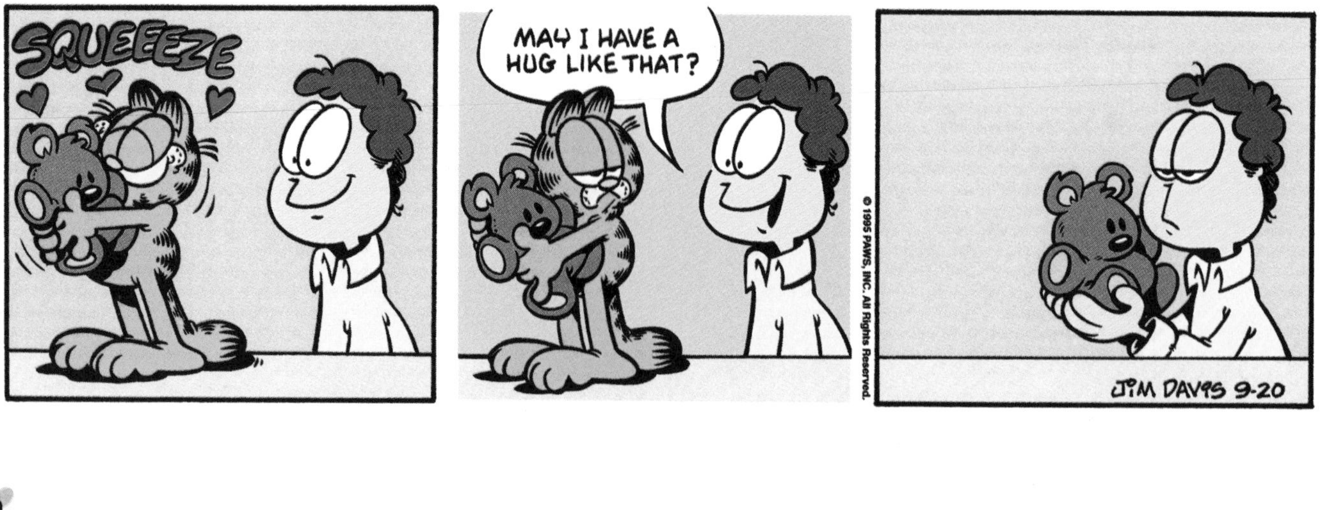
SQUEEEEZE
MAY I HAVE A HUG LIKE THAT?
© 1995 PAWS, INC. All Rights Reserved.
JIM DAVIS 9-20

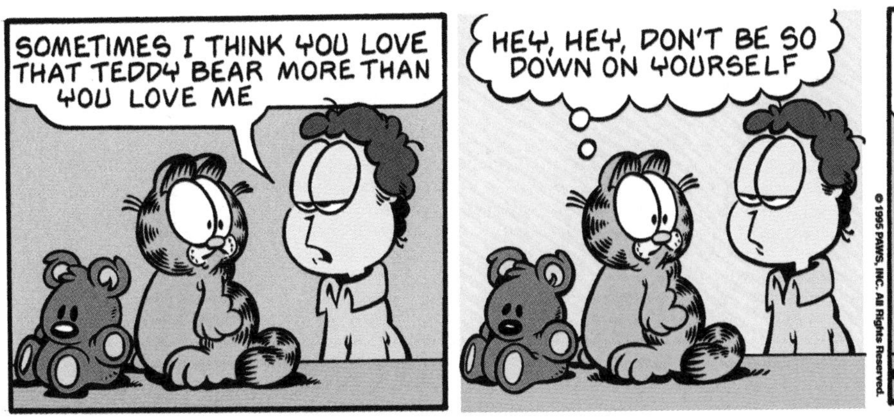
SOMETIMES I THINK YOU LOVE THAT TEDDY BEAR MORE THAN YOU LOVE ME
HEY, HEY, DON'T BE SO DOWN ON YOURSELF
AS LONG AS YOU CAN OPERATE THAT CAN OPENER, YOU HAVE A SPECIAL PLACE IN MY HEART
PAT PAT
JIM DAVIS 9-21
© 1995 PAWS, INC. All Rights Reserved.

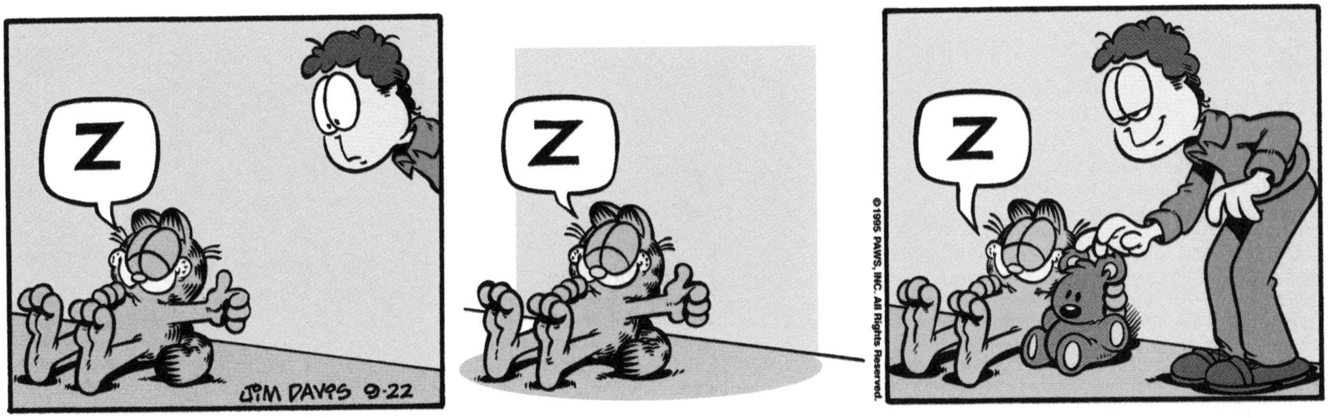
Z
JIM DAVIS 9-22
Z
Z
© 1995 PAWS, INC. All Rights Reserved.

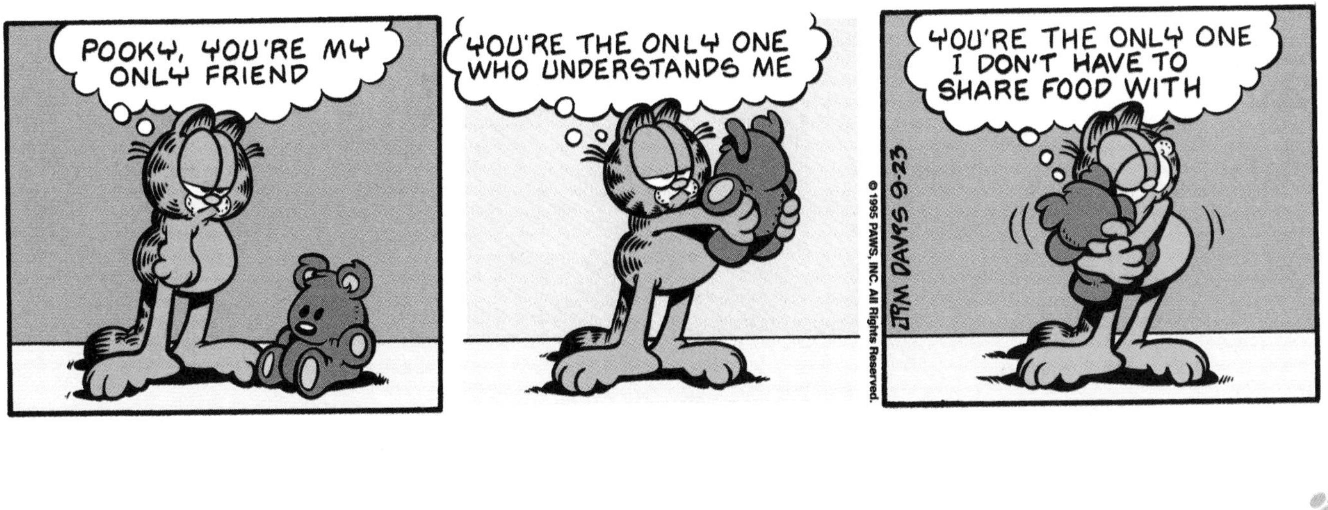
POOKY, YOU'RE MY ONLY FRIEND
YOU'RE THE ONLY ONE WHO UNDERSTANDS ME
JIM DAVIS 9-23
© 1995 PAWS, INC. All Rights Reserved.
YOU'RE THE ONLY ONE I DON'T HAVE TO SHARE FOOD WITH

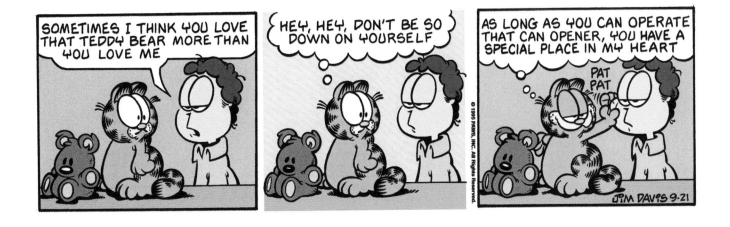

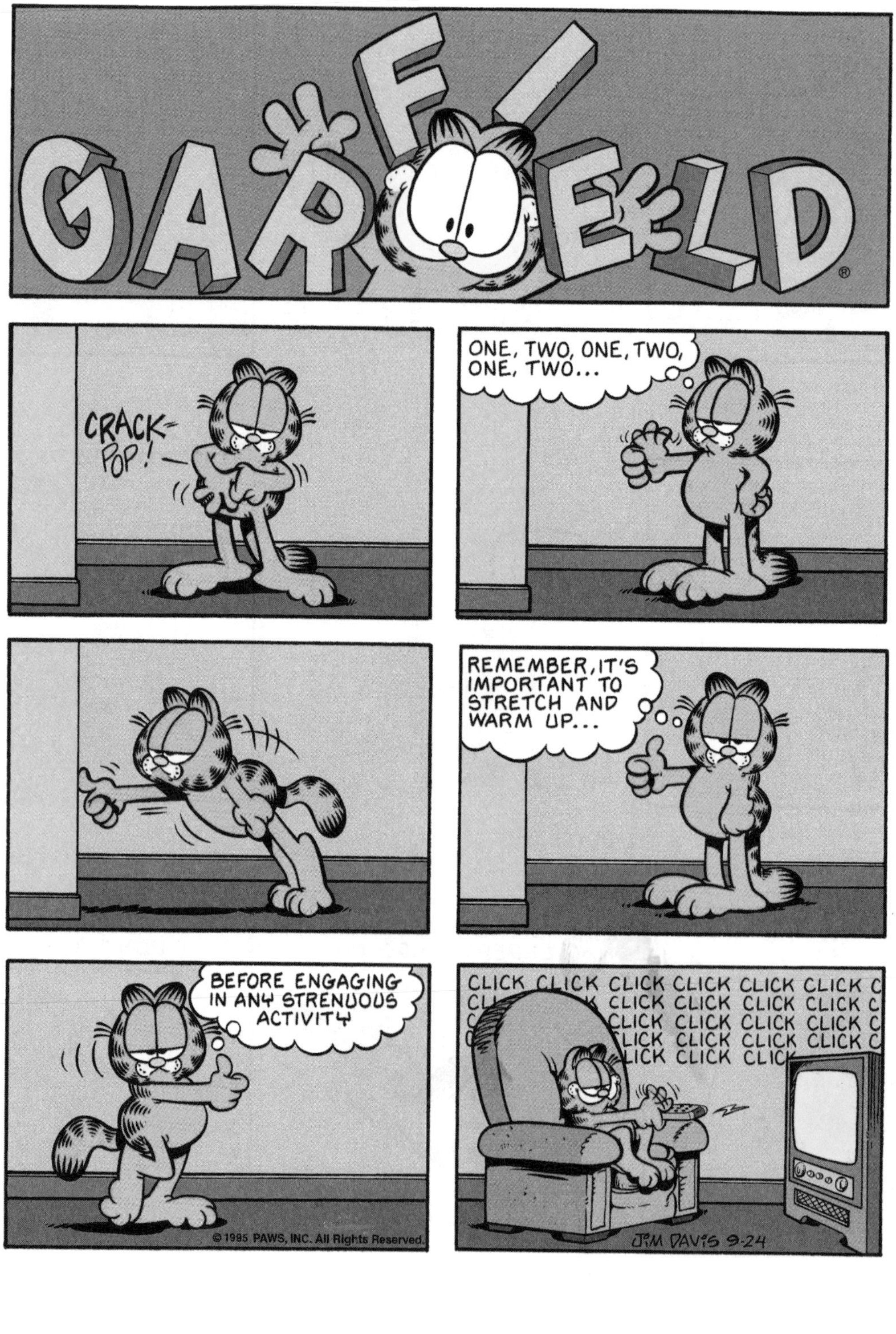
GARFIELD®
CRACK
POP!
ONE, TWO, ONE, TWO, ONE, TWO...
REMEMBER, IT'S IMPORTANT TO STRETCH AND WARM UP...
BEFORE ENGAGING IN ANY STRENUOUS ACTIVITY
CLICK CLICK CLICK CLICK CLICK CLICK
© 1995 PAWS, INC. All Rights Reserved.
JIM DAVIS 9-24

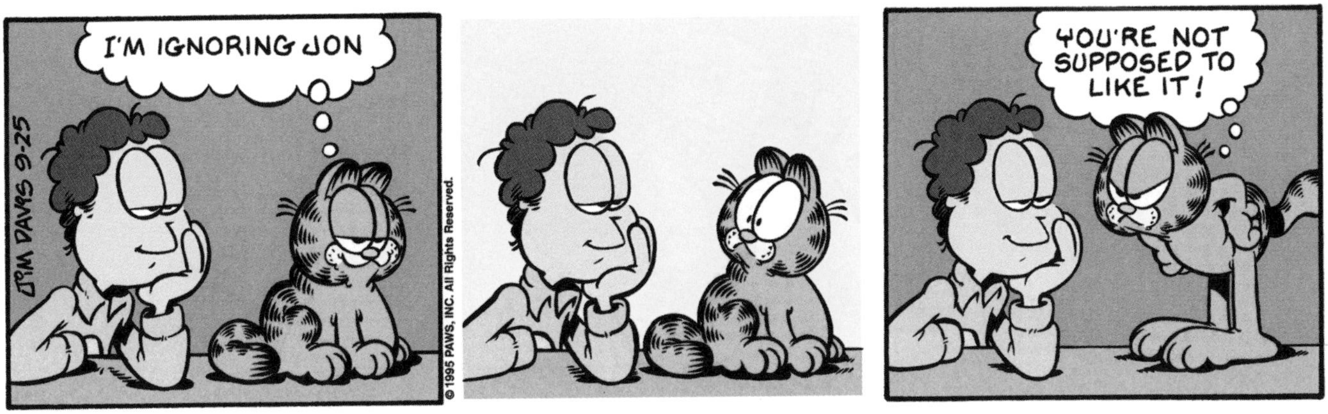
I'M IGNORING JON
JIM DAVIS 9-25
© 1995 PAWS, INC. All Rights Reserved.
YOU'RE NOT SUPPOSED TO LIKE IT!

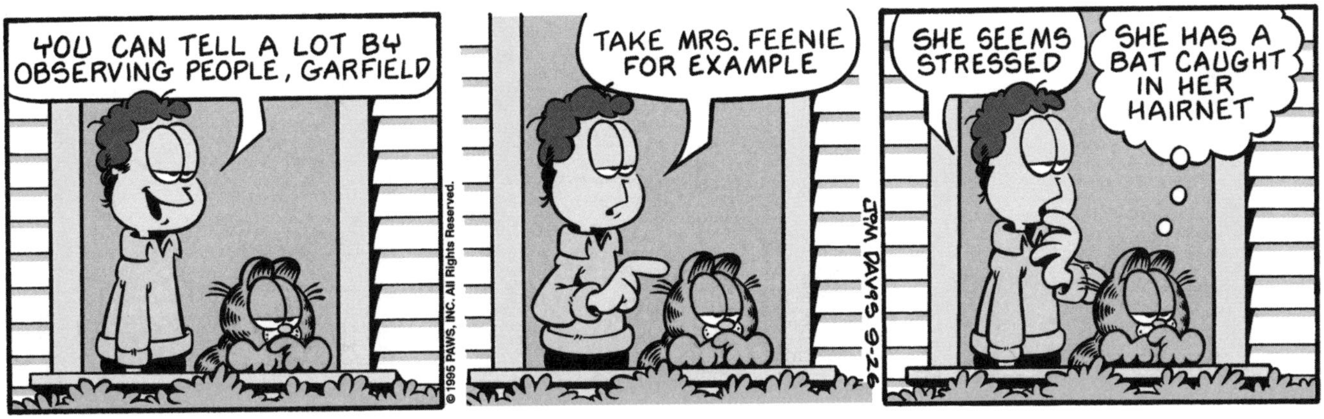
YOU CAN TELL A LOT BY OBSERVING PEOPLE, GARFIELD
© 1995 PAWS, INC. All Rights Reserved.
TAKE MRS. FEENIE FOR EXAMPLE
JIM DAVIS 9-26
SHE SEEMS STRESSED
SHE HAS A BAT CAUGHT IN HER HAIRNET

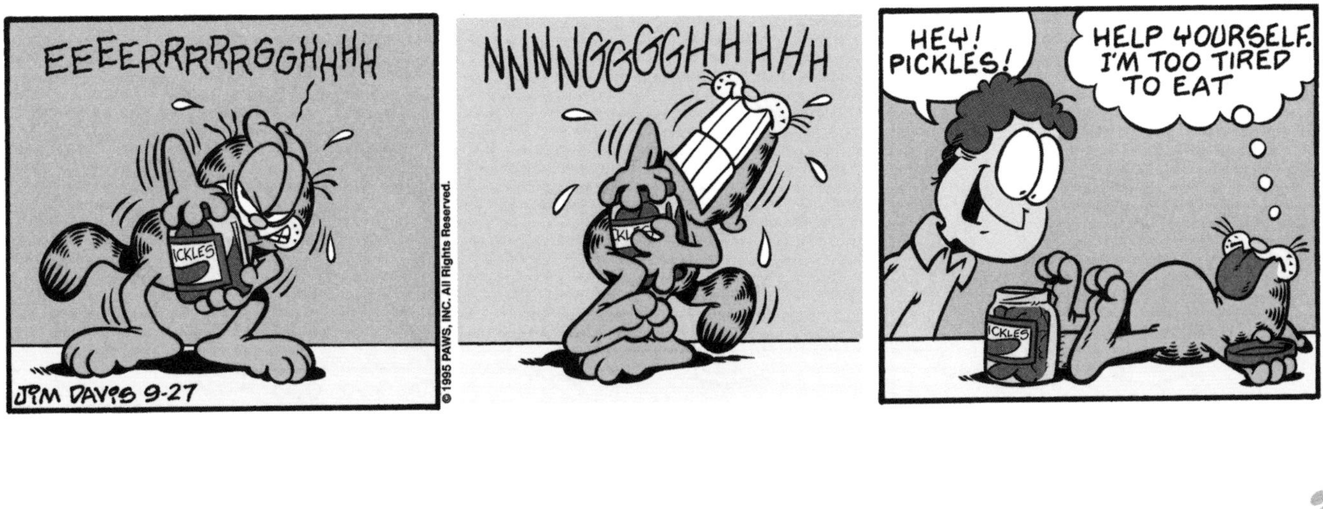
EEEERRRRRGGHHHH
JIM DAVIS 9-27
© 1995 PAWS, INC. All Rights Reserved.
NNNNGGGGHHHHH
HEY! PICKLES!
HELP YOURSELF. I'M TOO TIRED TO EAT

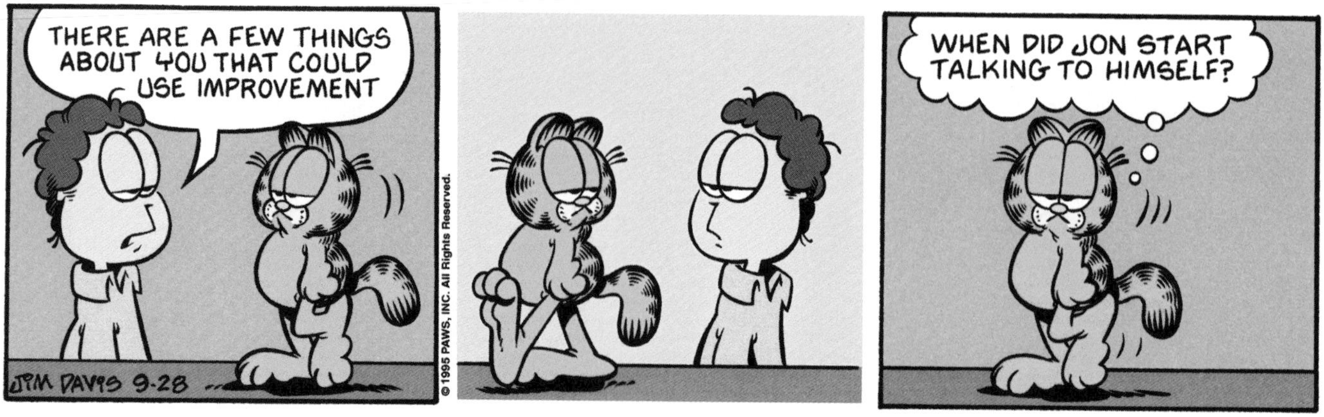
THERE ARE A FEW THINGS ABOUT YOU THAT COULD USE IMPROVEMENT
JIM DAVIS 9-28
© 1995 PAWS, INC. All Rights Reserved.
WHEN DID JON START TALKING TO HIMSELF?

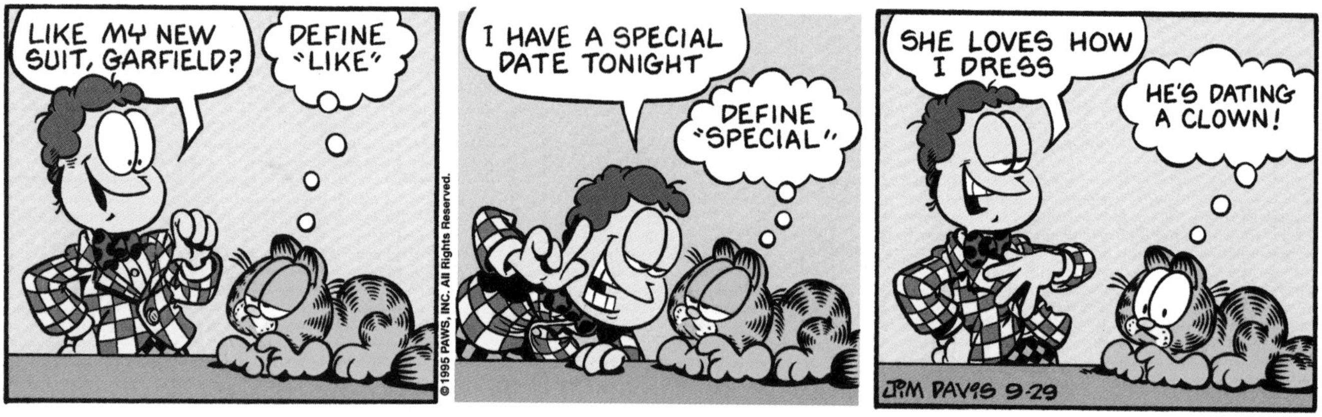
LIKE MY NEW SUIT, GARFIELD?
DEFINE "LIKE"
© 1995 PAWS, INC. All Rights Reserved.
I HAVE A SPECIAL DATE TONIGHT
DEFINE "SPECIAL"
SHE LOVES HOW I DRESS
HE'S DATING A CLOWN!
JIM DAVIS 9-29

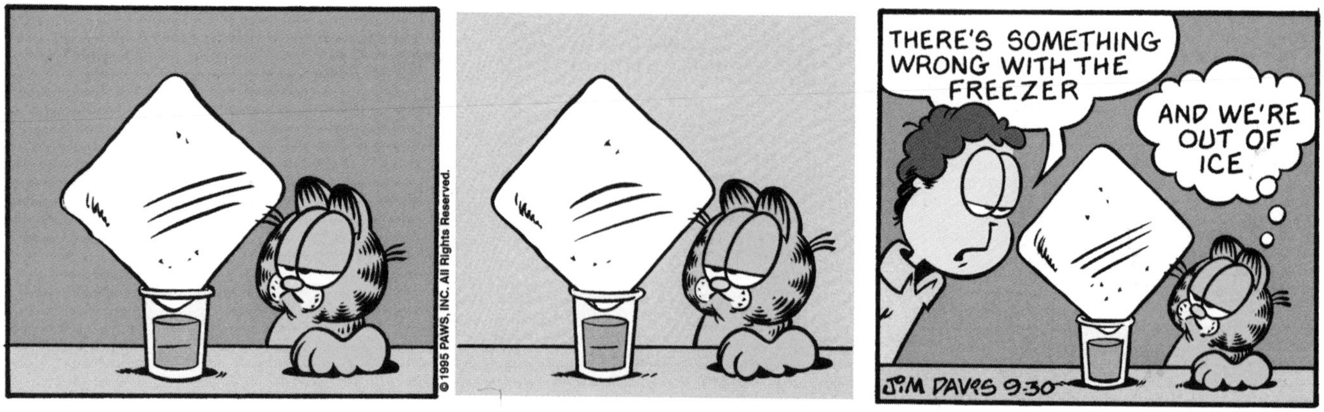
© 1995 PAWS, INC. All Rights Reserved.
THERE'S SOMETHING WRONG WITH THE FREEZER
AND WE'RE OUT OF ICE
JIM DAVIS 9-30

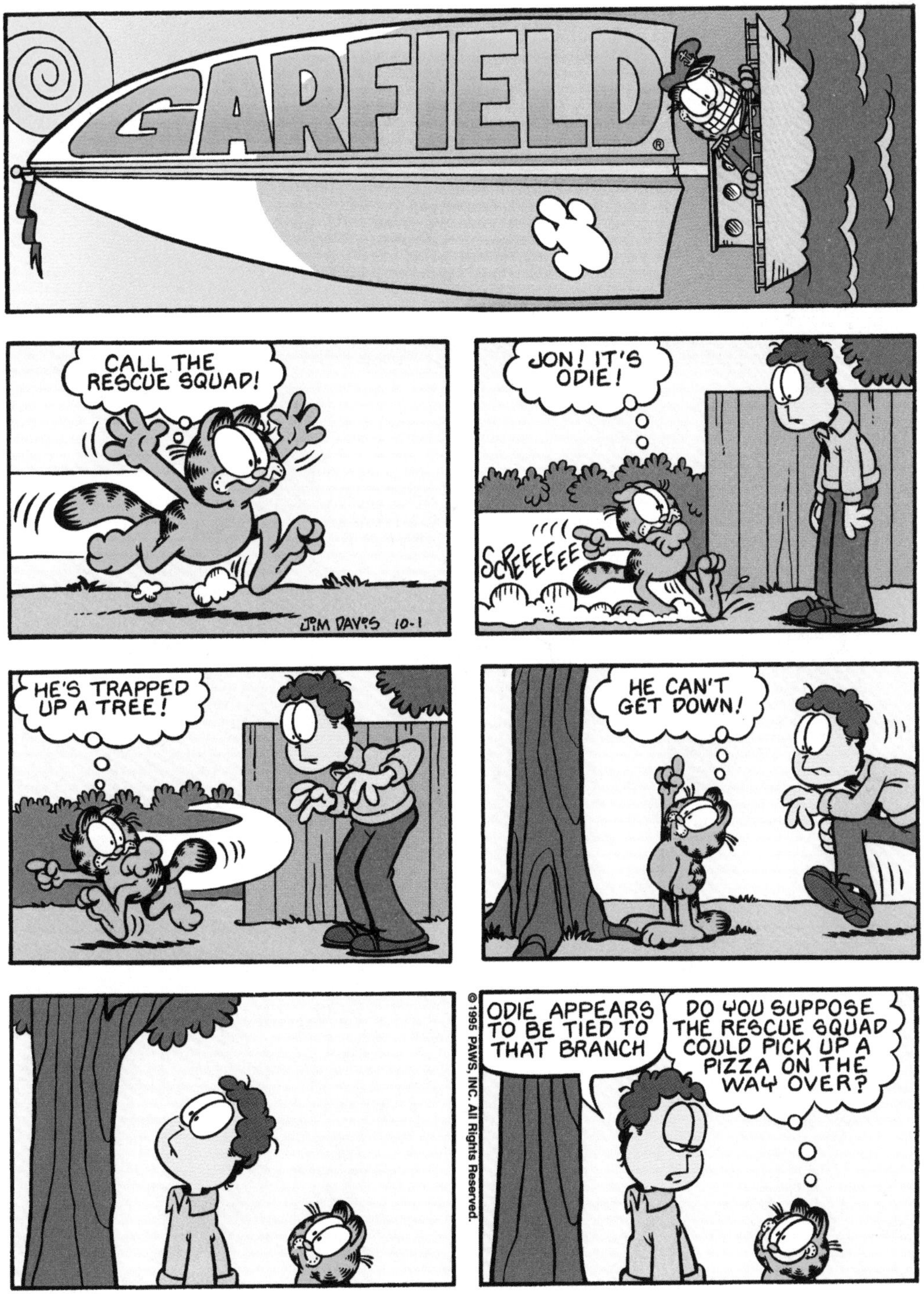
GARFIELD®
CALL THE RESCUE SQUAD!
JIM DAVIS 10-1
JON! IT'S ODIE!
SCREEEEEE
HE'S TRAPPED UP A TREE!
HE CAN'T GET DOWN!
ODIE APPEARS TO BE TIED TO THAT BRANCH
DO YOU SUPPOSE THE RESCUE SQUAD COULD PICK UP A PIZZA ON THE WAY OVER?

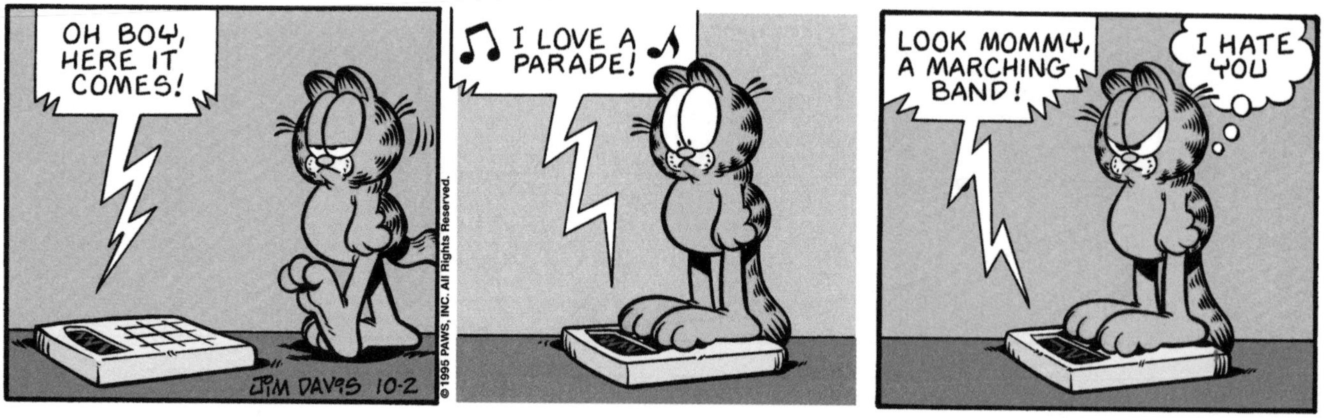
OH BOY, HERE IT COMES!
JIM DAVIS 10-2
© 1995 PAWS, INC. All Rights Reserved.
I LOVE A PARADE!
LOOK MOMMY, A MARCHING BAND!
I HATE YOU

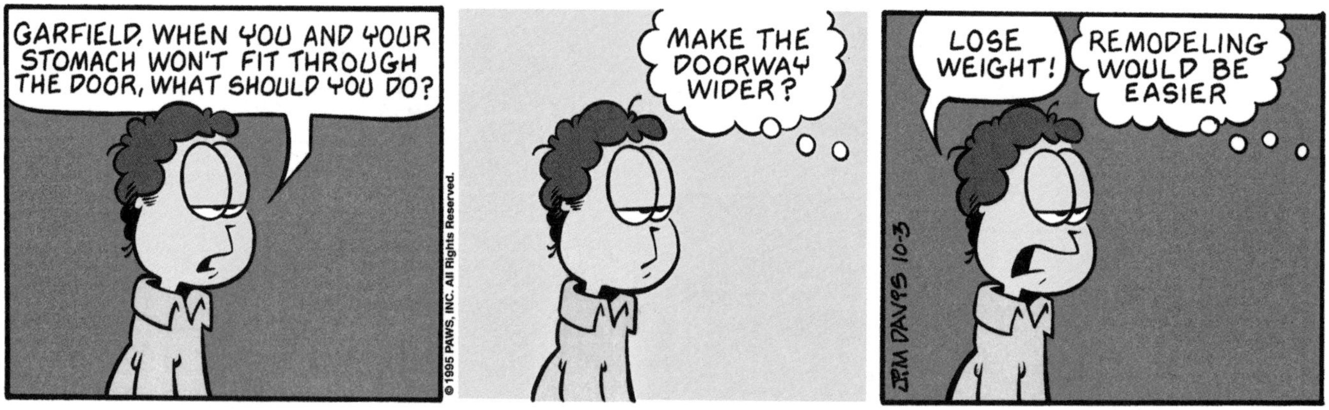
GARFIELD, WHEN YOU AND YOUR STOMACH WON'T FIT THROUGH THE DOOR, WHAT SHOULD YOU DO?
© 1995 PAWS, INC. All Rights Reserved.
MAKE THE DOORWAY WIDER?
LOSE WEIGHT!
REMODELING WOULD BE EASIER
JIM DAVIS 10-3

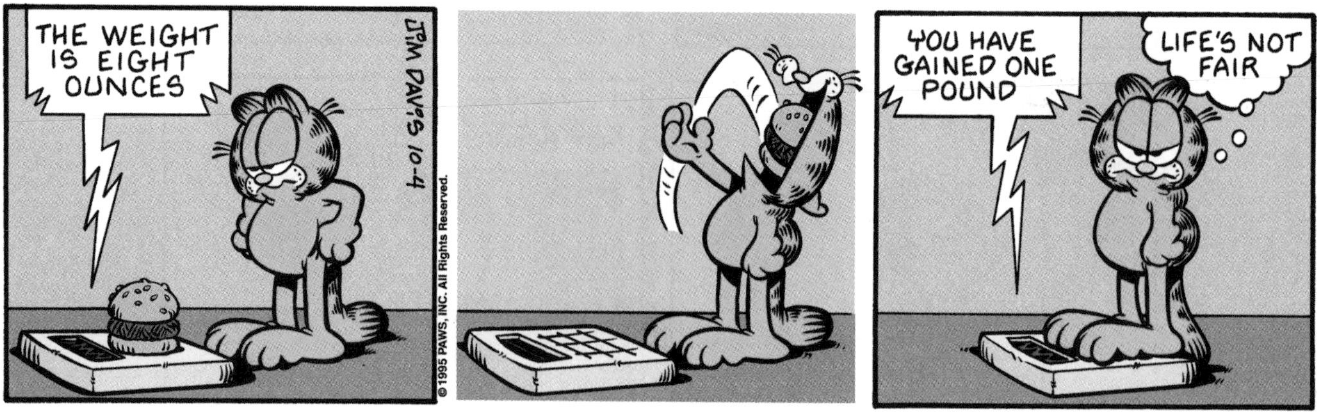
THE WEIGHT IS EIGHT OUNCES
JIM DAVIS 10-4
© 1995 PAWS, INC. All Rights Reserved.
YOU HAVE GAINED ONE POUND
LIFE'S NOT FAIR

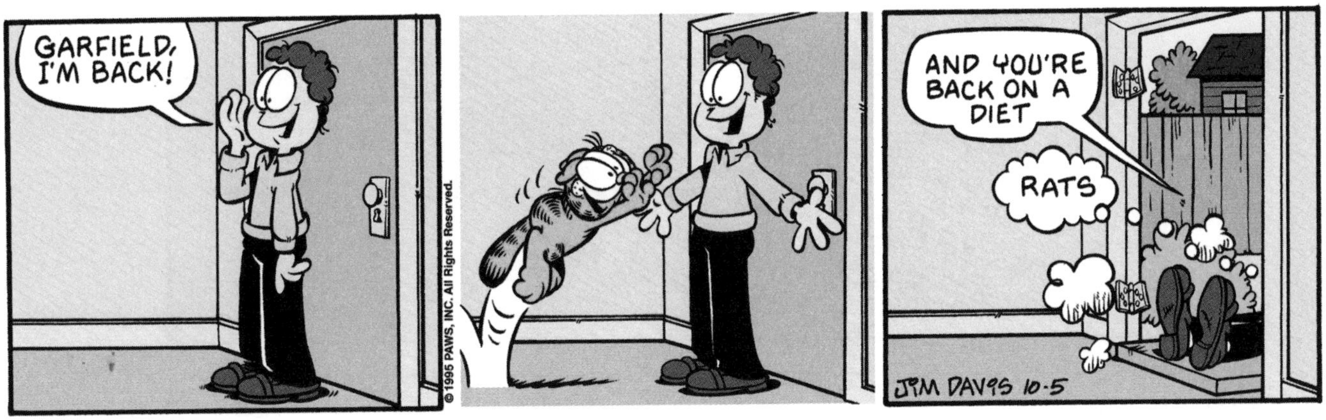
GARFIELD, I'M BACK!
AND YOU'RE BACK ON A DIET
RATS
JIM DAVIS 10-5
© 1995 PAWS, INC. All Rights Reserved.

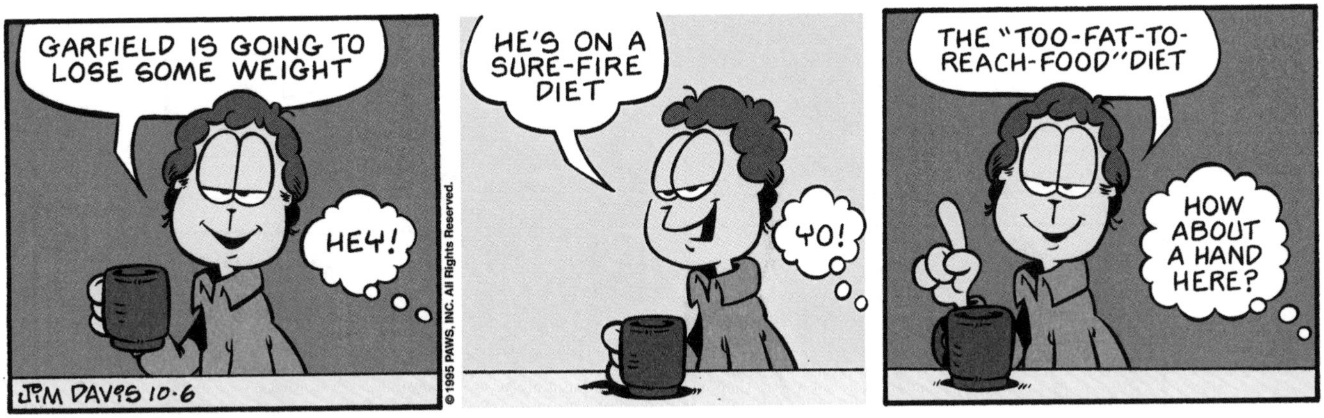
GARFIELD IS GOING TO LOSE SOME WEIGHT
HEY!
HE'S ON A SURE-FIRE DIET
YO!
THE "TOO-FAT-TO-REACH-FOOD" DIET
HOW ABOUT A HAND HERE?
JIM DAVIS 10-6
© 1995 PAWS, INC. All Rights Reserved.

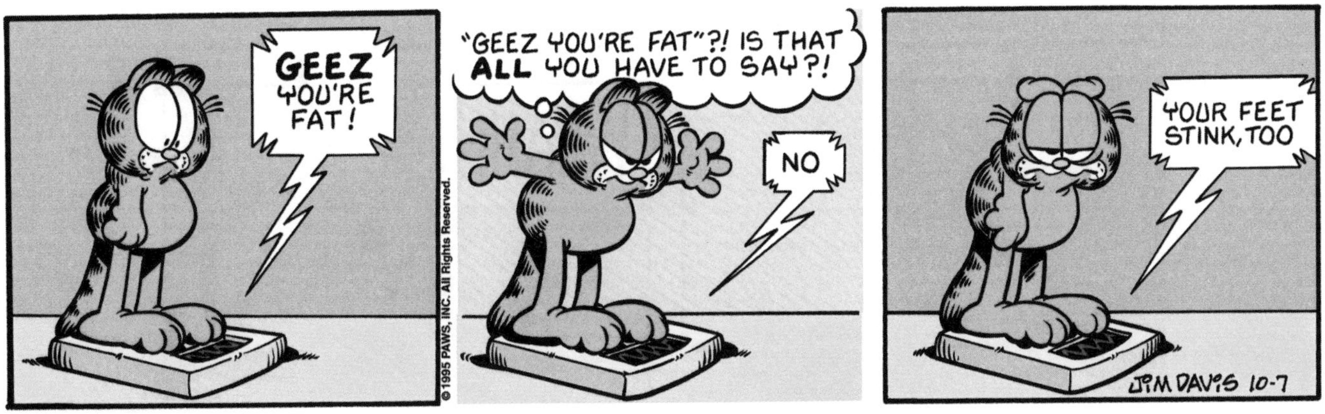
GEEZ YOU'RE FAT!
"GEEZ YOU'RE FAT"?! IS THAT ALL YOU HAVE TO SAY?!
NO
YOUR FEET STINK, TOO
JIM DAVIS 10-7
© 1995 PAWS, INC. All Rights Reserved.

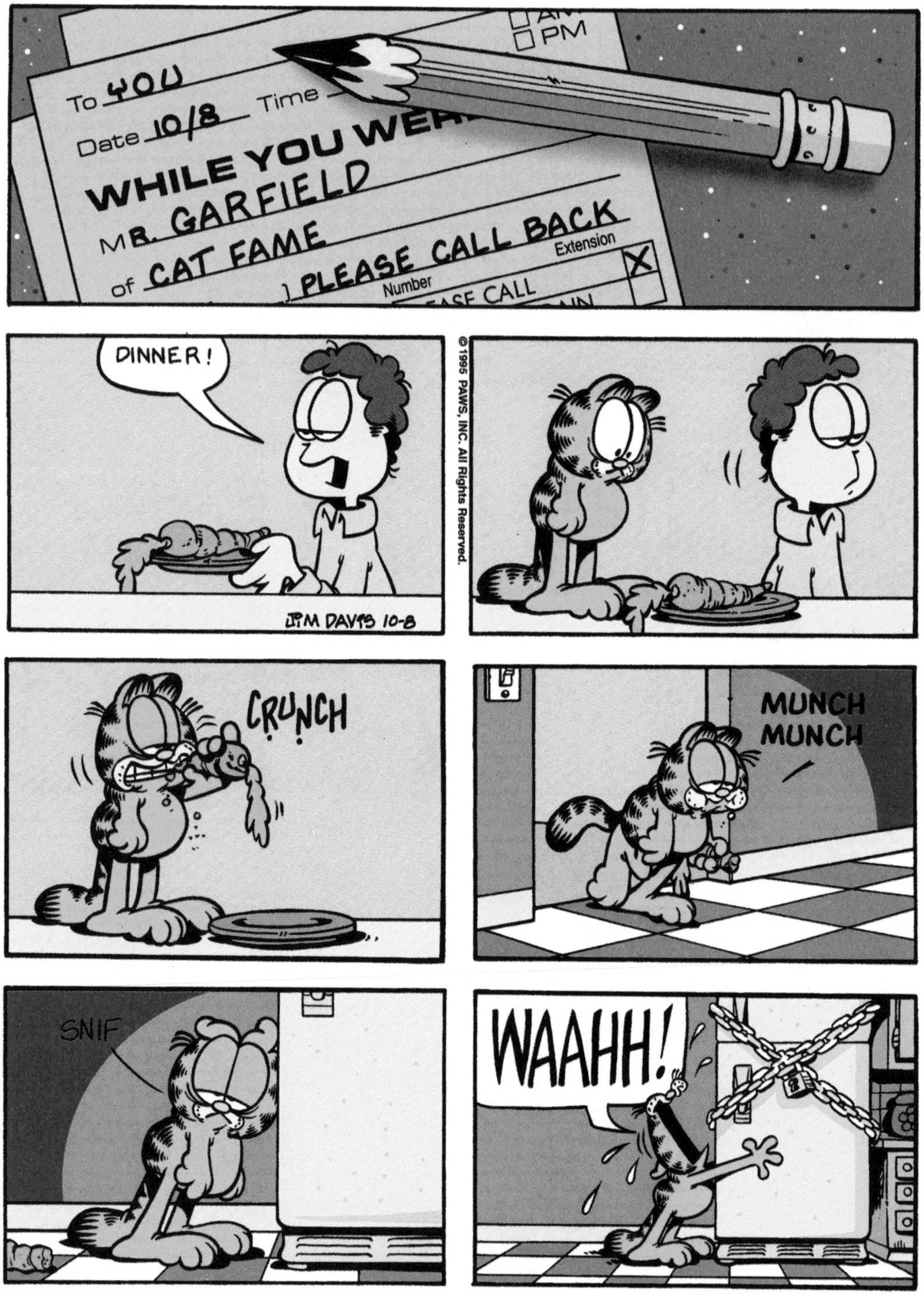

PM
To YOU
Date 10/8
Time
MR. GARFIELD
of CAT FAME
PLEASE CALL BACK
Number
Extension
DINNER!
JIM DAVIS 10-8
© 1995 PAWS, INC. All Rights Reserved.
CRUNCH
MUNCH
MUNCH
SNIF
WAAHH!

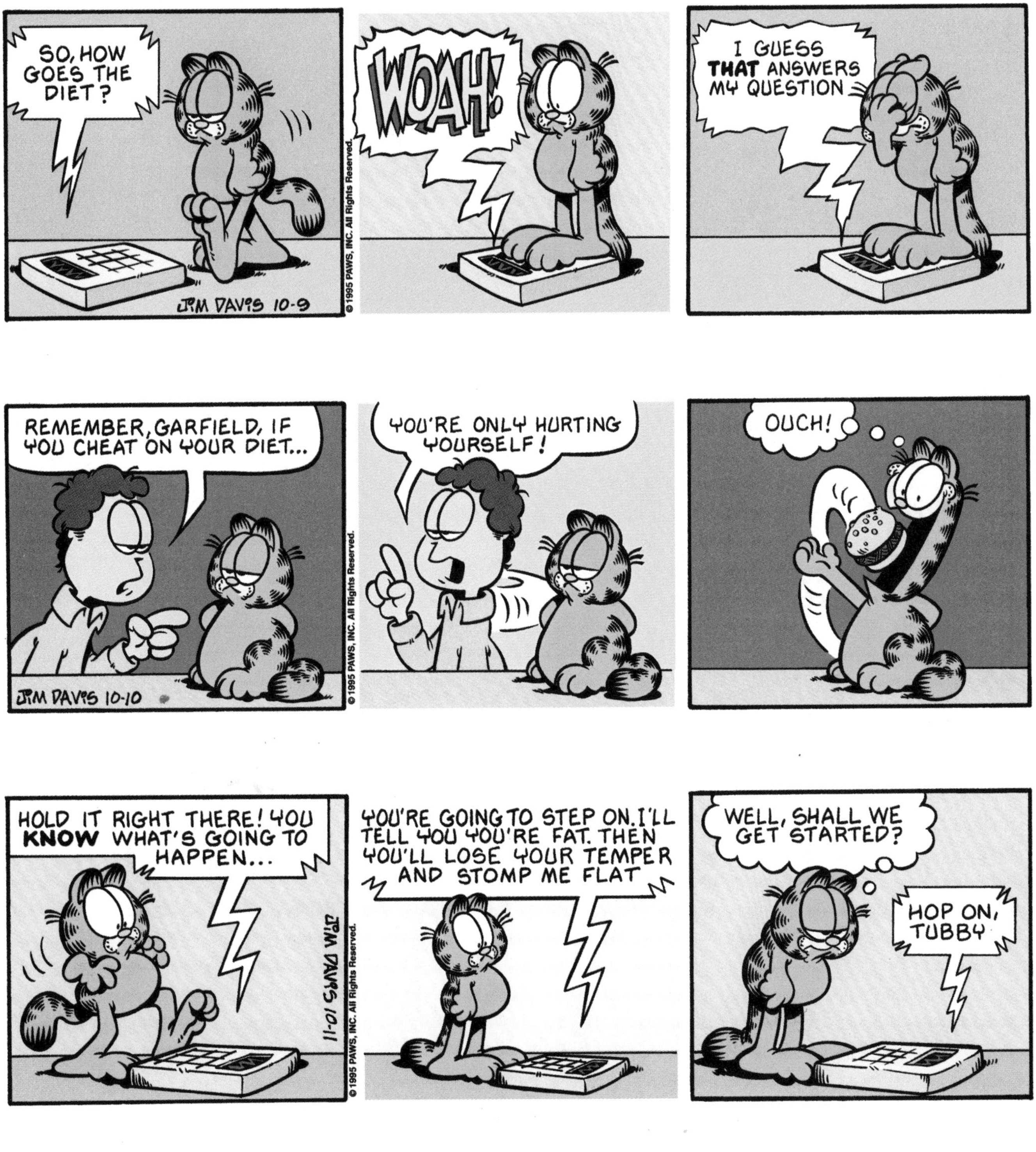
SO, HOW GOES THE DIET?
JIM DAVIS 10-9
WOAH!
© 1995 PAWS, INC. All Rights Reserved.
I GUESS THAT ANSWERS MY QUESTION
REMEMBER, GARFIELD, IF YOU CHEAT ON YOUR DIET...
JIM DAVIS 10-10
© 1995 PAWS, INC. All Rights Reserved.
YOU'RE ONLY HURTING YOURSELF!
OUCH!
HOLD IT RIGHT THERE! YOU KNOW WHAT'S GOING TO HAPPEN...
JIM DAVIS 10-11
© 1995 PAWS, INC. All Rights Reserved.
YOU'RE GOING TO STEP ON. I'LL TELL YOU YOU'RE FAT. THEN YOU'LL LOSE YOUR TEMPER AND STOMP ME FLAT
WELL, SHALL WE GET STARTED?
HOP ON, TUBBY

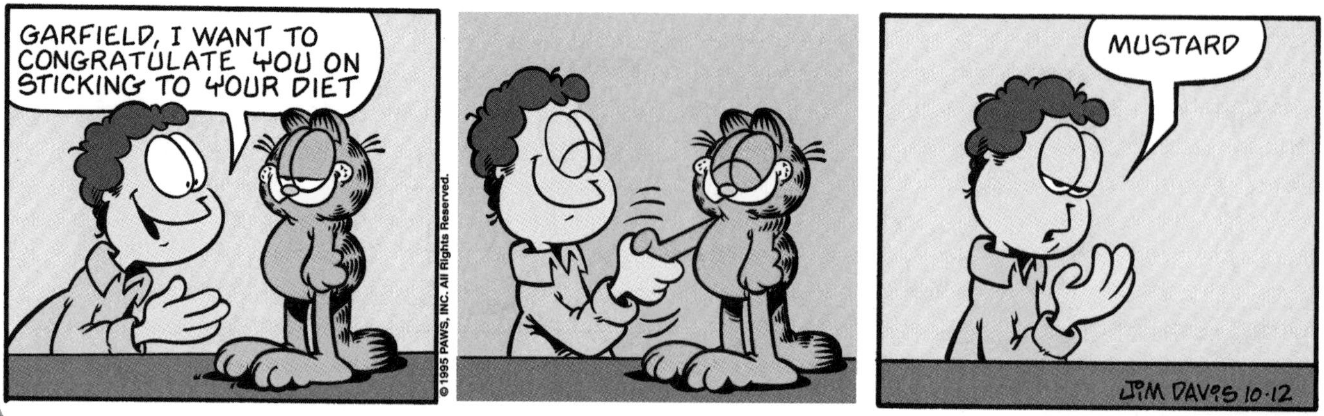
GARFIELD, I WANT TO CONGRATULATE YOU ON STICKING TO YOUR DIET
© 1995 PAWS, INC. All Rights Reserved.
MUSTARD
JIM DAVIS 10-12

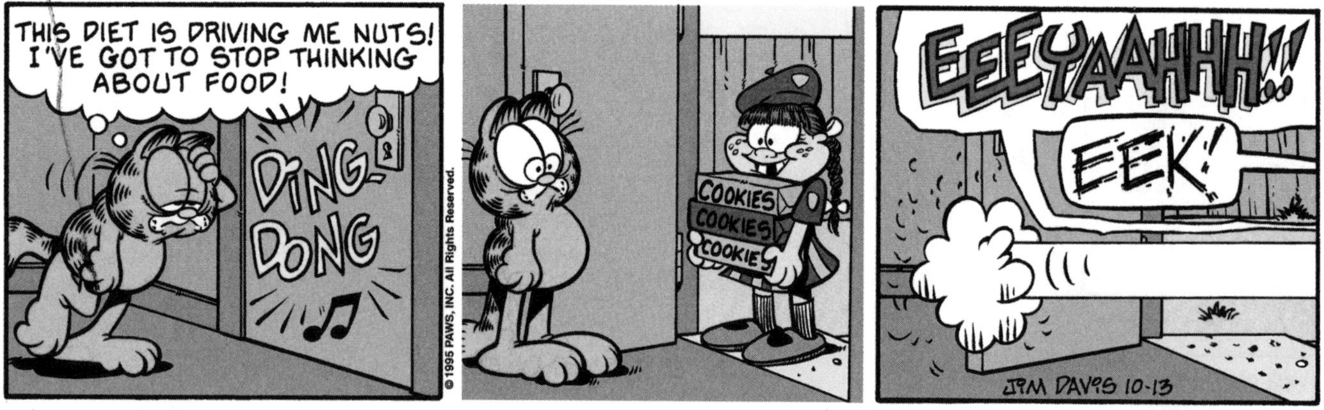
THIS DIET IS DRIVING ME NUTS! I'VE GOT TO STOP THINKING ABOUT FOOD!
DING-DONG
© 1995 PAWS, INC. All Rights Reserved.
COOKIES
COOKIES
COOKIES
EEEYAAHHH!!!
EEK!
JIM DAVIS 10-13

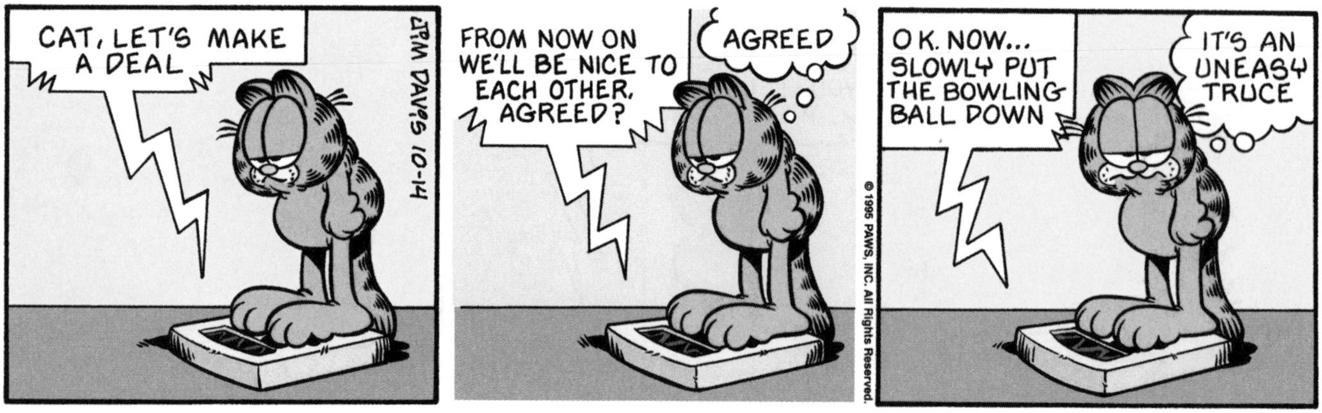
CAT, LET'S MAKE A DEAL
JIM DAVIS 10-14
FROM NOW ON WE'LL BE NICE TO EACH OTHER, AGREED?
AGREED
© 1995 PAWS, INC. All Rights Reserved.
O.K. NOW... SLOWLY PUT THE BOWLING BALL DOWN
IT'S AN UNEASY TRUCE

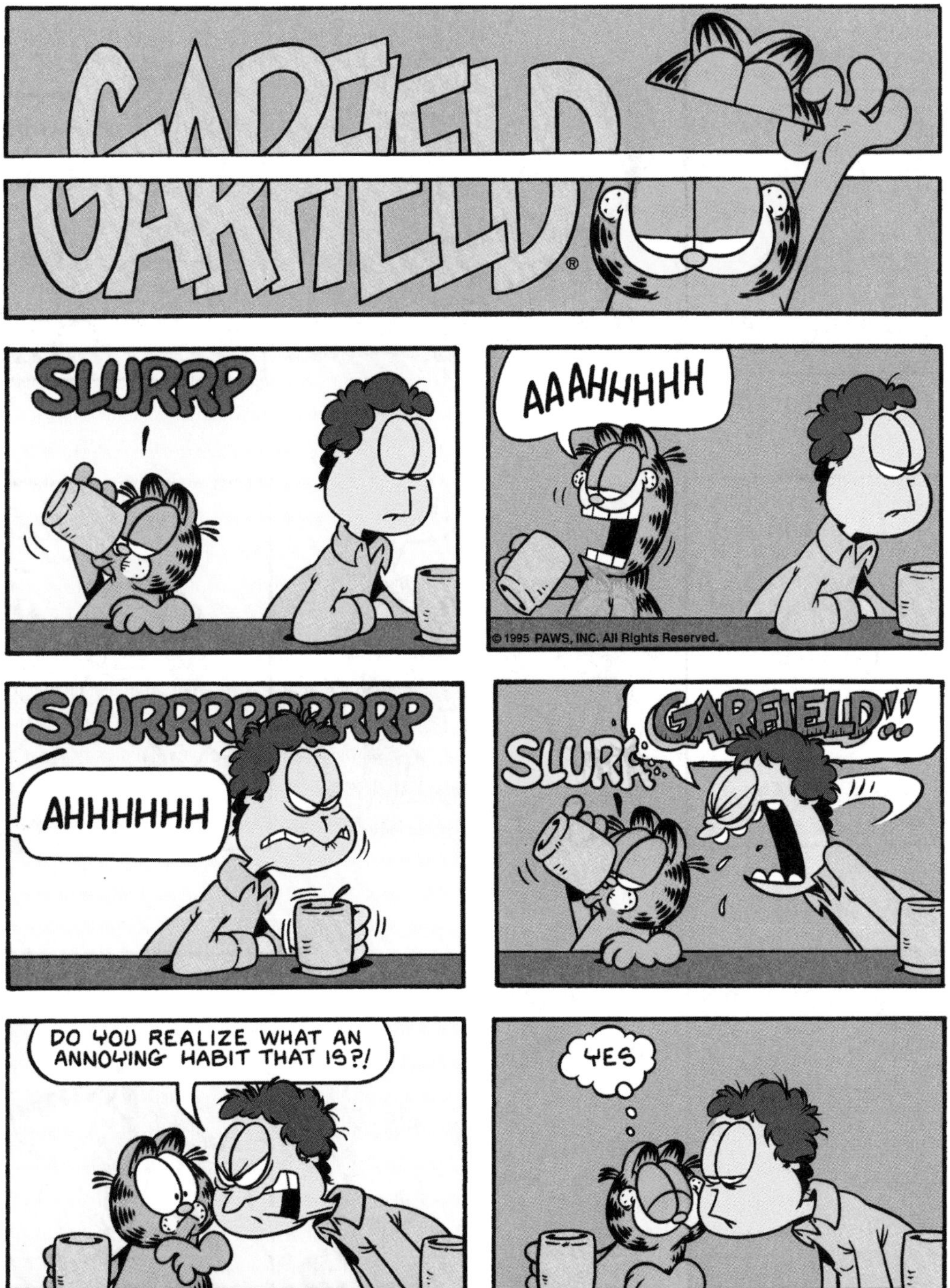
GARFIELD®
SLURRP
AAAHHHHH
© 1995 PAWS, INC. All Rights Reserved.
SLURRRPPPPRRP
AHHHHHH
SLURR
GARFIELD!!
DO YOU REALIZE WHAT AN ANNOYING HABIT THAT IS?!
YES
JIM DAVIS 10-15

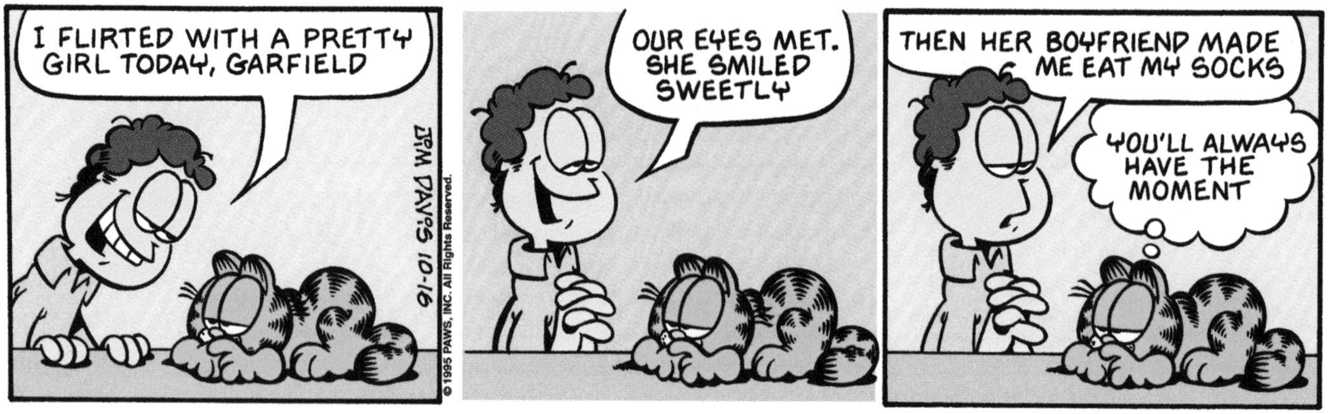
I FLIRTED WITH A PRETTY GIRL TODAY, GARFIELD
JIM DAVIS 10-16
© 1995 PAWS, INC. All Rights Reserved.
OUR EYES MET. SHE SMILED SWEETLY
THEN HER BOYFRIEND MADE ME EAT MY SOCKS
YOU'LL ALWAYS HAVE THE MOMENT

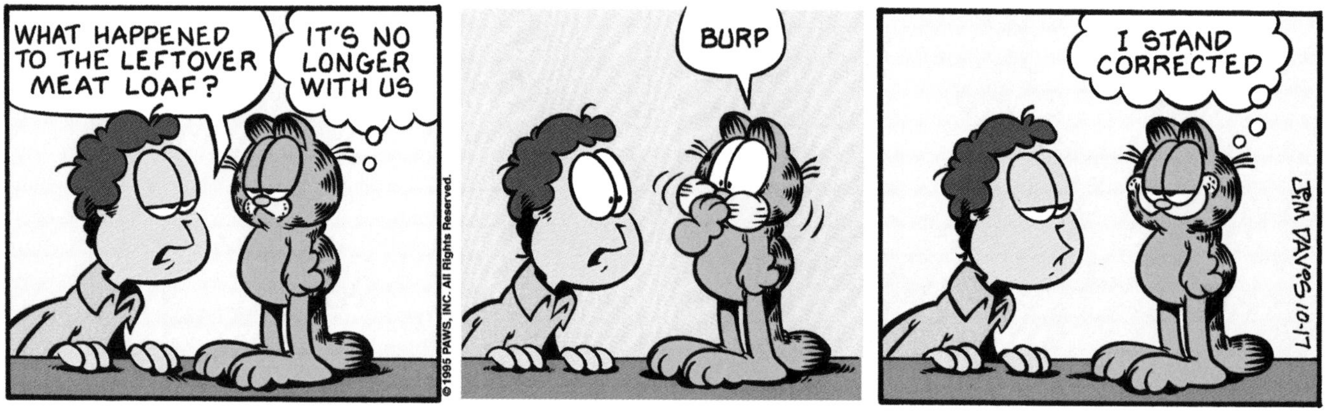
WHAT HAPPENED TO THE LEFTOVER MEAT LOAF?
IT'S NO LONGER WITH US
© 1995 PAWS, INC. All Rights Reserved.
BURP
I STAND CORRECTED
JIM DAVIS 10-17

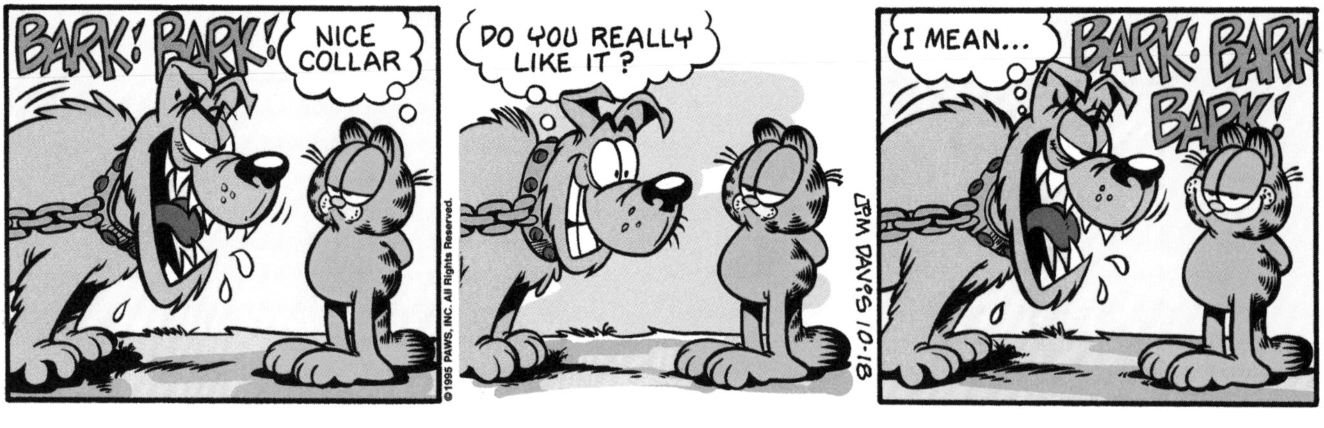
BARK! BARK!
NICE COLLAR
© 1995 PAWS, INC. All Rights Reserved.
DO YOU REALLY LIKE IT?
JIM DAVIS 10-18
I MEAN...
BARK! BARK BARK!

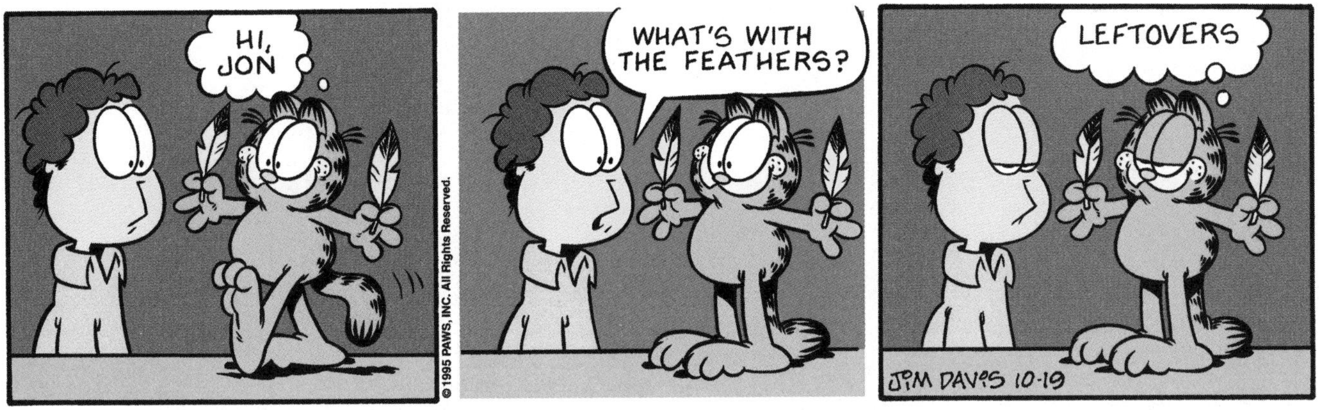
HI, JON
WHAT'S WITH THE FEATHERS?
LEFTOVERS
© 1995 PAWS, INC. All Rights Reserved.
JIM DAVIS 10-19

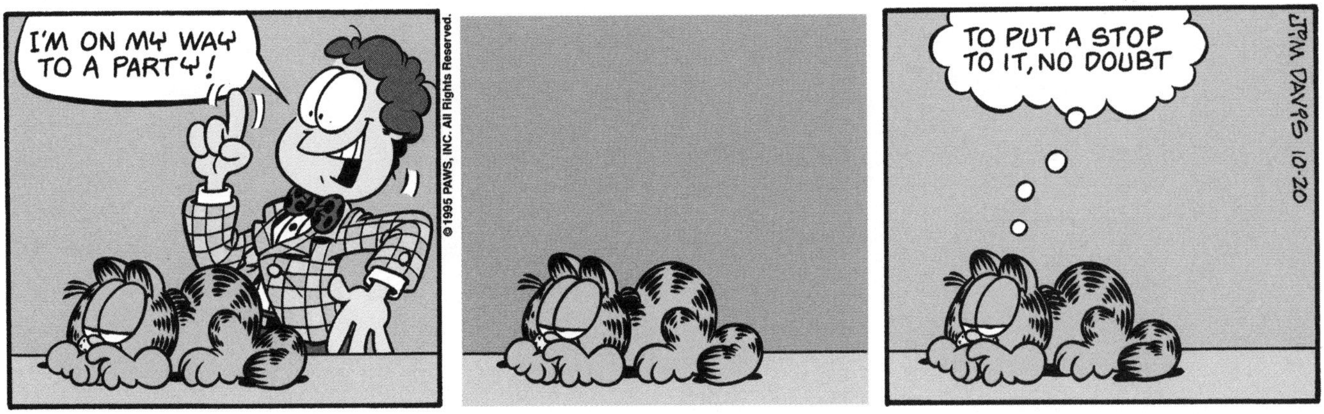
I'M ON MY WAY TO A PARTY!
TO PUT A STOP TO IT, NO DOUBT
© 1995 PAWS, INC. All Rights Reserved.
JIM DAVIS 10-20

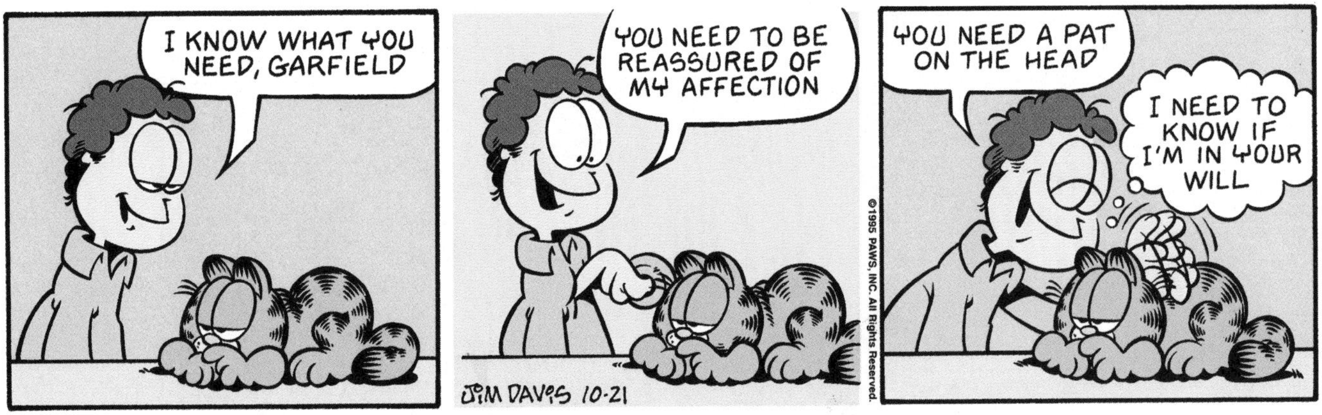
I KNOW WHAT YOU NEED, GARFIELD
YOU NEED TO BE REASSURED OF MY AFFECTION
YOU NEED A PAT ON THE HEAD
I NEED TO KNOW IF I'M IN YOUR WILL
© 1995 PAWS, INC. All Rights Reserved.
JIM DAVIS 10-21

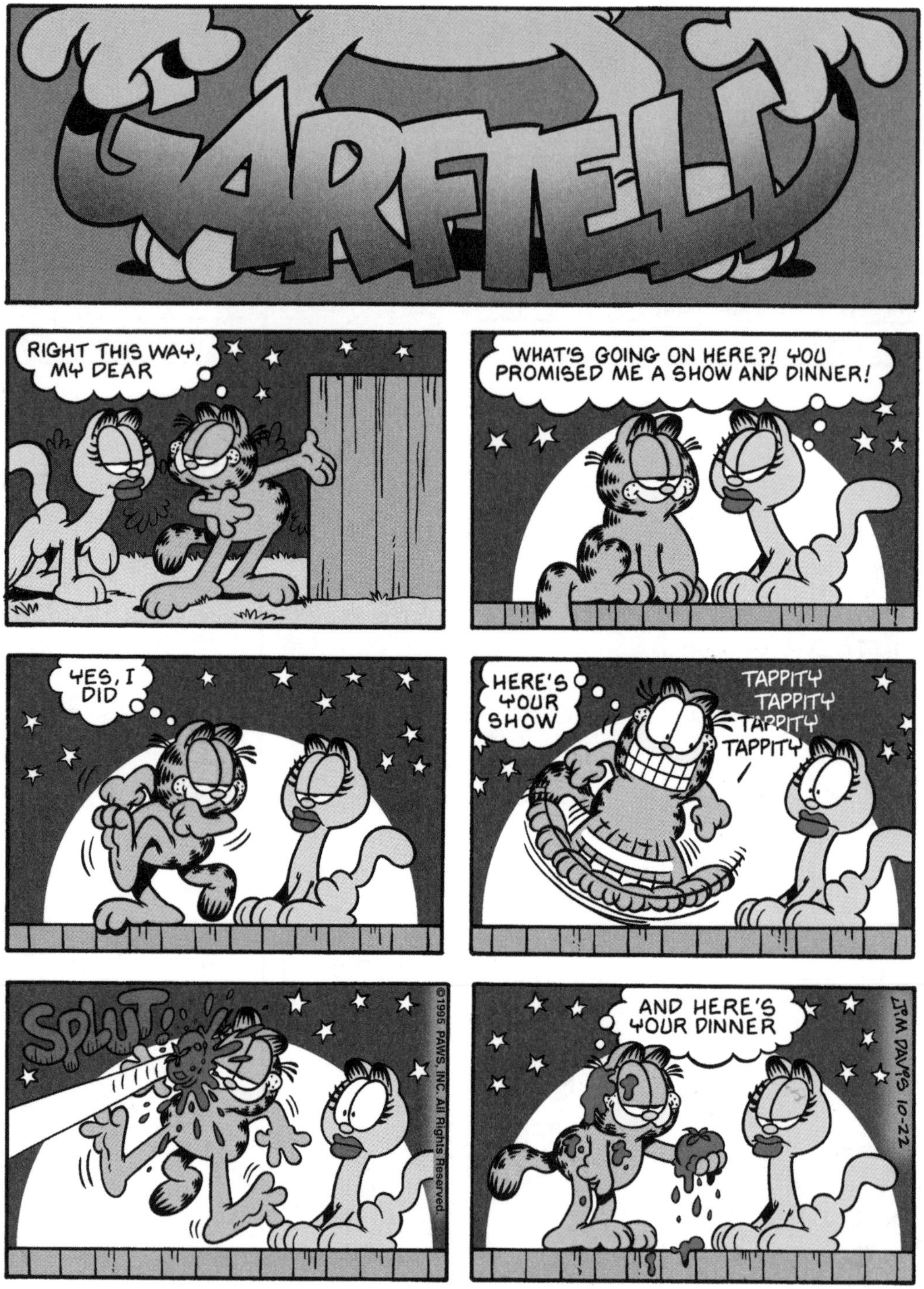
GARFIELD
RIGHT THIS WAY, MY DEAR
WHAT'S GOING ON HERE?! YOU PROMISED ME A SHOW AND DINNER!
YES, I DID
HERE'S YOUR SHOW
TAPPITY TAPPITY TAPPITY TAPPITY
SPLUT!
©1995 PAWS, INC. All Rights Reserved.
AND HERE'S YOUR DINNER
JIM DAVIS 10-22

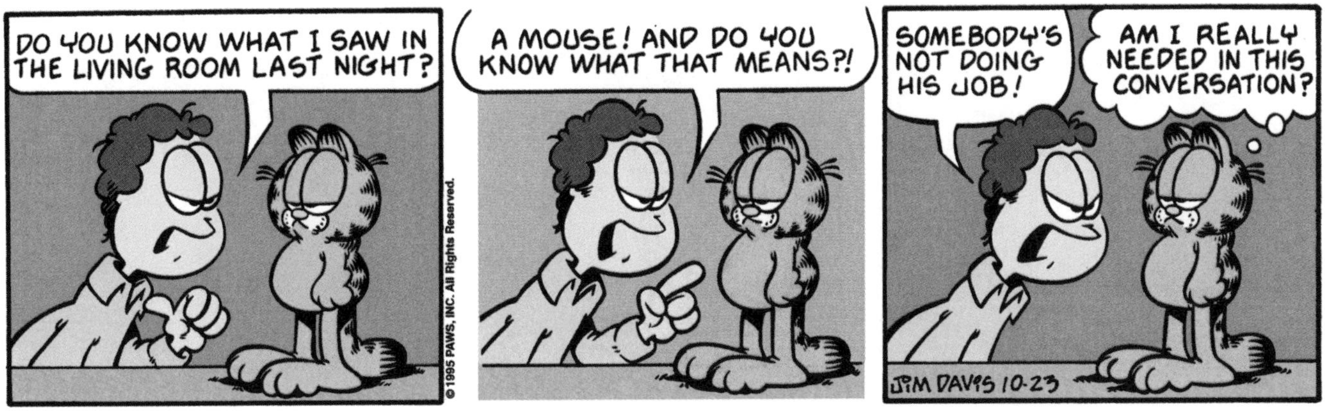
DO YOU KNOW WHAT I SAW IN THE LIVING ROOM LAST NIGHT?
© 1995 PAWS, INC. All Rights Reserved.
A MOUSE! AND DO YOU KNOW WHAT THAT MEANS?!
SOMEBODY'S NOT DOING HIS JOB!
AM I REALLY NEEDED IN THIS CONVERSATION?
JIM DAVIS 10-23

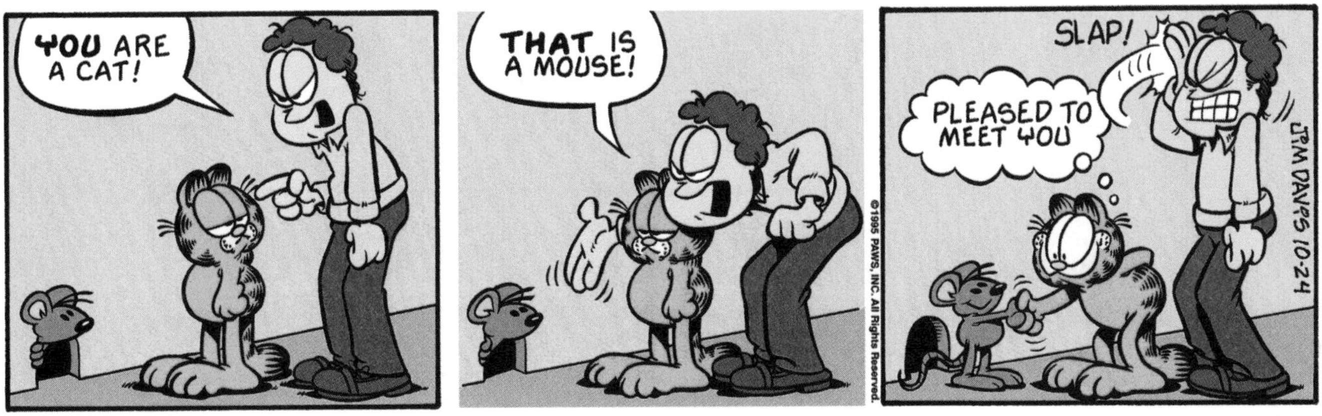
YOU ARE A CAT!
THAT IS A MOUSE!
© 1995 PAWS, INC. All Rights Reserved.
SLAP!
PLEASED TO MEET YOU
JIM DAVIS 10-24

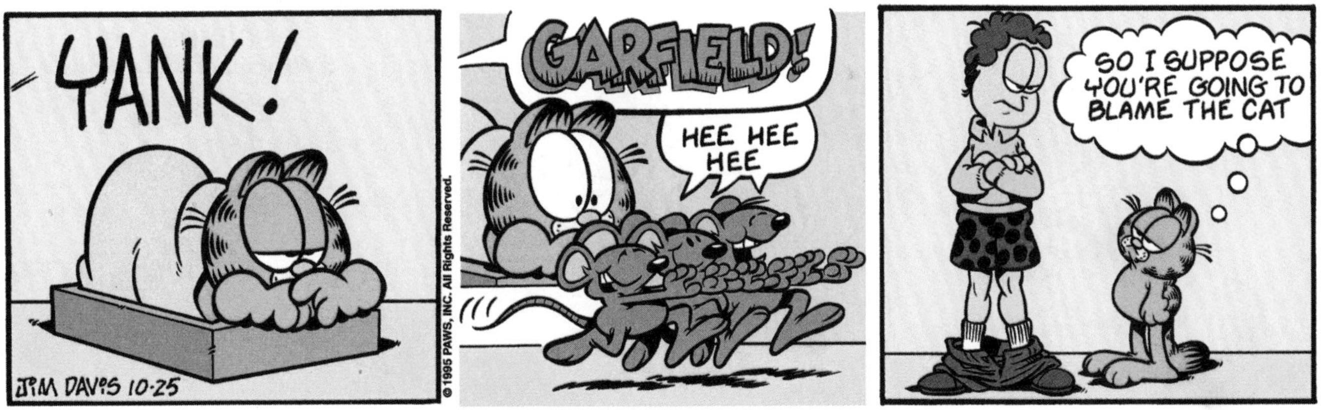
YANK!
JIM DAVIS 10-25
© 1995 PAWS, INC. All Rights Reserved.
GARFIELD!
HEE HEE HEE
SO I SUPPOSE YOU'RE GOING TO BLAME THE CAT

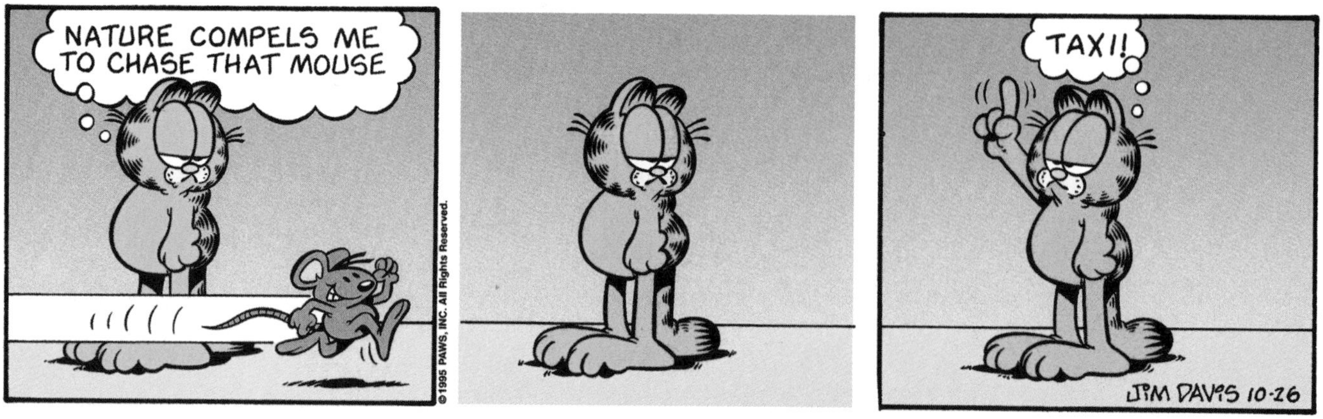
NATURE COMPELS ME TO CHASE THAT MOUSE
©1995 PAWS, INC. All Rights Reserved.
TAXI!
JIM DAVIS 10-26

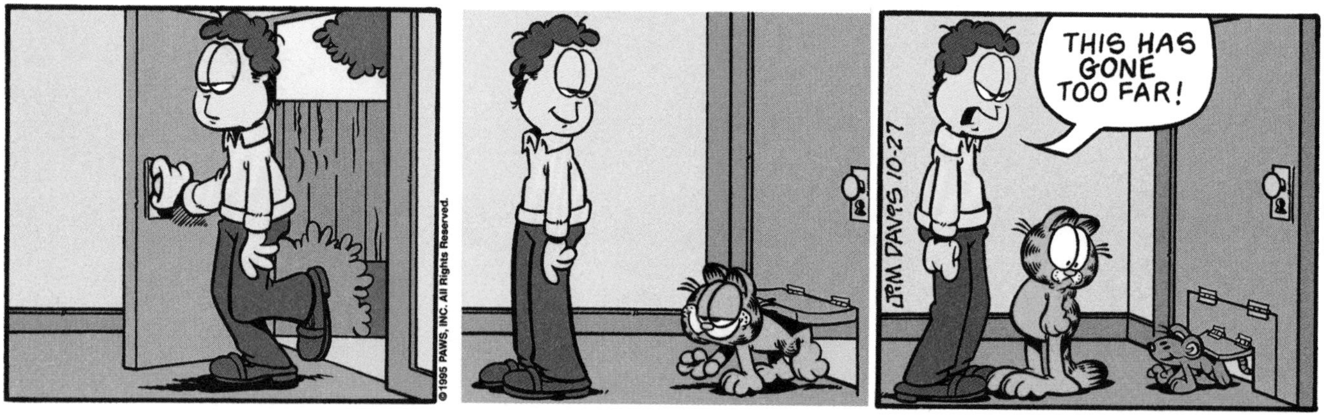
©1995 PAWS, INC. All Rights Reserved.
JIM DAVIS 10-27
THIS HAS GONE TOO FAR!

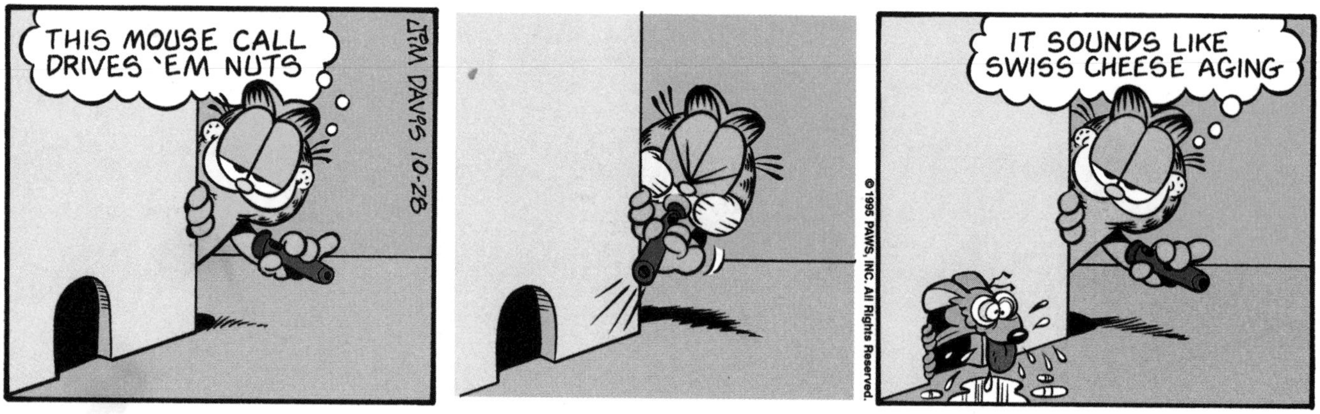
THIS MOUSE CALL DRIVES 'EM NUTS
JIM DAVIS 10-28
©1995 PAWS, INC. All Rights Reserved.
IT SOUNDS LIKE SWISS CHEESE AGING

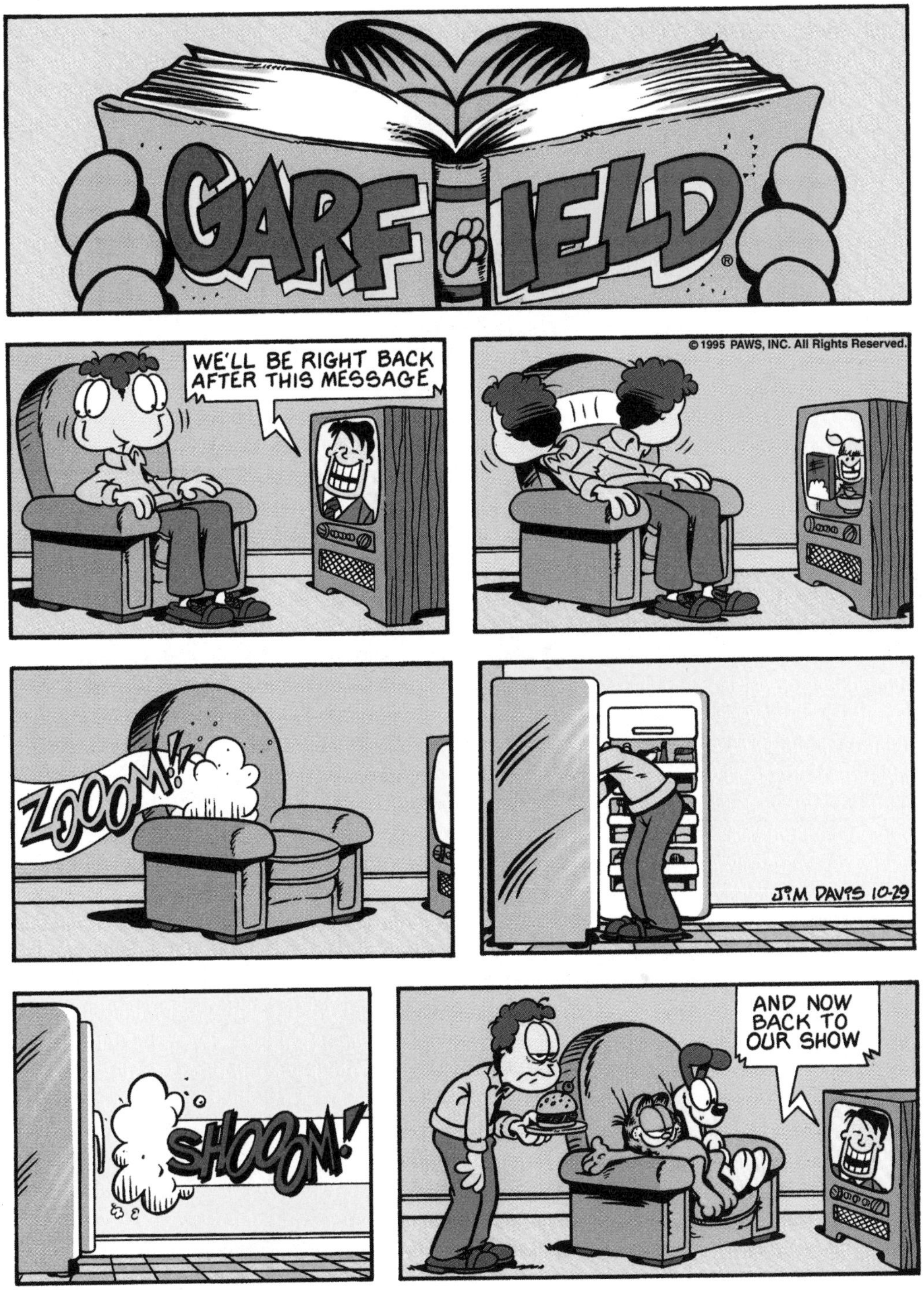
GARFIELD®
© 1995 PAWS, INC. All Rights Reserved.
WE'LL BE RIGHT BACK AFTER THIS MESSAGE
ZOOOM!
JIM DAVIS 10-29
SHOOOM!
AND NOW BACK TO OUR SHOW

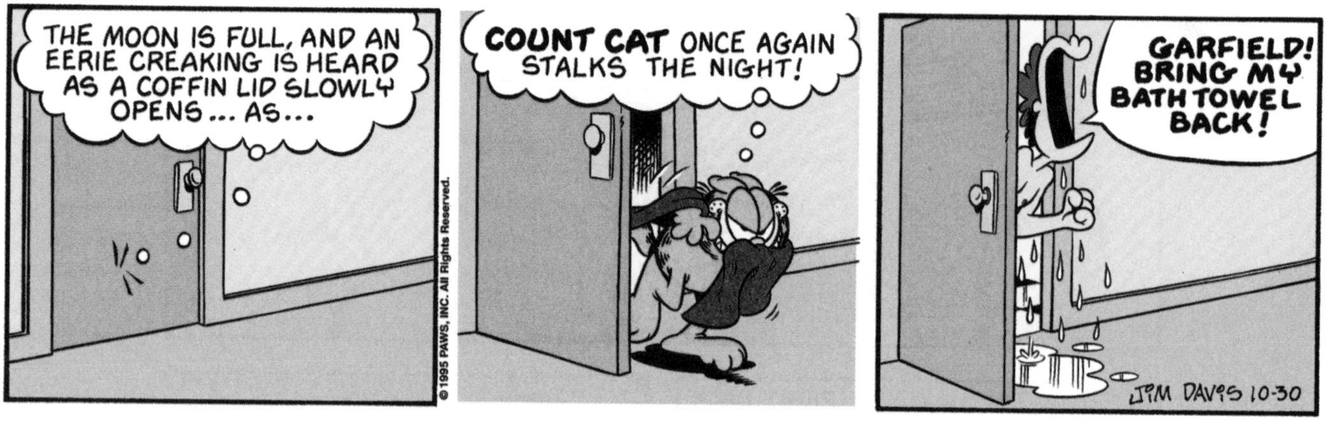
THE MOON IS FULL, AND AN EERIE CREAKING IS HEARD AS A COFFIN LID SLOWLY OPENS... AS...
© 1995 PAWS, INC. All Rights Reserved.
COUNT CAT ONCE AGAIN STALKS THE NIGHT!
GARFIELD! BRING MY BATH TOWEL BACK!
JIM DAVIS 10-30

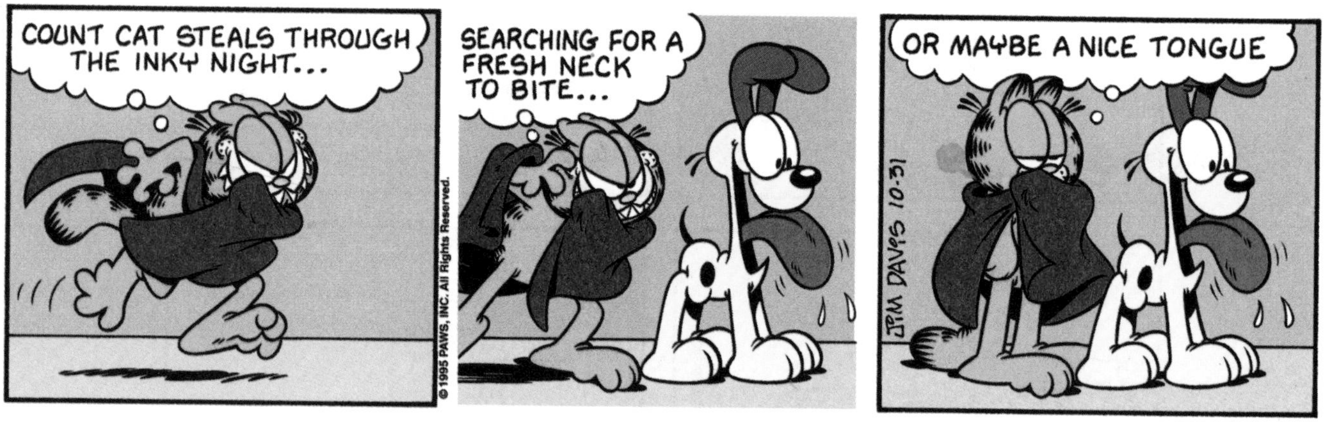
COUNT CAT STEALS THROUGH THE INKY NIGHT...
© 1995 PAWS, INC. All Rights Reserved.
SEARCHING FOR A FRESH NECK TO BITE...
OR MAYBE A NICE TONGUE
JIM DAVIS 10-31

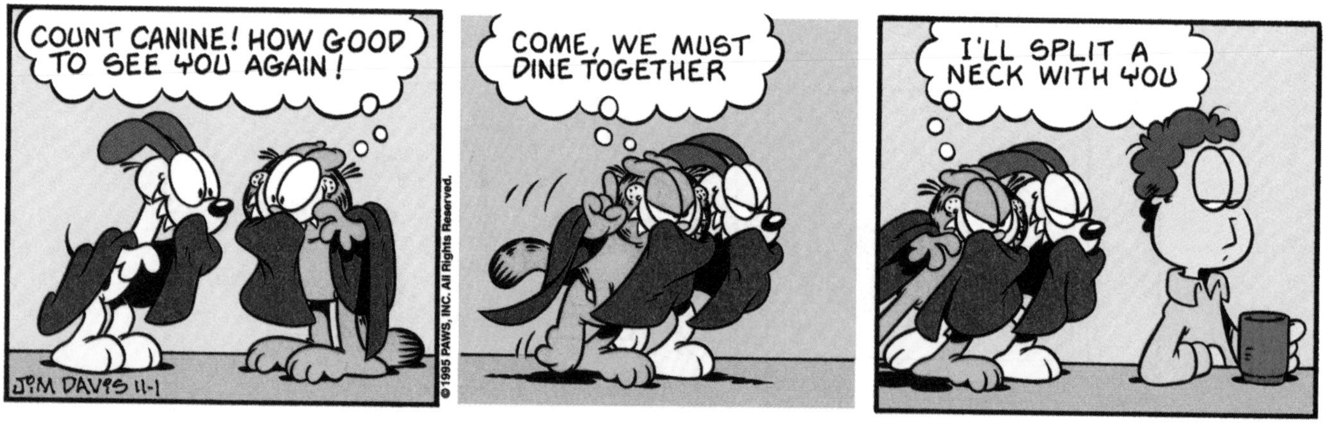
COUNT CANINE! HOW GOOD TO SEE YOU AGAIN!
JIM DAVIS 11-1
© 1995 PAWS, INC. All Rights Reserved.
COME, WE MUST DINE TOGETHER
I'LL SPLIT A NECK WITH YOU

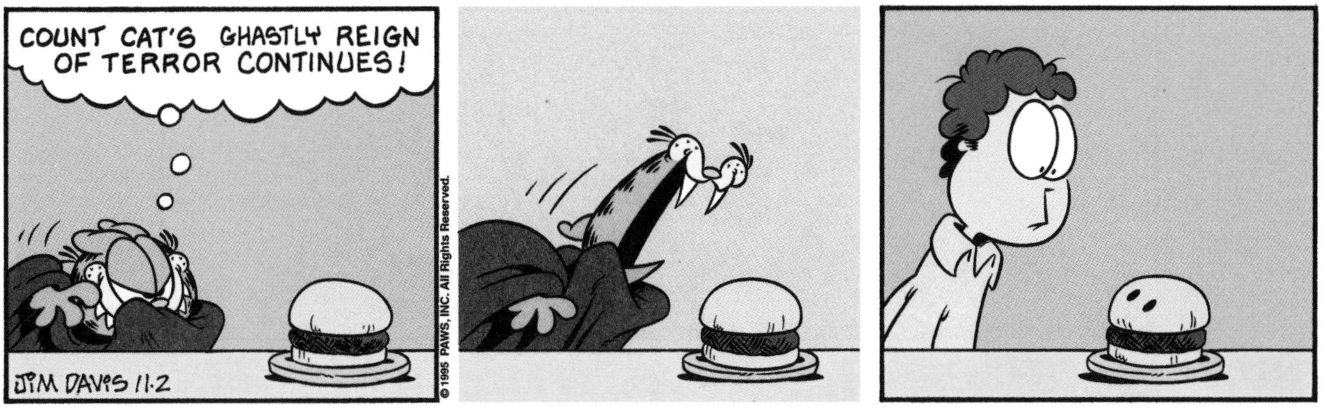
COUNT CAT'S GHASTLY REIGN OF TERROR CONTINUES!
JIM DAVIS 11·2
© 1995 PAWS, INC. All Rights Reserved.

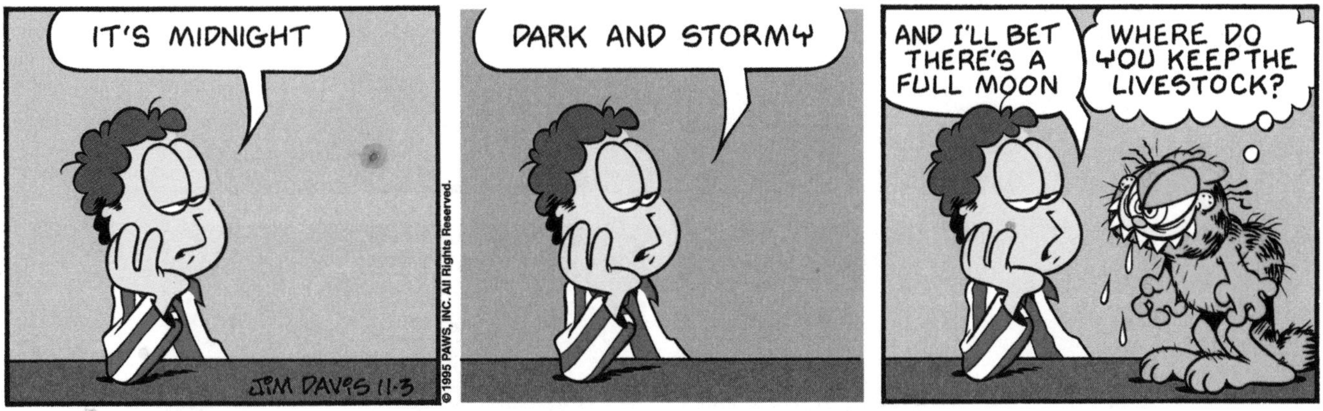
IT'S MIDNIGHT
JIM DAVIS 11·3
© 1995 PAWS, INC. All Rights Reserved.
DARK AND STORMY
AND I'LL BET THERE'S A FULL MOON
WHERE DO YOU KEEP THE LIVESTOCK?

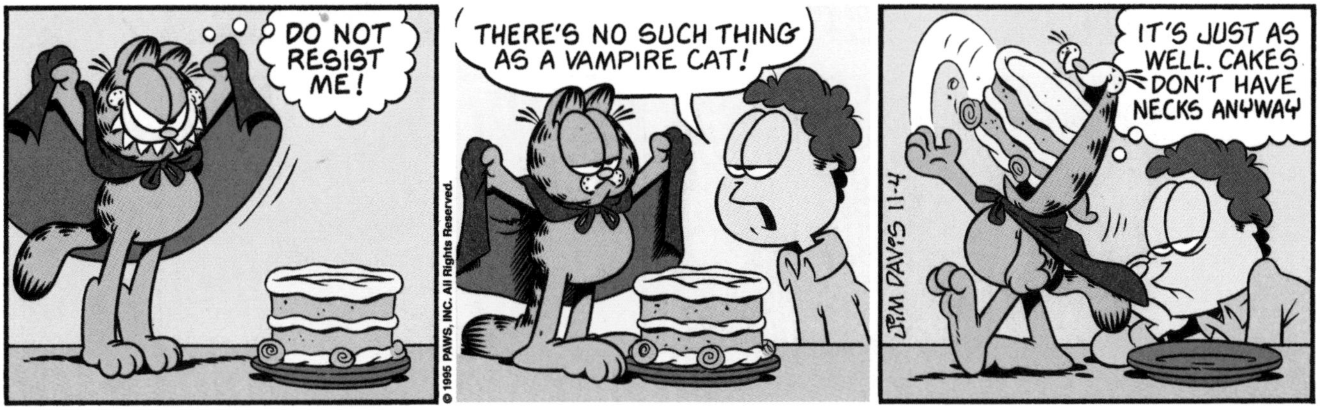
DO NOT RESIST ME!
© 1995 PAWS, INC. All Rights Reserved.
THERE'S NO SUCH THING AS A VAMPIRE CAT!
JIM DAVIS 11·4
IT'S JUST AS WELL. CAKES DON'T HAVE NECKS ANYWAY

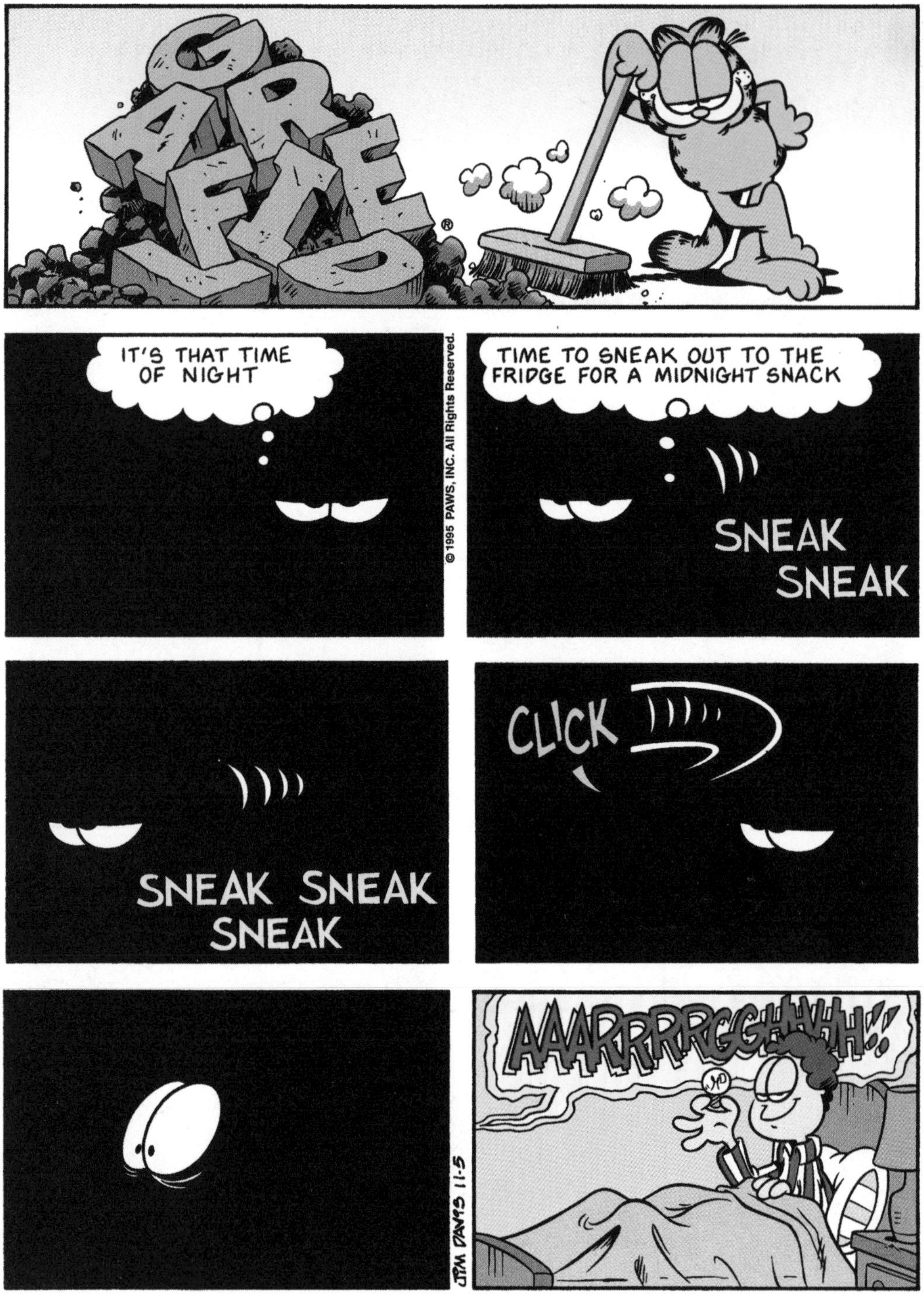
GARFIELD®
IT'S THAT TIME OF NIGHT
© 1995 PAWS, INC. All Rights Reserved.
TIME TO SNEAK OUT TO THE FRIDGE FOR A MIDNIGHT SNACK
SNEAK SNEAK
SNEAK SNEAK SNEAK
CLICK
JIM DAVIS 11-5
AAARRRRGGHHHH!!

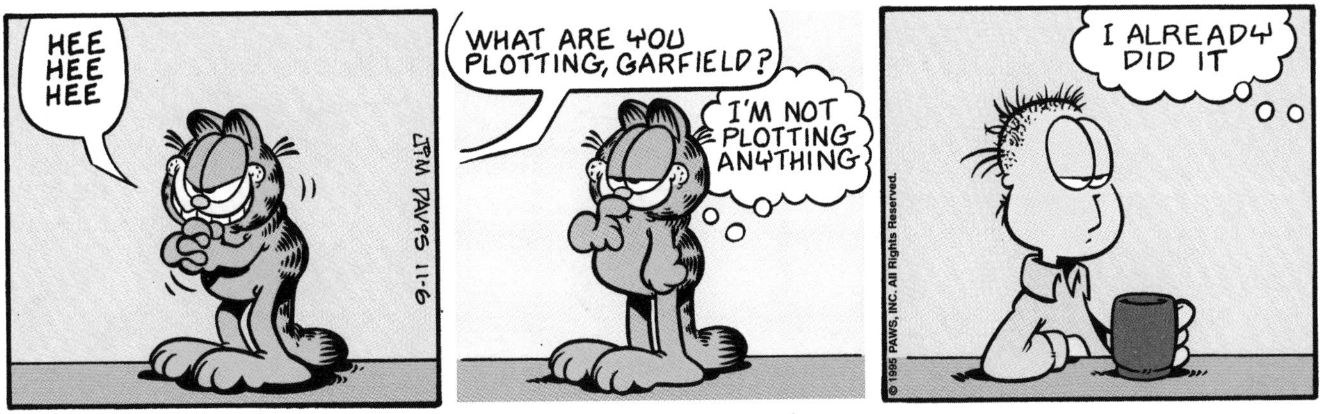
HEE HEE HEE
JIM DAVIS 11-6
WHAT ARE YOU PLOTTING, GARFIELD?
I'M NOT PLOTTING ANYTHING
© 1995 PAWS, INC. All Rights Reserved.
I ALREADY DID IT

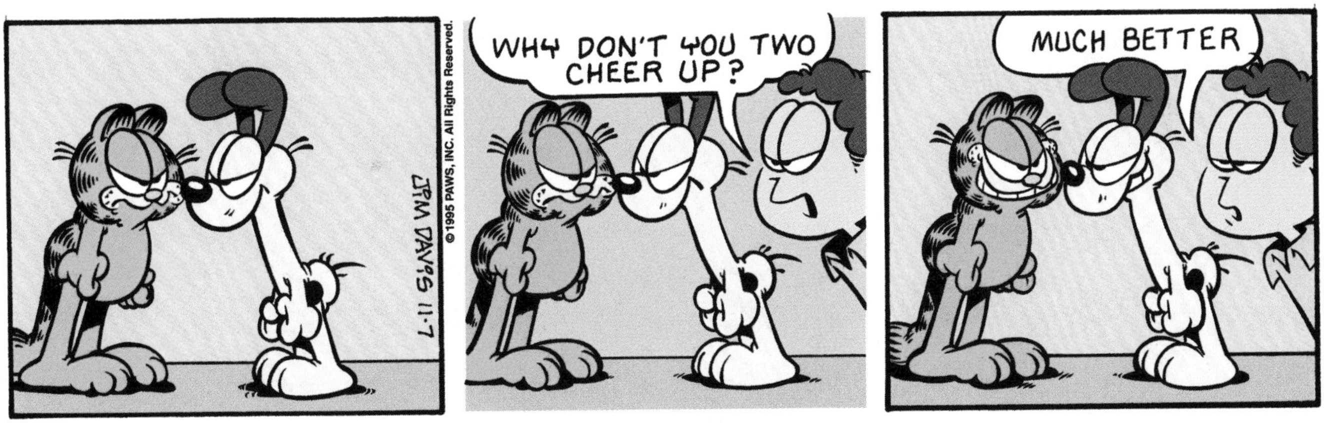
© 1995 PAWS, INC. All Rights Reserved.
JIM DAVIS 11-7
WHY DON'T YOU TWO CHEER UP?
MUCH BETTER

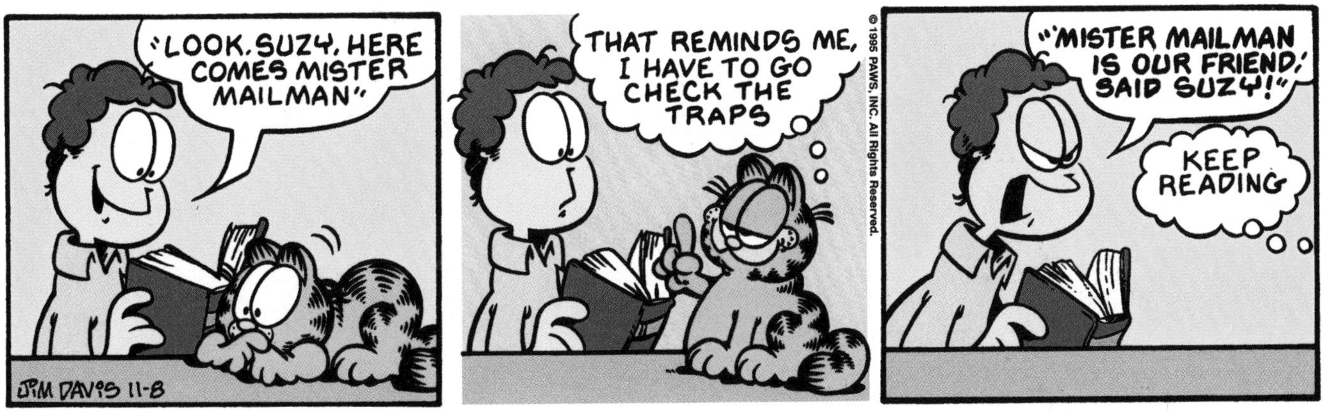
"LOOK, SUZY, HERE COMES MISTER MAILMAN"
JIM DAVIS 11-8
THAT REMINDS ME, I HAVE TO GO CHECK THE TRAPS
© 1995 PAWS, INC. All Rights Reserved.
"'MISTER MAILMAN IS OUR FRIEND,' SAID SUZY!"
KEEP READING

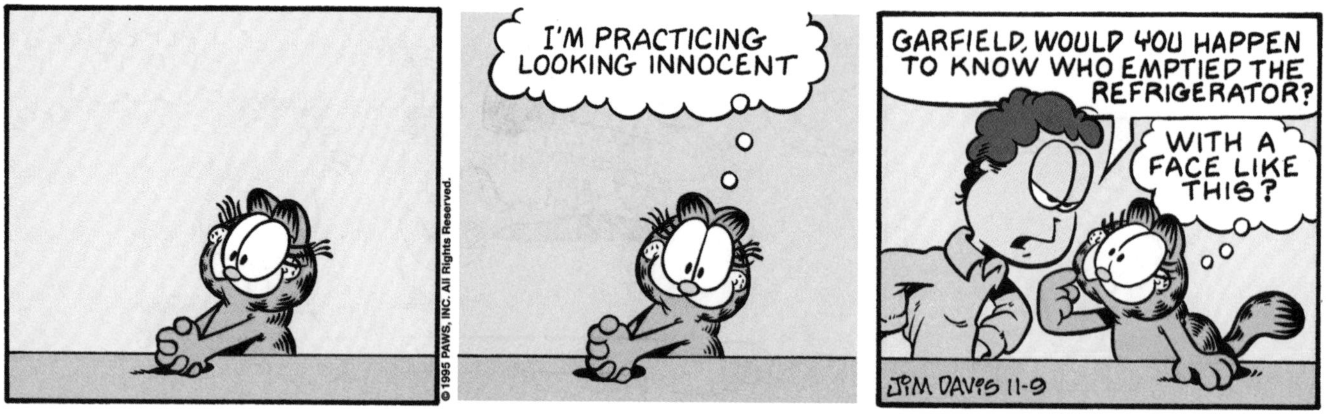
I'M PRACTICING LOOKING INNOCENT
GARFIELD, WOULD YOU HAPPEN TO KNOW WHO EMPTIED THE REFRIGERATOR?
WITH A FACE LIKE THIS?
© 1995 PAWS, INC. All Rights Reserved.
JIM DAVIS 11-9

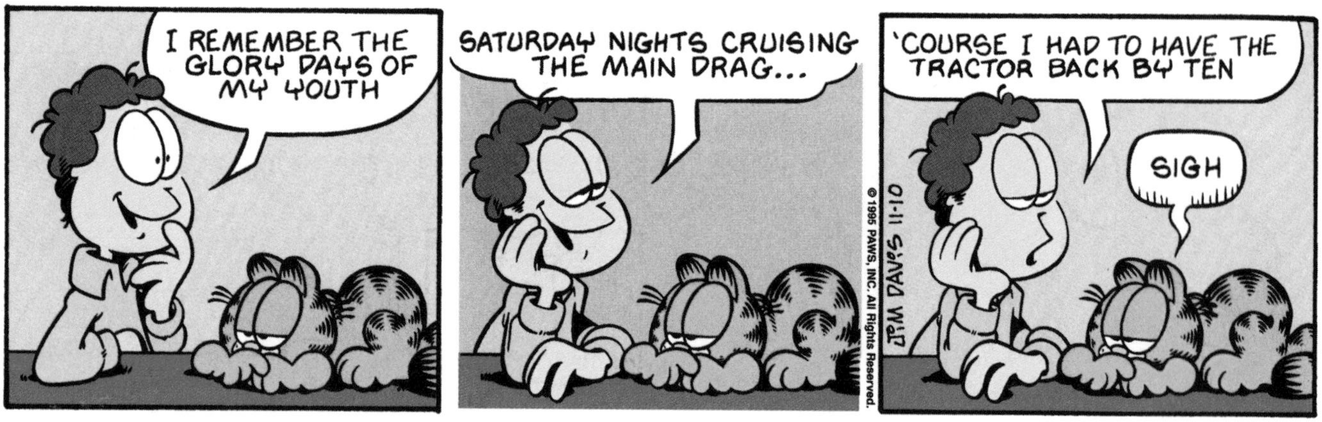
I REMEMBER THE GLORY DAYS OF MY YOUTH
SATURDAY NIGHTS CRUISING THE MAIN DRAG...
'COURSE I HAD TO HAVE THE TRACTOR BACK BY TEN
SIGH
© 1995 PAWS, INC. All Rights Reserved.
JIM DAVIS 11-10

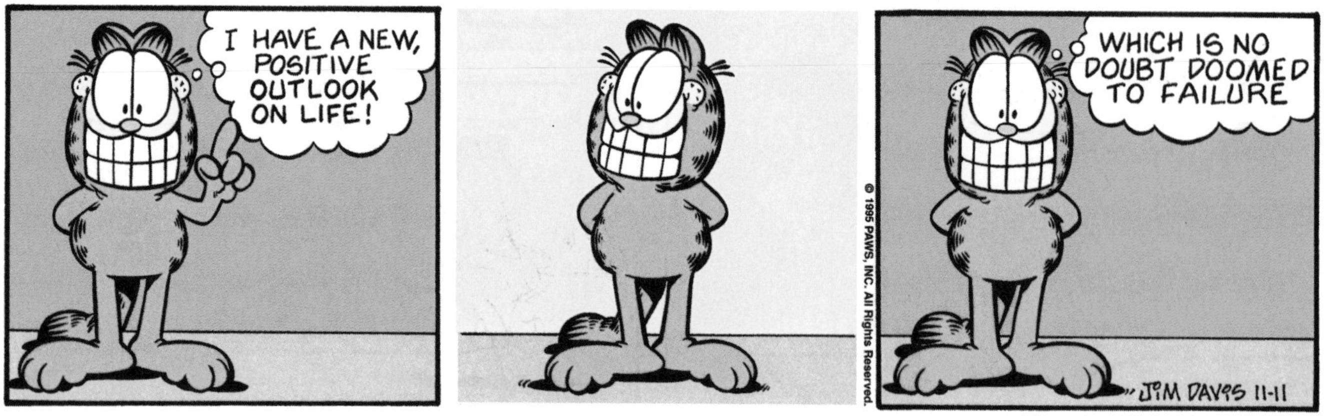
I HAVE A NEW, POSITIVE OUTLOOK ON LIFE!
WHICH IS NO DOUBT DOOMED TO FAILURE
© 1995 PAWS, INC. All Rights Reserved.
JIM DAVIS 11-11

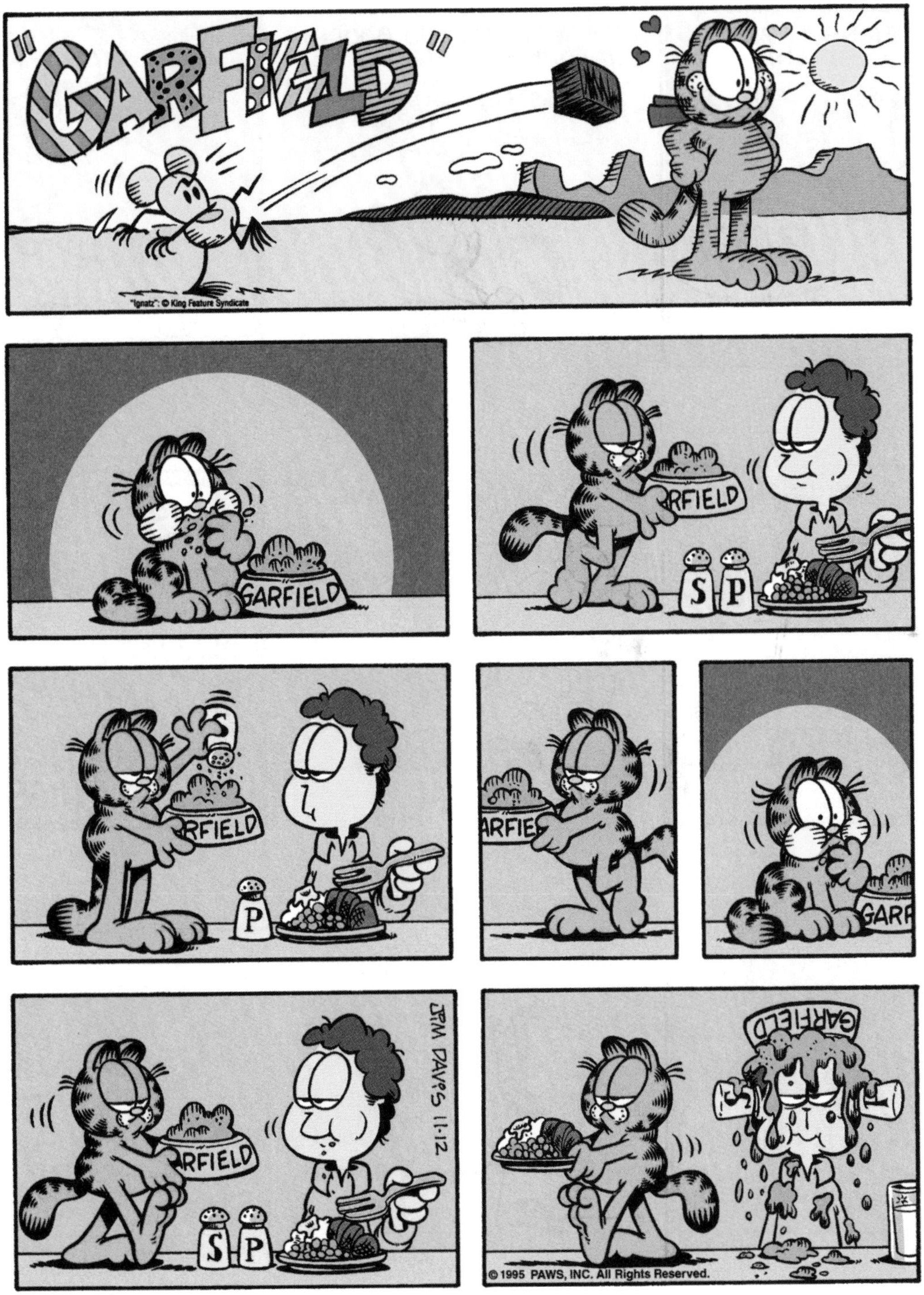
"GARFIELD"
"Ignatz": © King Feature Syndicate
GARFIELD
RFIELD
S
P
RFIELD
ARFIE
GARF
JPM DAVIS 11-12
RFIELD
GARFIELD
© 1995 PAWS, INC. All Rights Reserved.

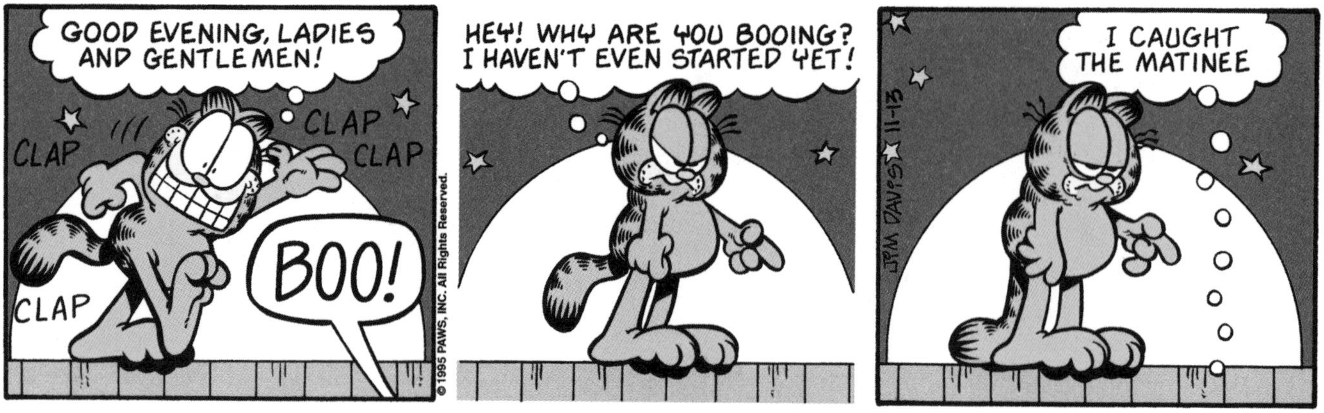
GOOD EVENING, LADIES AND GENTLEMEN!
CLAP
CLAP
CLAP
CLAP
BOO!
© 1995 PAWS, INC. All Rights Reserved.
HEY! WHY ARE YOU BOOING? I HAVEN'T EVEN STARTED YET!
JIM DAVIS 11-13
I CAUGHT THE MATINEE

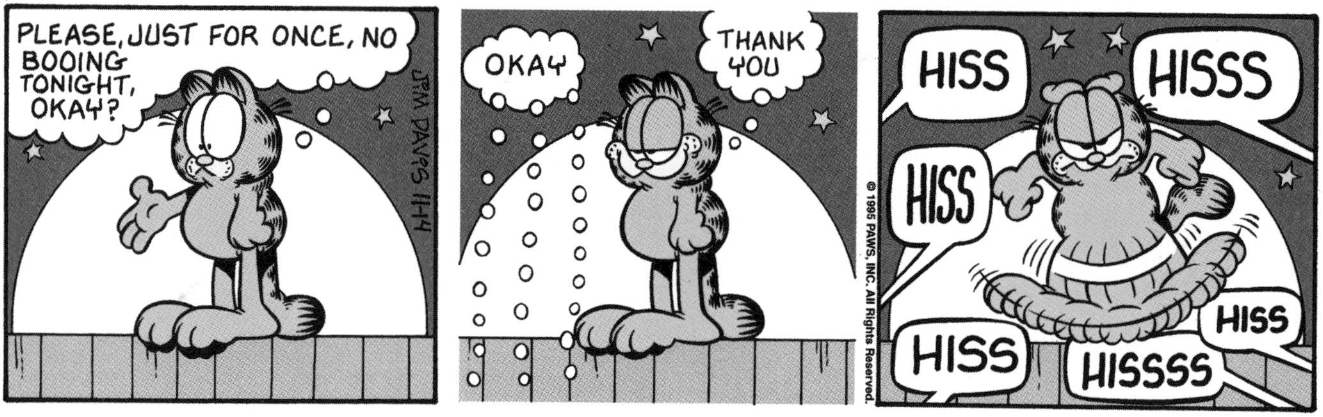
PLEASE, JUST FOR ONCE, NO BOOING TONIGHT, OKAY?
JIM DAVIS 11-14
OKAY
THANK YOU
© 1995 PAWS, INC. All Rights Reserved.
HISS
HISSS
HISS
HISS
HISSSS
HISS

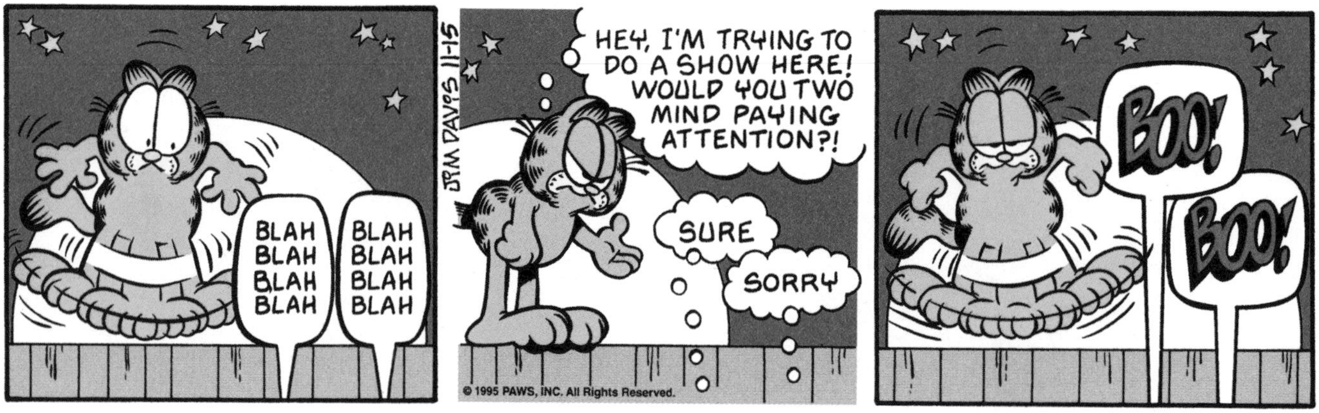
BLAH BLAH BLAH BLAH
BLAH BLAH BLAH BLAH
JIM DAVIS 11-15
HEY, I'M TRYING TO DO A SHOW HERE! WOULD YOU TWO MIND PAYING ATTENTION?!
SURE
SORRY
© 1995 PAWS, INC. All Rights Reserved.
BOO!
BOO!

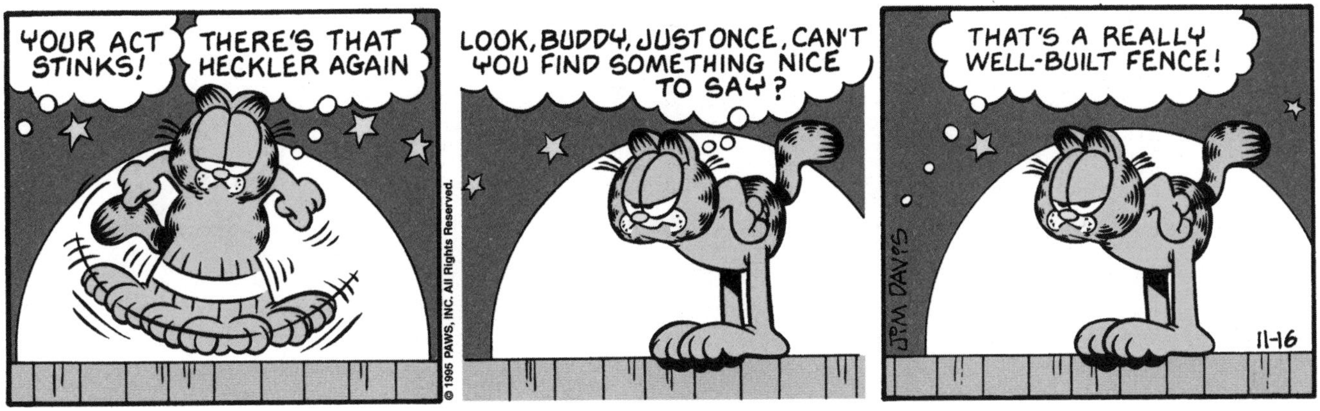
YOUR ACT STINKS!
THERE'S THAT HECKLER AGAIN
LOOK, BUDDY, JUST ONCE, CAN'T YOU FIND SOMETHING NICE TO SAY?
© 1995 PAWS, INC. All Rights Reserved.
THAT'S A REALLY WELL-BUILT FENCE!
JIM DAVIS
11-16

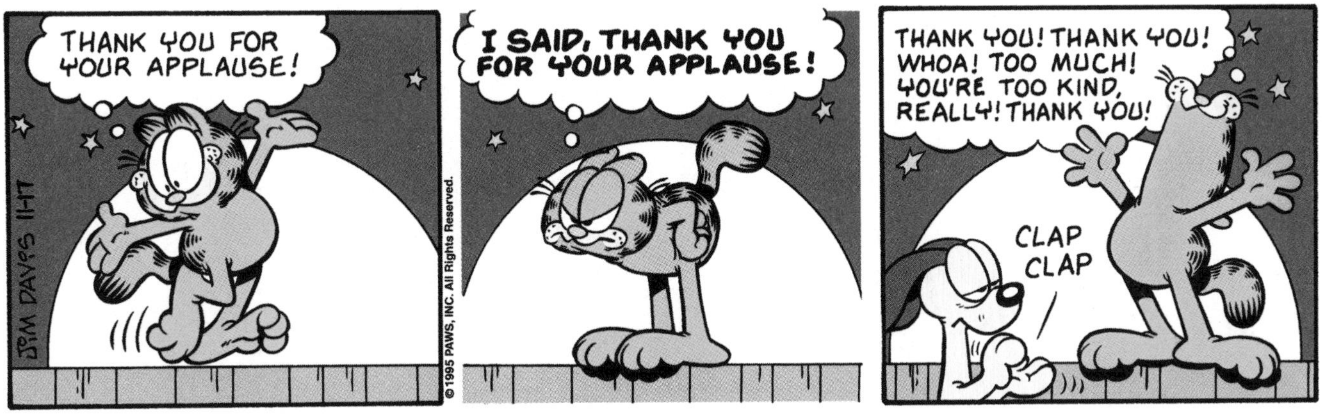
THANK YOU FOR YOUR APPLAUSE!
JIM DAVIS 11-17
© 1995 PAWS, INC. All Rights Reserved.
I SAID, THANK YOU FOR YOUR APPLAUSE!
THANK YOU! THANK YOU! WHOA! TOO MUCH! YOU'RE TOO KIND, REALLY! THANK YOU!
CLAP CLAP

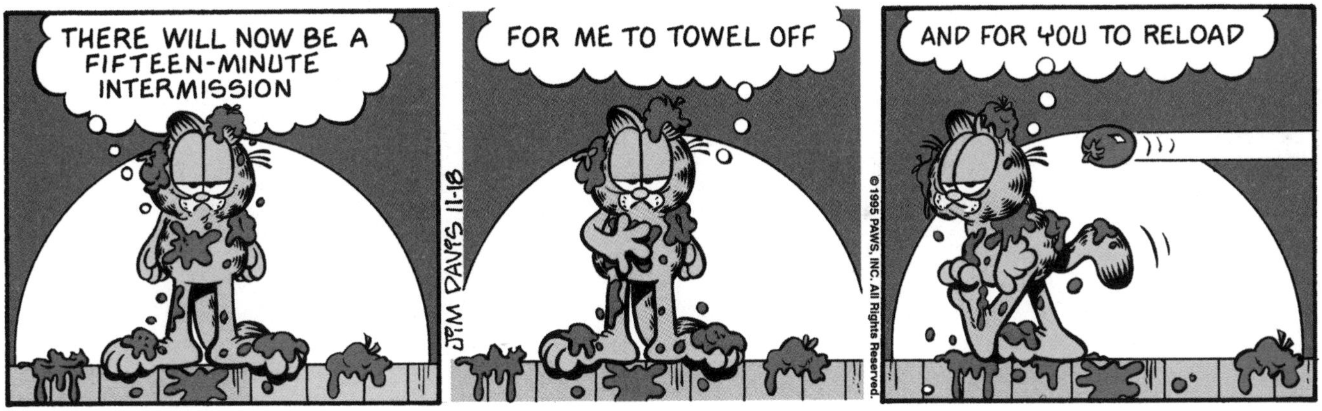
THERE WILL NOW BE A FIFTEEN-MINUTE INTERMISSION
JIM DAVIS 11-18
FOR ME TO TOWEL OFF
© 1995 PAWS, INC. All Rights Reserved.
AND FOR YOU TO RELOAD

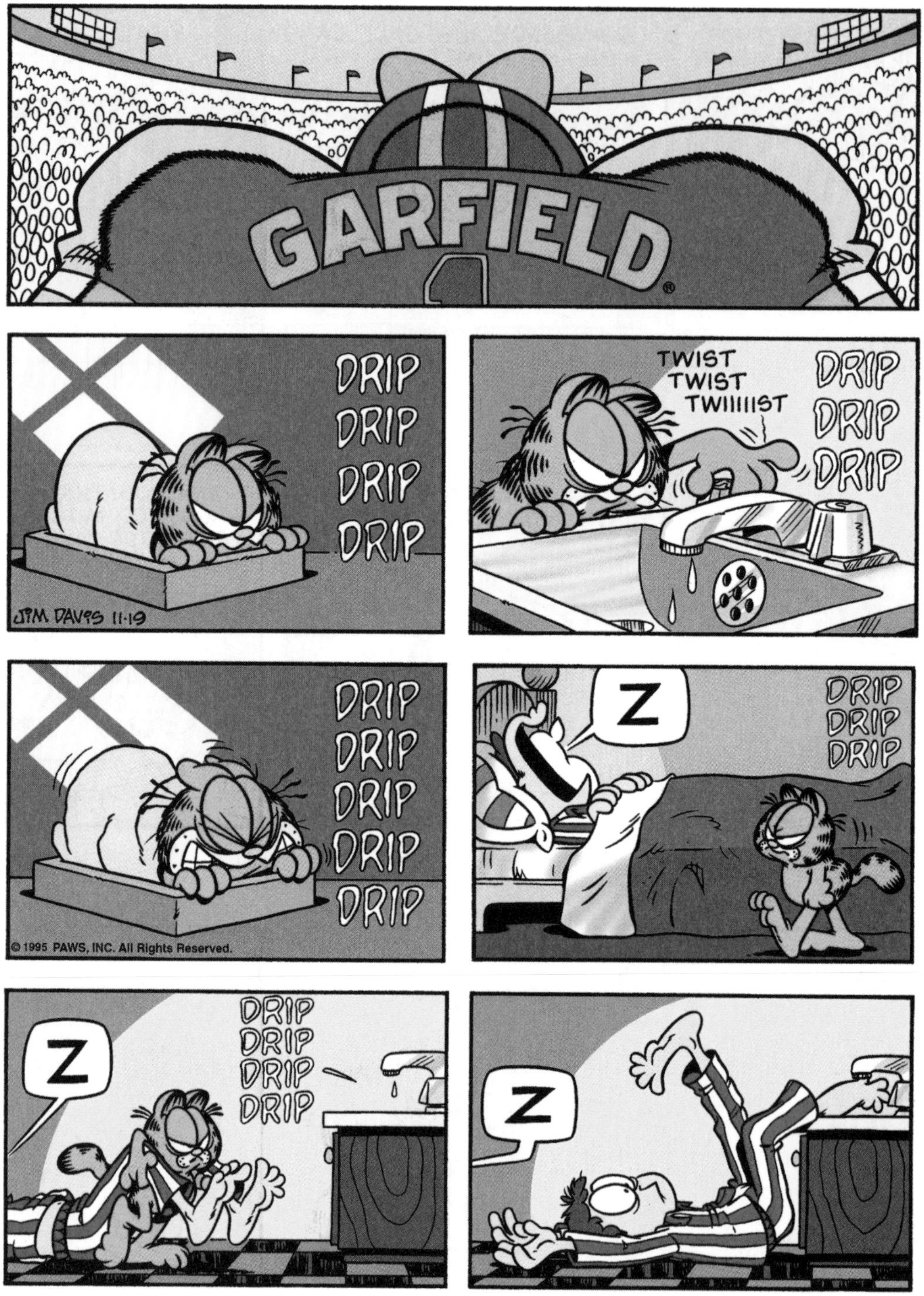
GARFIELD®
DRIP DRIP DRIP DRIP
JIM DAVIS 11-19
TWIST TWIST TWIIIIIST
DRIP DRIP DRIP
DRIP DRIP DRIP DRIP DRIP
© 1995 PAWS, INC. All Rights Reserved.
Z
DRIP DRIP DRIP
Z
DRIP DRIP DRIP DRIP
Z

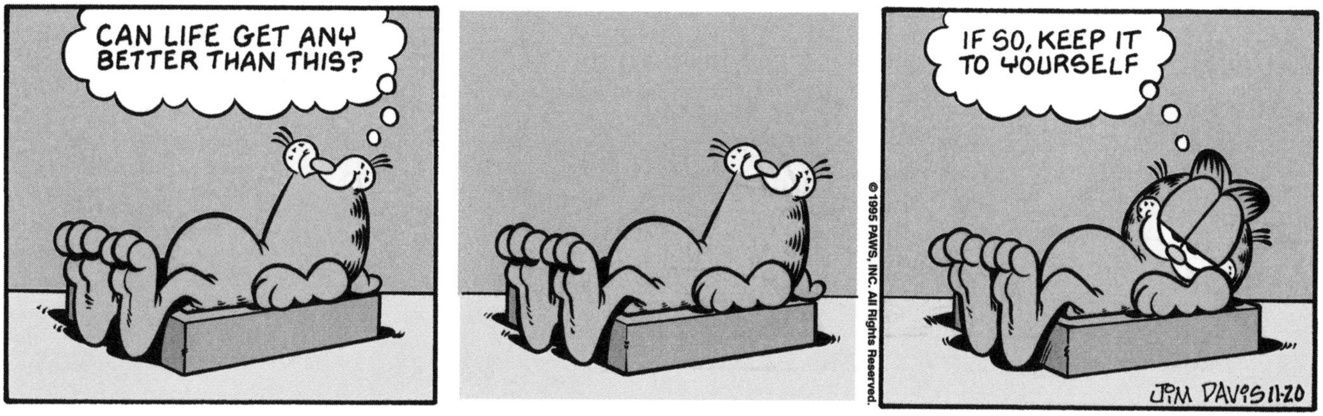
CAN LIFE GET ANY BETTER THAN THIS?
IF SO, KEEP IT TO YOURSELF
JIM DAVIS 11-20
© 1995 PAWS, INC. All Rights Reserved.

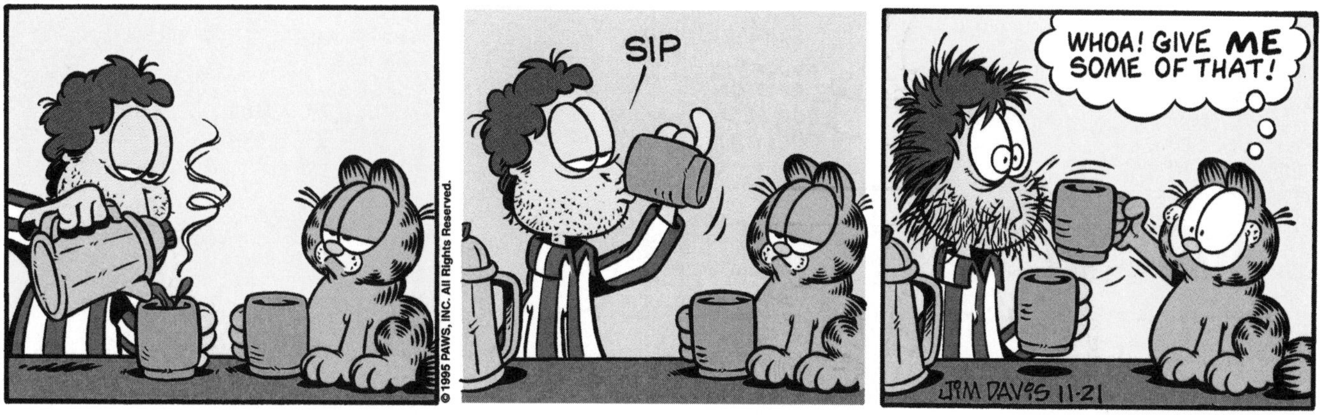
SIP
WHOA! GIVE **ME** SOME OF THAT!
JIM DAVIS 11-21
© 1995 PAWS, INC. All Rights Reserved.

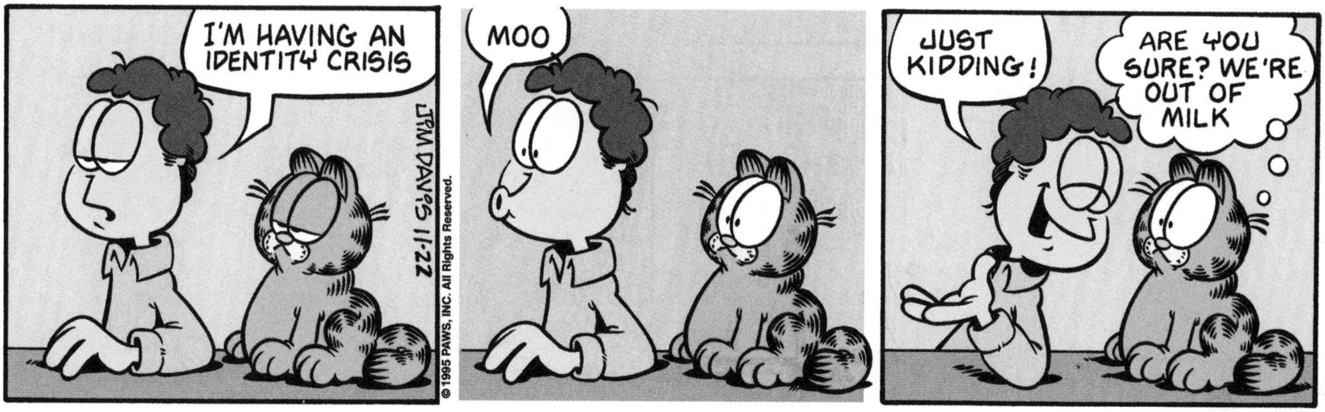
I'M HAVING AN IDENTITY CRISIS
MOO
JUST KIDDING!
ARE YOU SURE? WE'RE OUT OF MILK
JIM DAVIS 11-22
© 1995 PAWS, INC. All Rights Reserved.

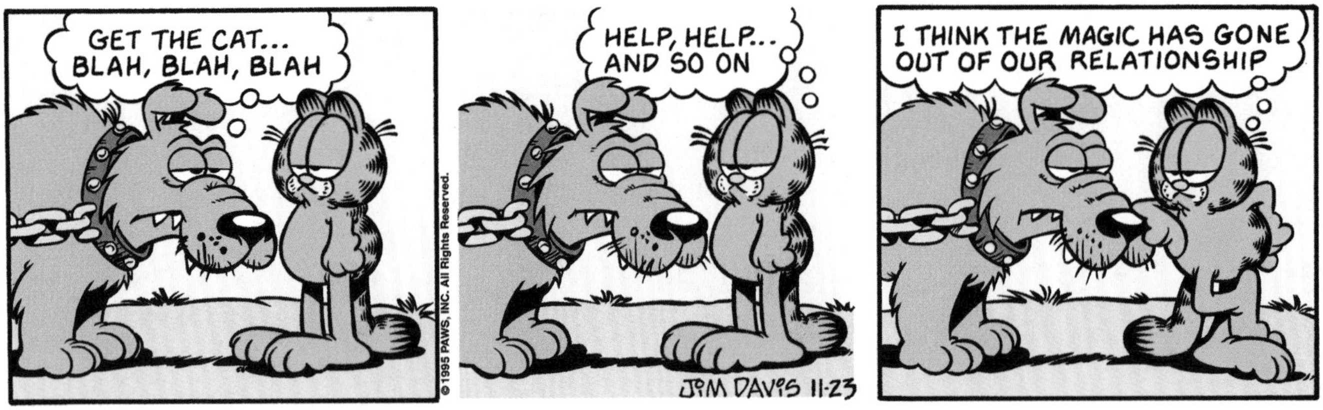
GET THE CAT... BLAH, BLAH, BLAH
© 1995 PAWS, INC. All Rights Reserved.
HELP, HELP... AND SO ON
JIM DAVIS 11-23
I THINK THE MAGIC HAS GONE OUT OF OUR RELATIONSHIP

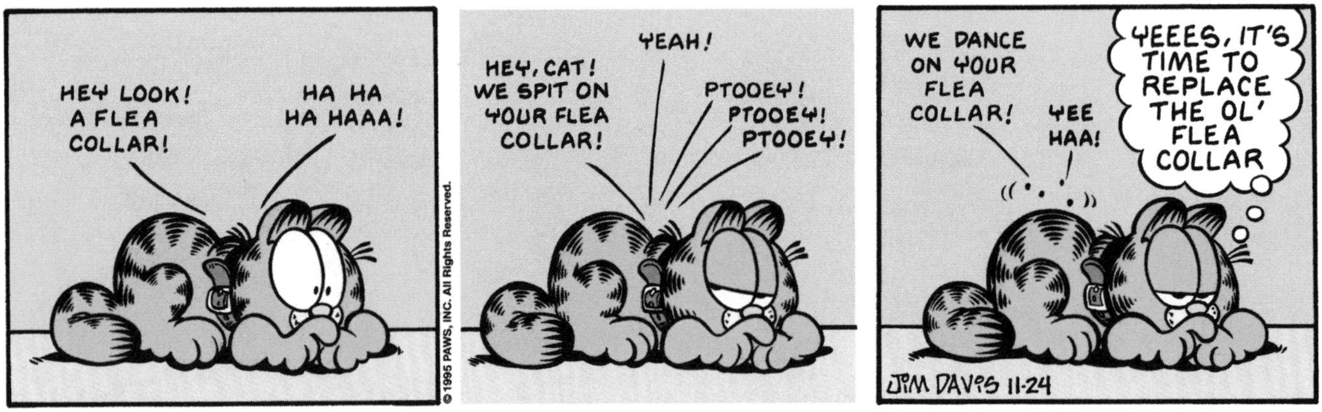
HEY LOOK! A FLEA COLLAR!
HA HA HA HAAA!
© 1995 PAWS, INC. All Rights Reserved.
HEY, CAT! WE SPIT ON YOUR FLEA COLLAR!
YEAH!
PTOOEY! PTOOEY! PTOOEY!
WE DANCE ON YOUR FLEA COLLAR!
YEE HAA!
YEEES, IT'S TIME TO REPLACE THE OL' FLEA COLLAR
JIM DAVIS 11-24

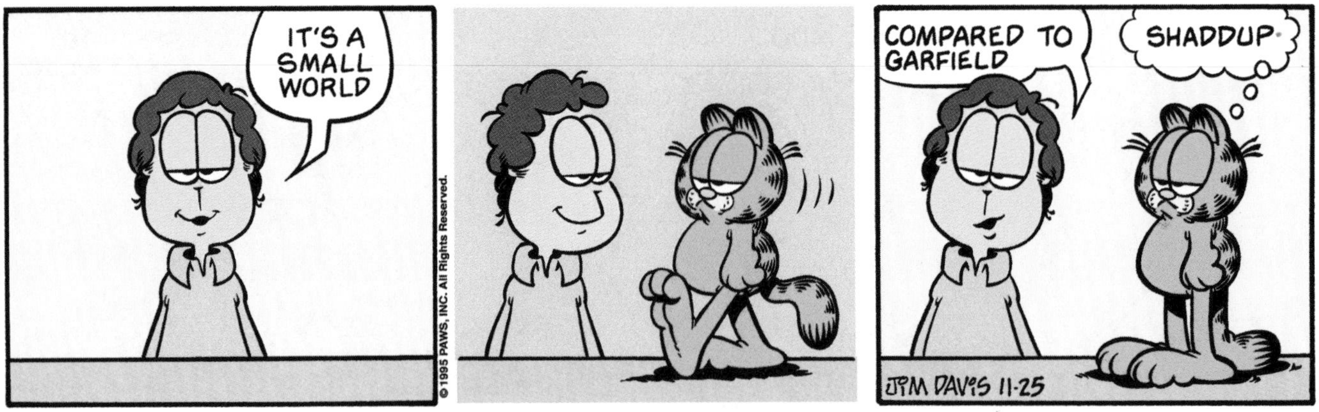
IT'S A SMALL WORLD
© 1995 PAWS, INC. All Rights Reserved.
COMPARED TO GARFIELD
SHADDUP
JIM DAVIS 11-25

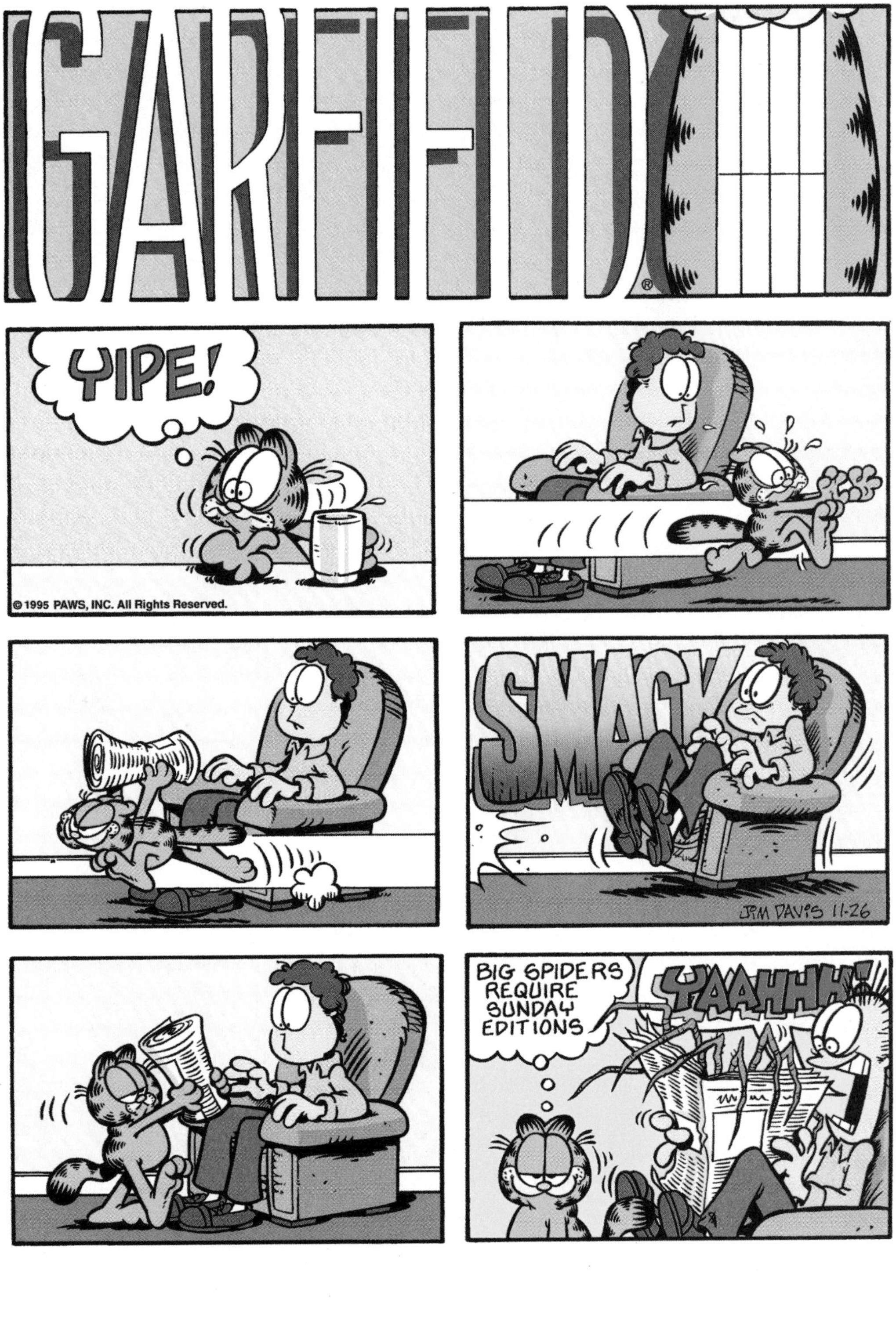
GARFIELD
YIPE!
© 1995 PAWS, INC. All Rights Reserved.
SMACK
JIM DAVIS 11-26
BIG SPIDERS REQUIRE SUNDAY EDITIONS
YAAHHH!

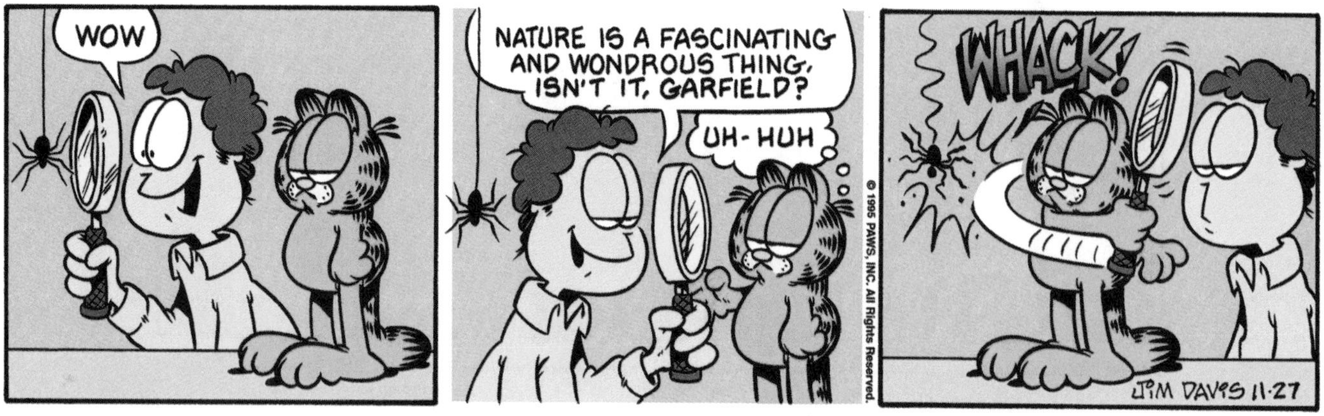
WOW
NATURE IS A FASCINATING AND WONDROUS THING, ISN'T IT, GARFIELD?
UH-HUH
© 1995 PAWS, INC. All Rights Reserved.
WHACK!
JIM DAVIS 11-27

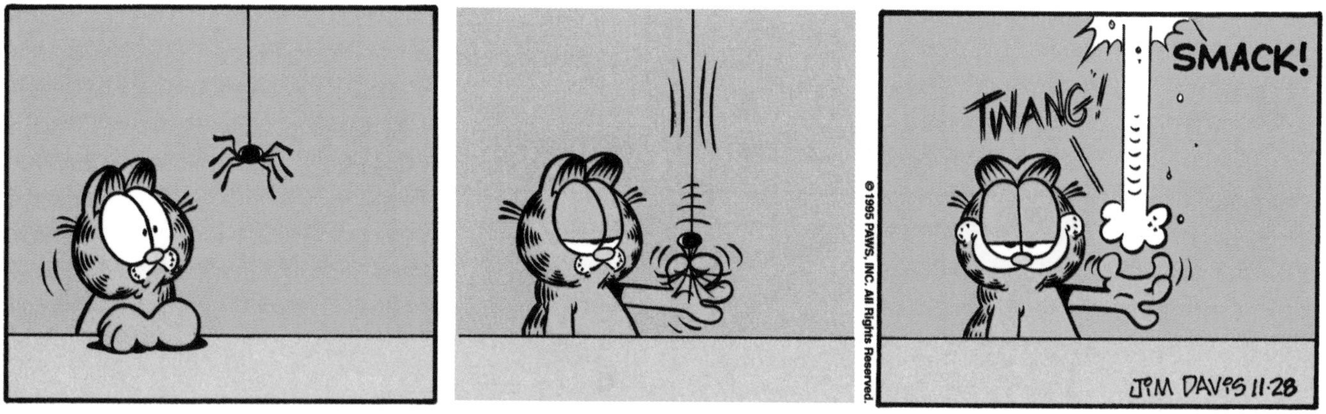
© 1995 PAWS, INC. All Rights Reserved.
TWANG!
SMACK!
JIM DAVIS 11-28

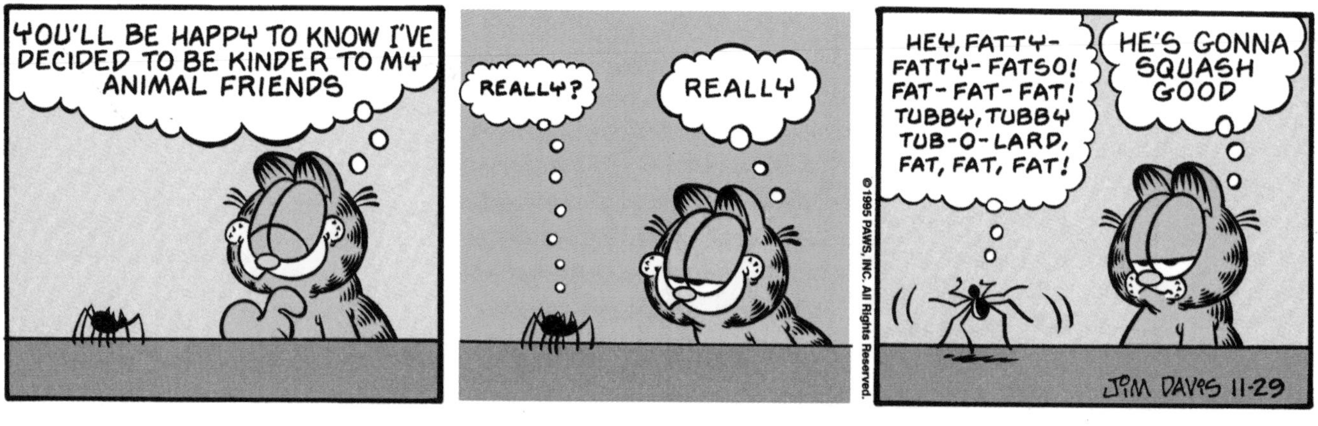
YOU'LL BE HAPPY TO KNOW I'VE DECIDED TO BE KINDER TO MY ANIMAL FRIENDS
REALLY?
REALLY
© 1995 PAWS, INC. All Rights Reserved.
HEY, FATTY-FATTY-FATSO! FAT-FAT-FAT! TUBBY, TUBBY TUB-O-LARD, FAT, FAT, FAT!
HE'S GONNA SQUASH GOOD
JIM DAVIS 11-29

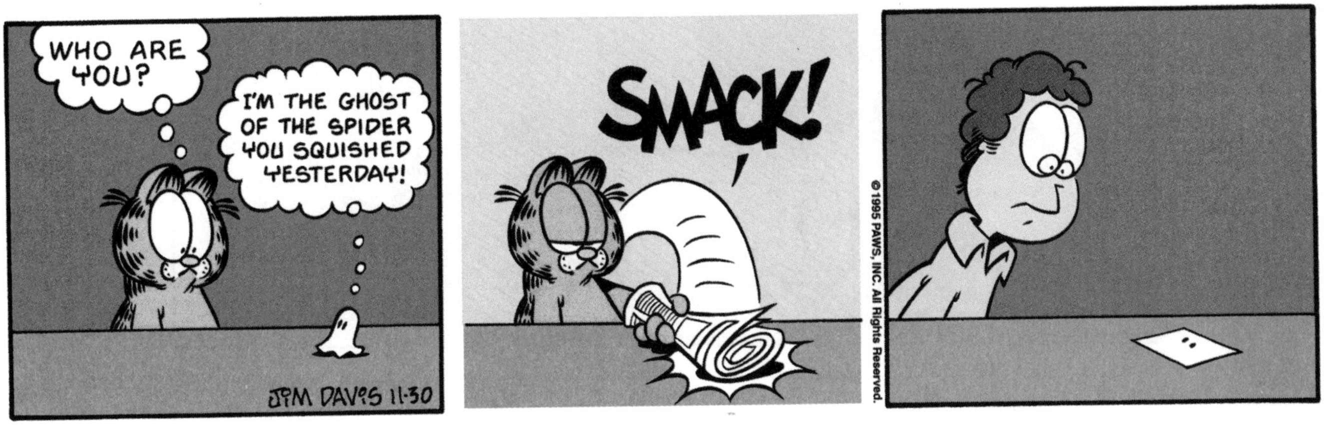
WHO ARE YOU?
I'M THE GHOST OF THE SPIDER YOU SQUISHED YESTERDAY!
JIM DAVIS 11-30
SMACK!
© 1995 PAWS, INC. All Rights Reserved.

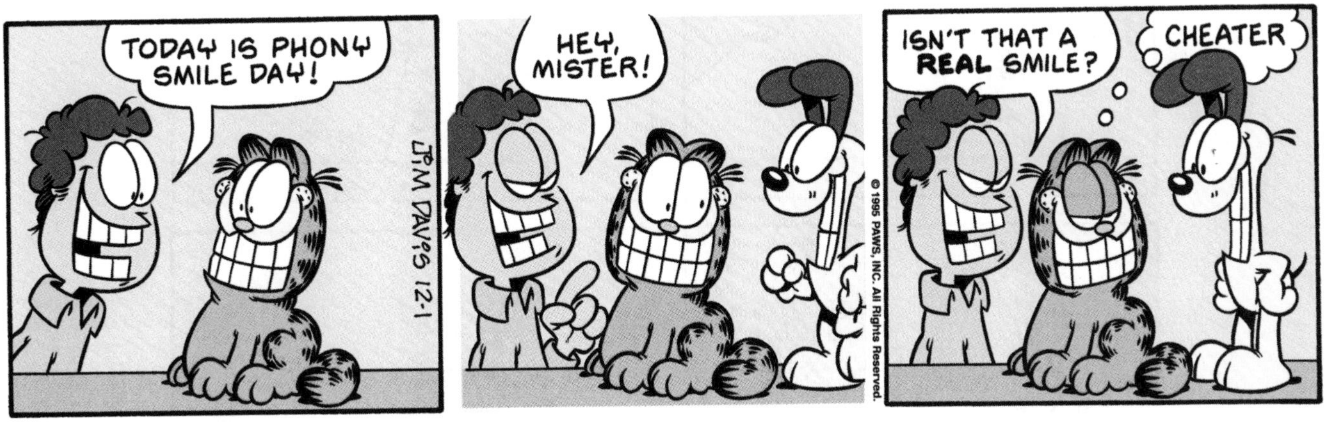
TODAY IS PHONY SMILE DAY!
JIM DAVIS 12-1
HEY, MISTER!
© 1995 PAWS, INC. All Rights Reserved.
ISN'T THAT A **REAL** SMILE?
CHEATER

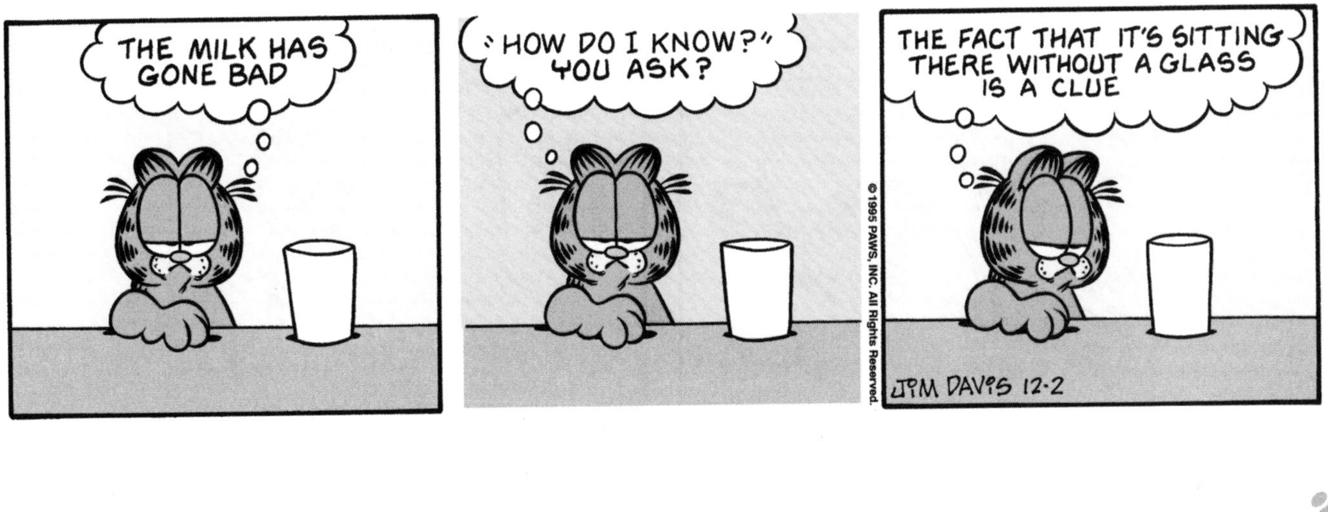
THE MILK HAS GONE BAD
"HOW DO I KNOW?" YOU ASK?
© 1995 PAWS, INC. All Rights Reserved.
THE FACT THAT IT'S SITTING THERE WITHOUT A GLASS IS A CLUE
JIM DAVIS 12-2

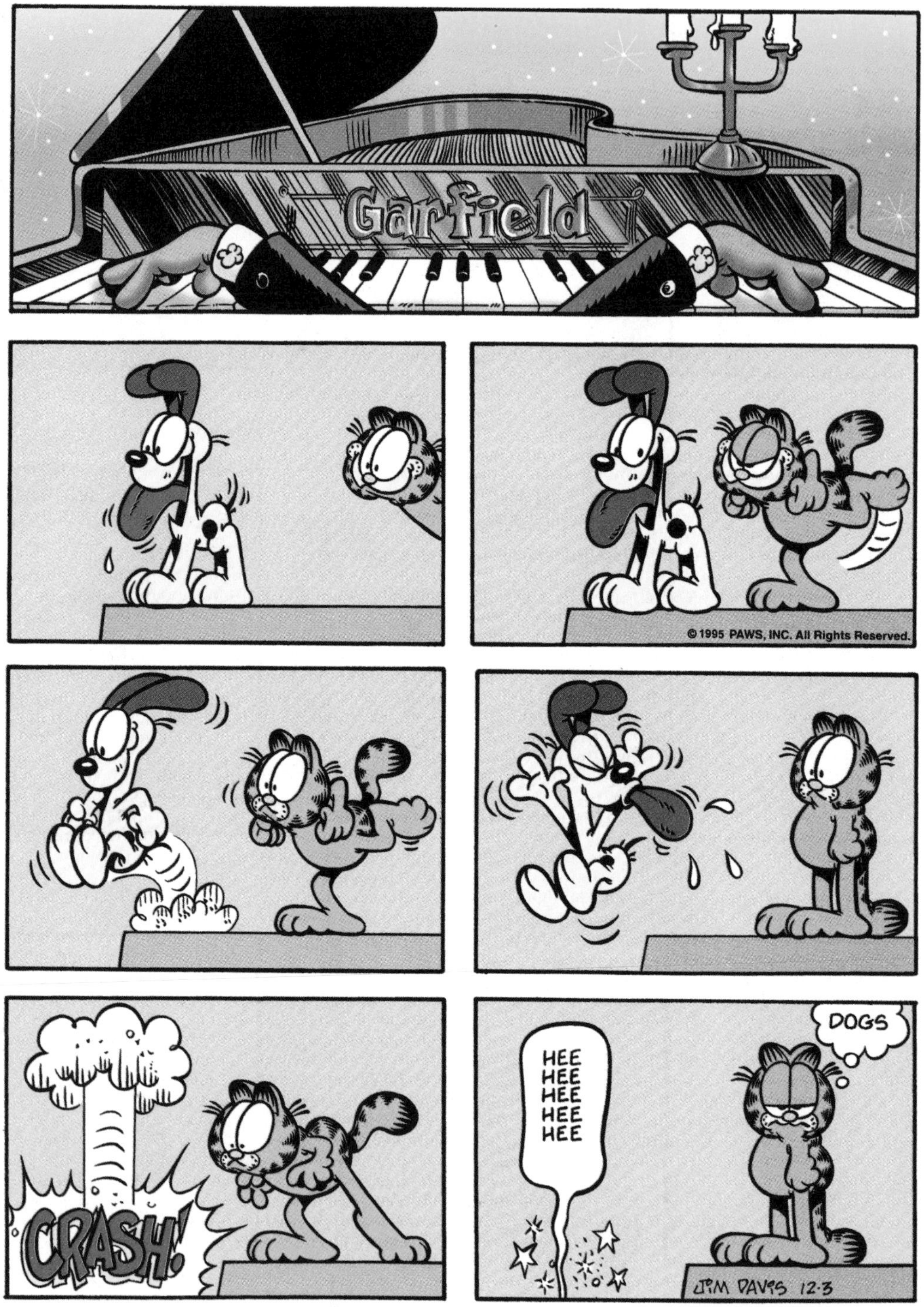
Garfield
© 1995 PAWS, INC. All Rights Reserved.
CRASH!
HEE HEE HEE HEE HEE
DOGS
JIM DAVIS 12-3

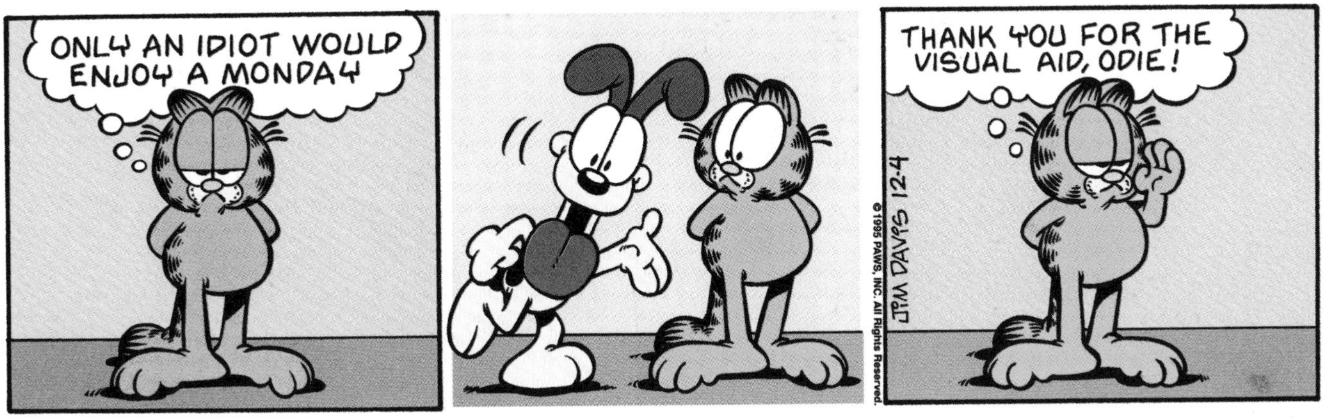
ONLY AN IDIOT WOULD ENJOY A MONDAY
THANK YOU FOR THE VISUAL AID, ODIE!
JIM DAVIS 12-4
© 1995 PAWS, INC. All Rights Reserved.

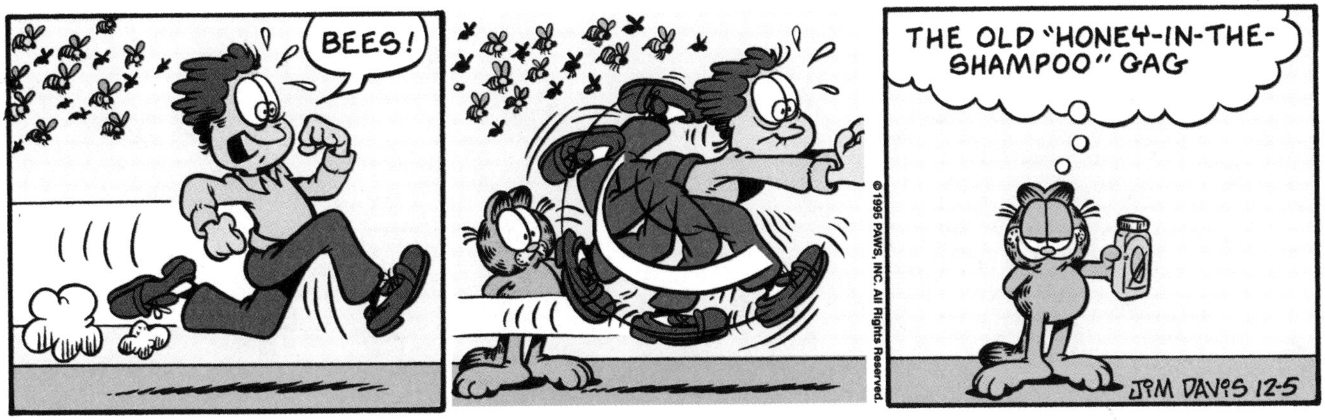
BEES!
THE OLD "HONEY-IN-THE-SHAMPOO" GAG
JIM DAVIS 12-5
© 1995 PAWS, INC. All Rights Reserved.

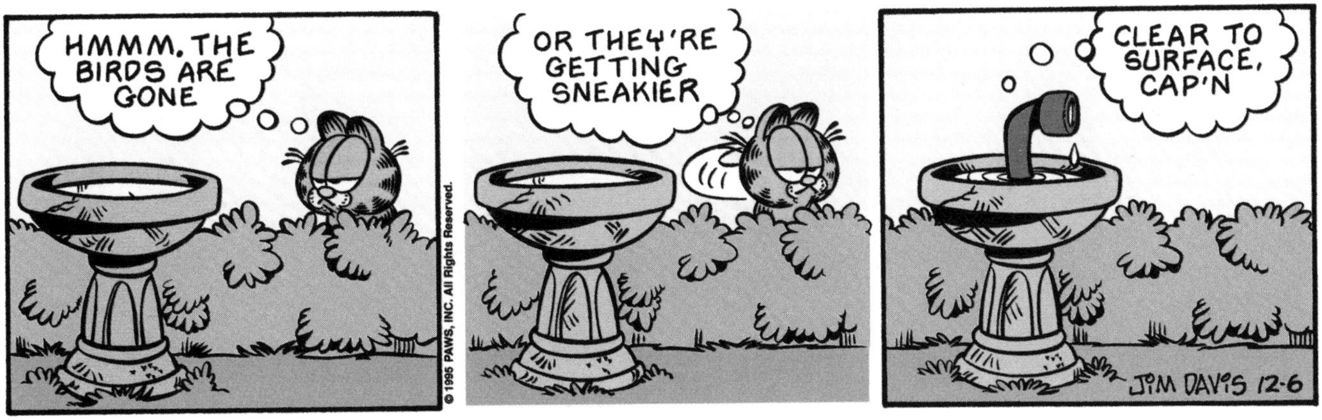
HMMM. THE BIRDS ARE GONE
OR THEY'RE GETTING SNEAKIER
CLEAR TO SURFACE, CAP'N
JIM DAVIS 12-6
© 1995 PAWS, INC. All Rights Reserved.

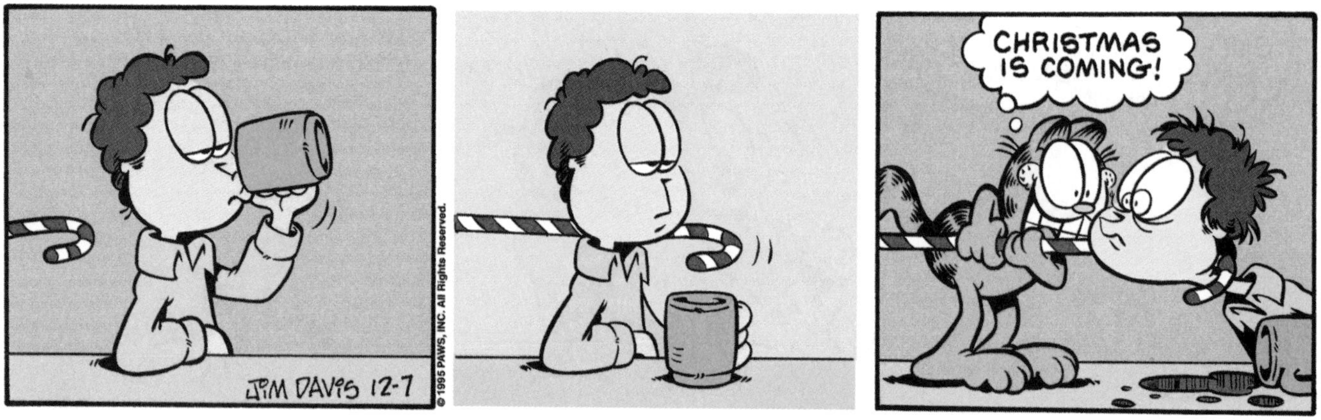
JIM DAVIS 12-7
© 1995 PAWS, INC. All Rights Reserved.
CHRISTMAS IS COMING!

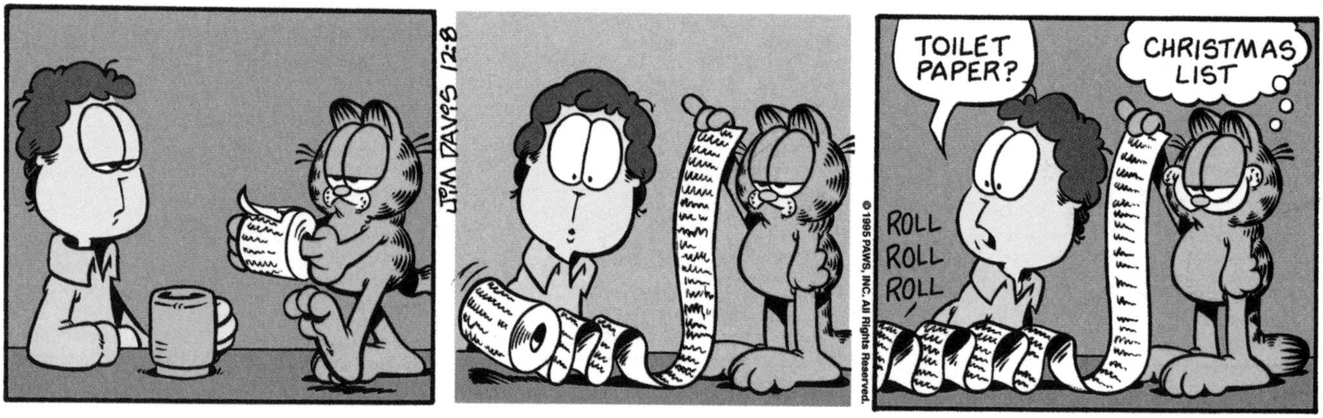
JIM DAVIS 12-8
© 1995 PAWS, INC. All Rights Reserved.
TOILET PAPER?
ROLL ROLL ROLL
CHRISTMAS LIST

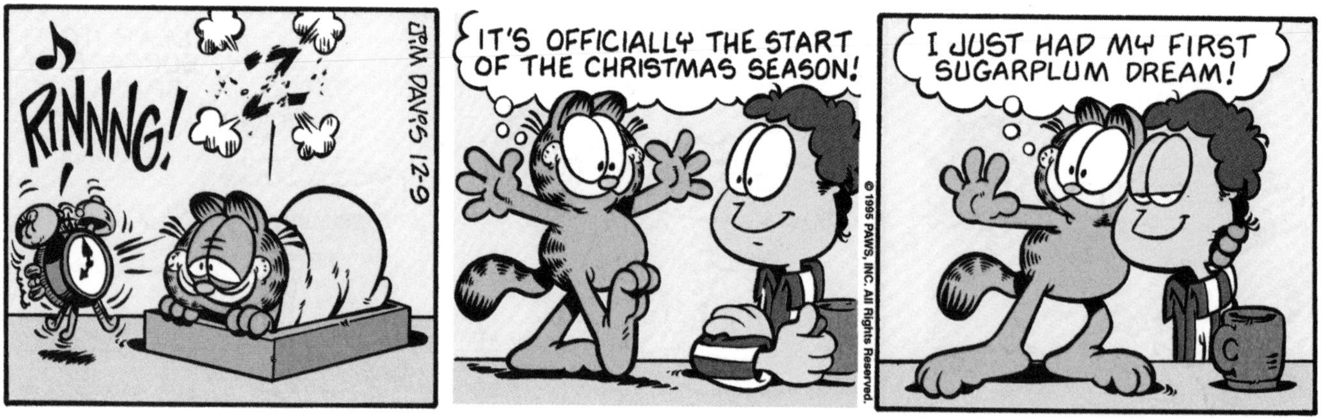
RINNNG!
JIM DAVIS 12-9
IT'S OFFICIALLY THE START OF THE CHRISTMAS SEASON!
© 1995 PAWS, INC. All Rights Reserved.
I JUST HAD MY FIRST SUGARPLUM DREAM!

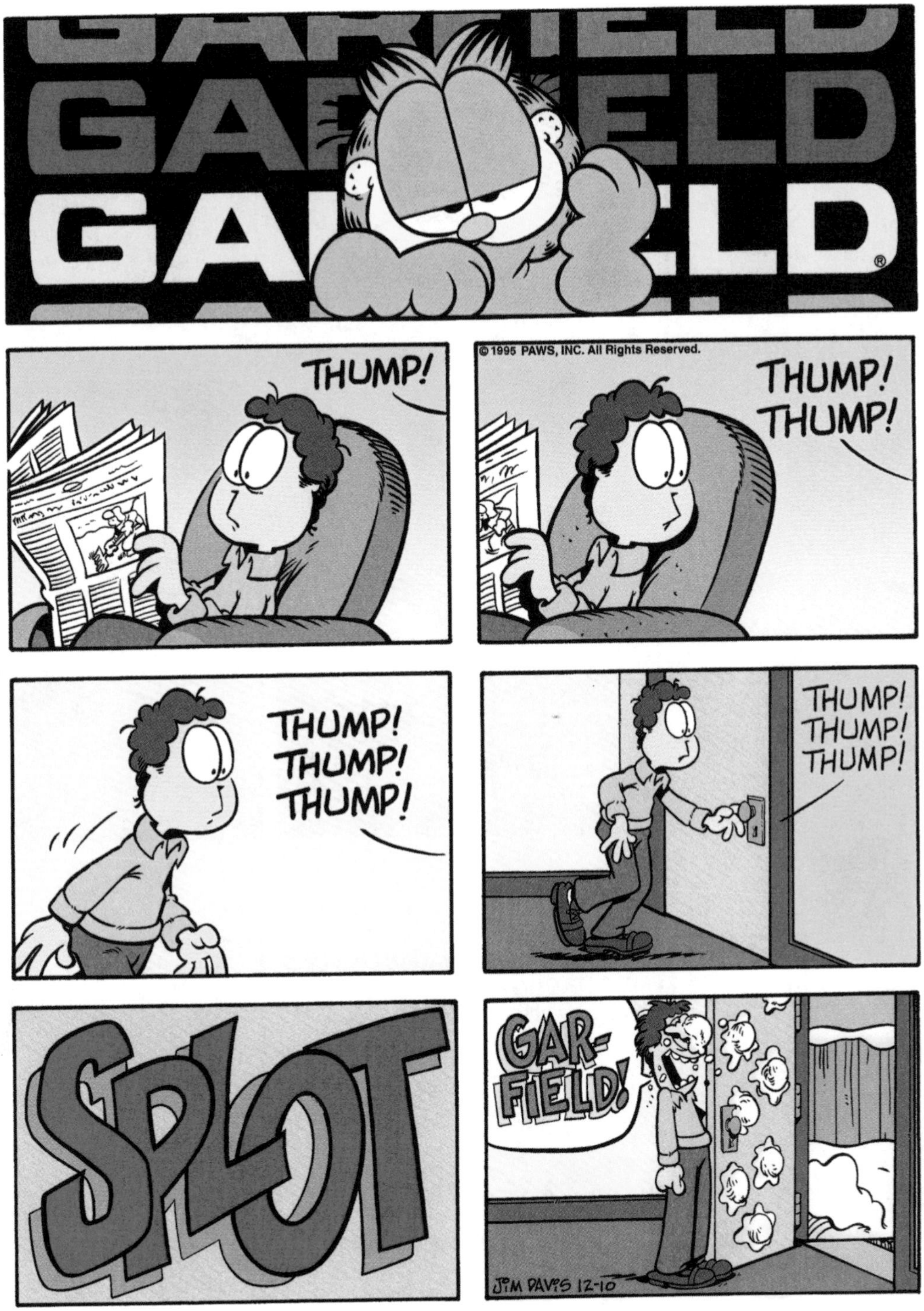
GARFIELD
© 1995 PAWS, INC. All Rights Reserved.
THUMP!
THUMP! THUMP!
THUMP! THUMP! THUMP!
THUMP! THUMP! THUMP!
SPLOT
GAR-FIELD!
JIM DAVIS 12-10

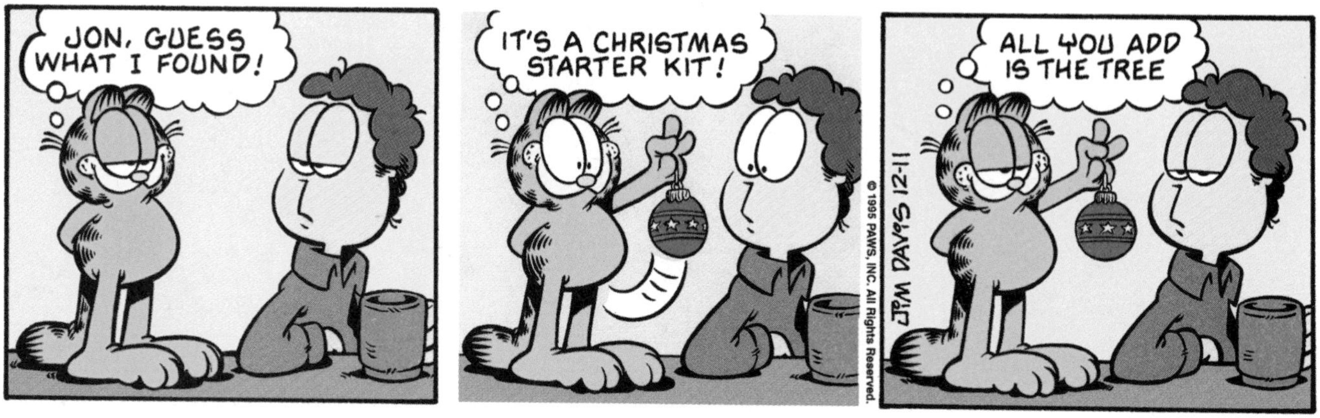
JON, GUESS WHAT I FOUND!
IT'S A CHRISTMAS STARTER KIT!
ALL YOU ADD IS THE TREE
© 1995 PAWS, INC. All Rights Reserved.
JIM DAVIS 12-11

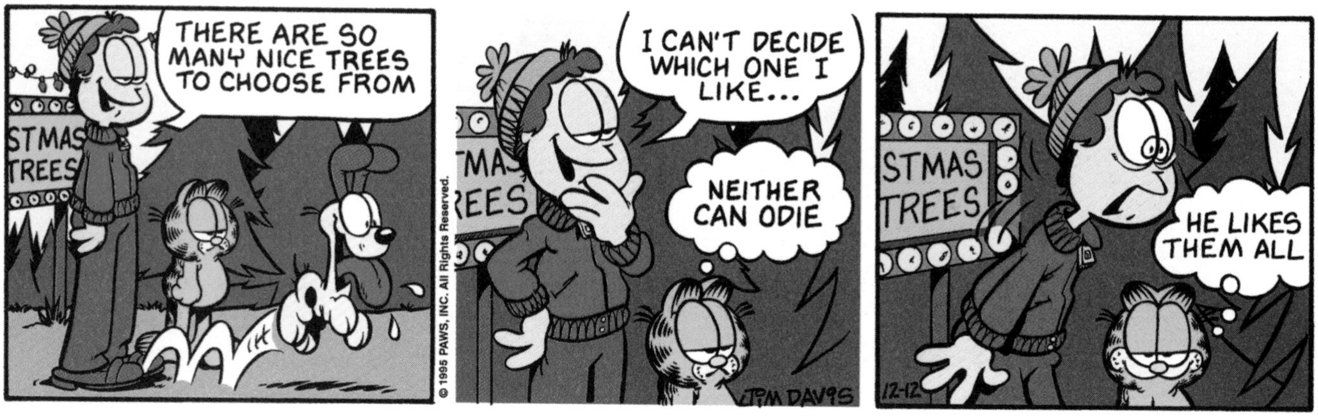
THERE ARE SO MANY NICE TREES TO CHOOSE FROM
STMAS TREES
I CAN'T DECIDE WHICH ONE I LIKE...
NEITHER CAN ODIE
HE LIKES THEM ALL
© 1995 PAWS, INC. All Rights Reserved.
JIM DAVIS 12-12

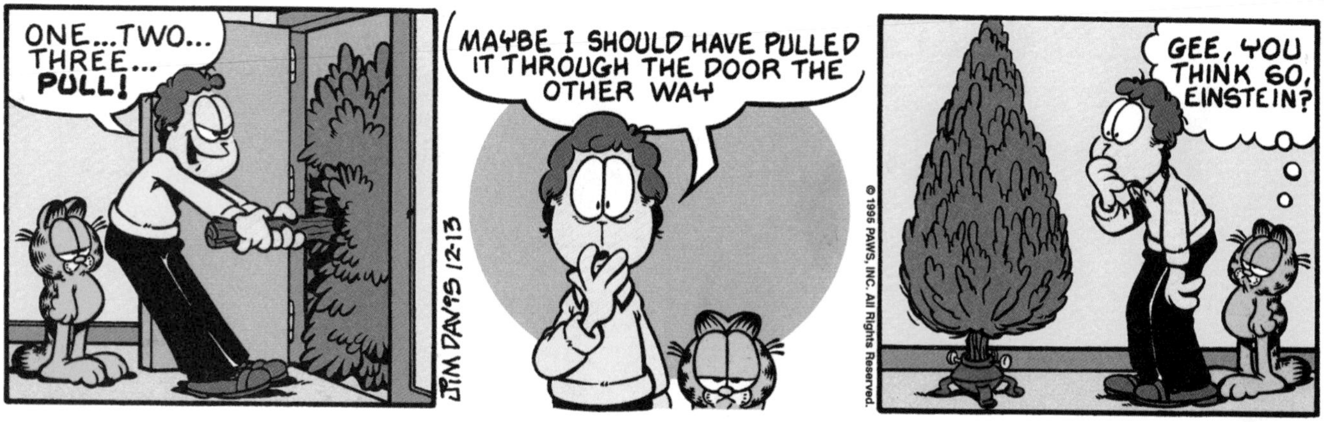
ONE...TWO... THREE... PULL!
MAYBE I SHOULD HAVE PULLED IT THROUGH THE DOOR THE OTHER WAY
GEE, YOU THINK SO, EINSTEIN?
JIM DAVIS 12-13
© 1995 PAWS, INC. All Rights Reserved.

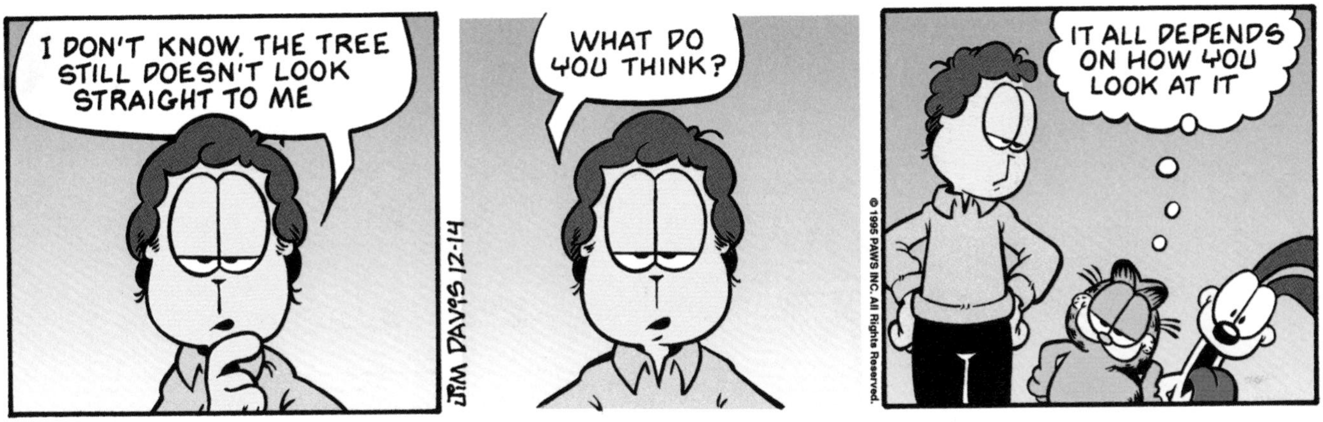
I DON'T KNOW. THE TREE STILL DOESN'T LOOK STRAIGHT TO ME
WHAT DO YOU THINK?
IT ALL DEPENDS ON HOW YOU LOOK AT IT
JIM DAVIS 12-14
© 1995 PAWS INC. All Rights Reserved.

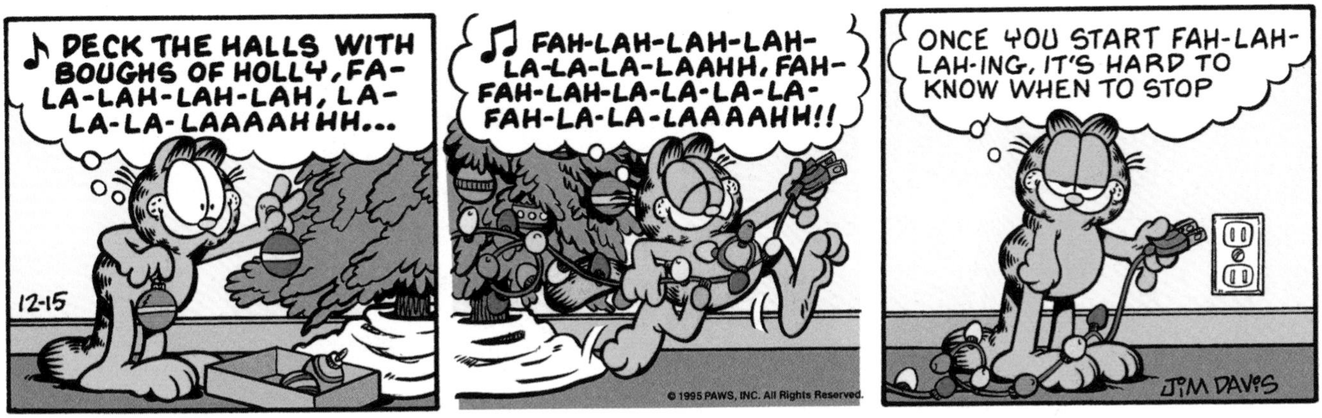
♪ DECK THE HALLS WITH BOUGHS OF HOLLY, FA-LA-LAH-LAH-LAH, LA-LA-LA-LAAAAHHH...
♫ FAH-LAH-LAH-LAH-LA-LA-LA-LAAHH, FAH-FAH-LAH-LA-LA-LA-LA-FAH-LA-LA-LAAAAHH!!
ONCE YOU START FAH-LAH-LAH-ING, IT'S HARD TO KNOW WHEN TO STOP
12-15
© 1995 PAWS, INC. All Rights Reserved.
JIM DAVIS

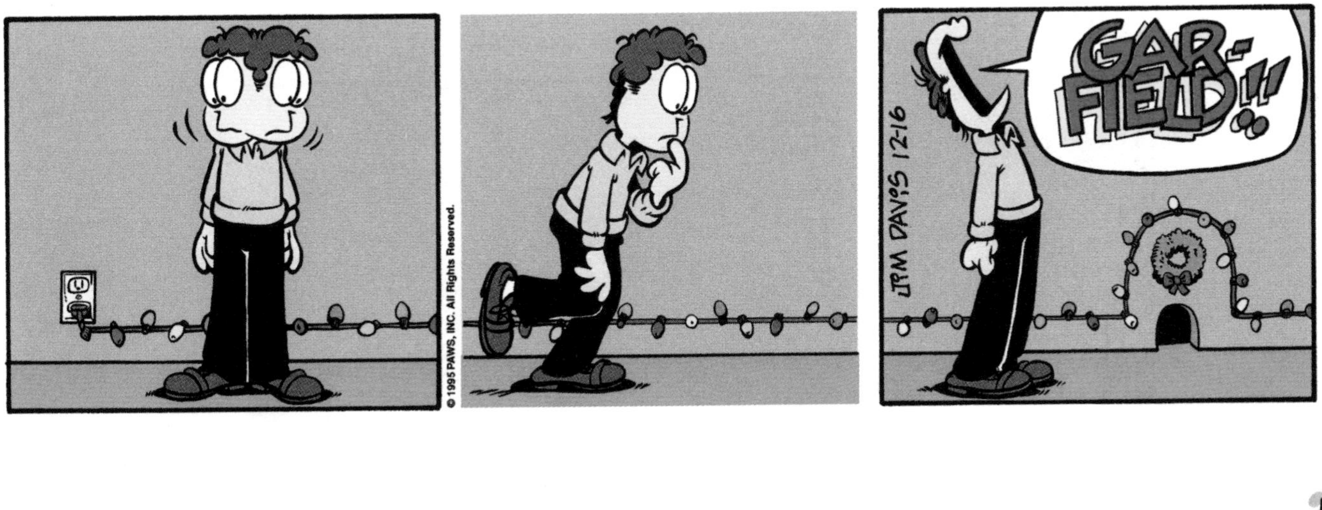
© 1995 PAWS, INC. All Rights Reserved.
JIM DAVIS 12-16
GAR-FIELD!!!

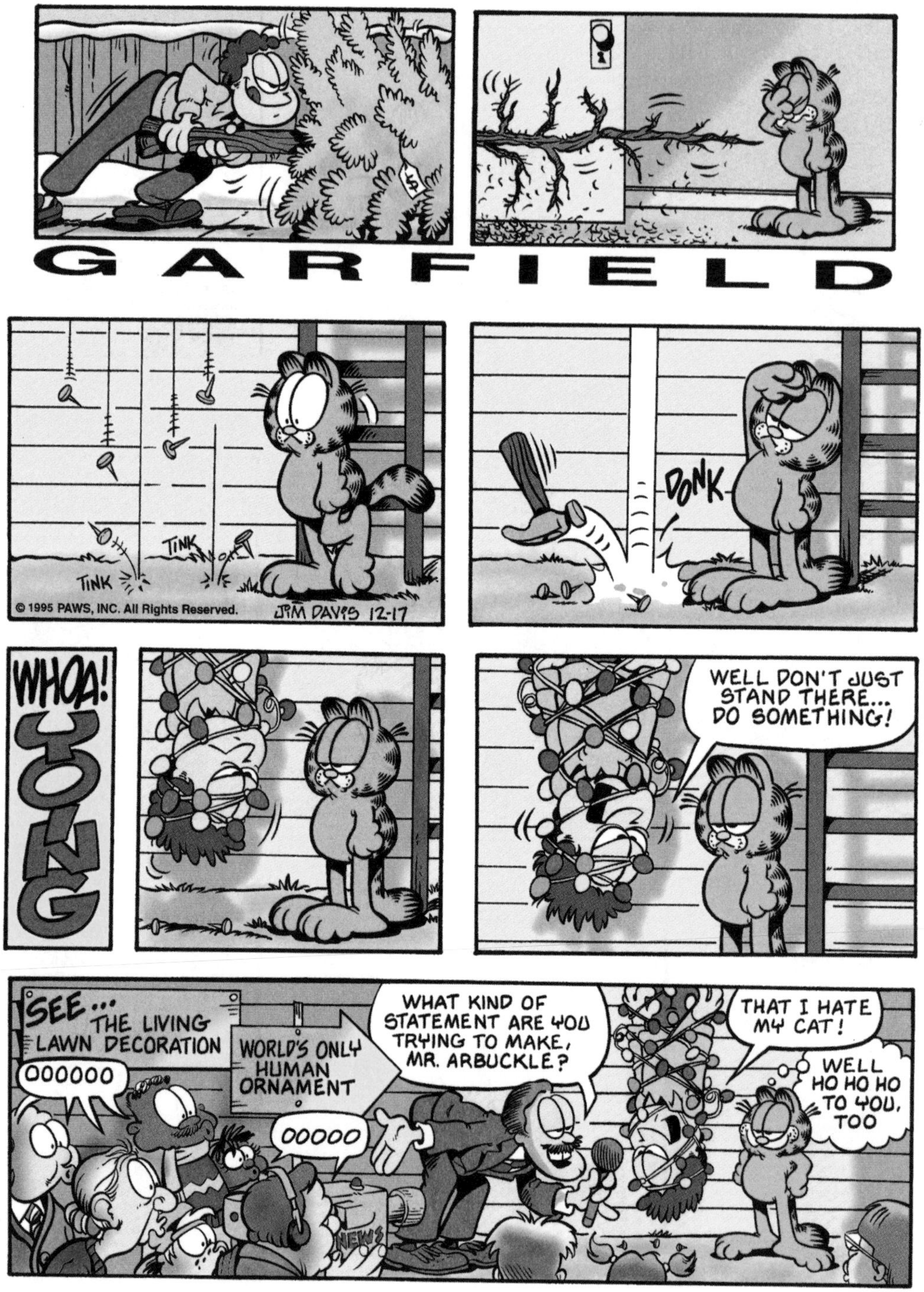
GARFIELD
TINK
TINK
© 1995 PAWS, INC. All Rights Reserved.
JIM DAVIS 12-17
DONK
WHOA!
YOING
WELL DON'T JUST STAND THERE... DO SOMETHING!
SEE... THE LIVING LAWN DECORATION
WORLD'S ONLY HUMAN ORNAMENT
OOOOOO
WHAT KIND OF STATEMENT ARE YOU TRYING TO MAKE, MR. ARBUCKLE?
THAT I HATE MY CAT!
OOOOO
WELL HO HO HO TO YOU, TOO
NEWS

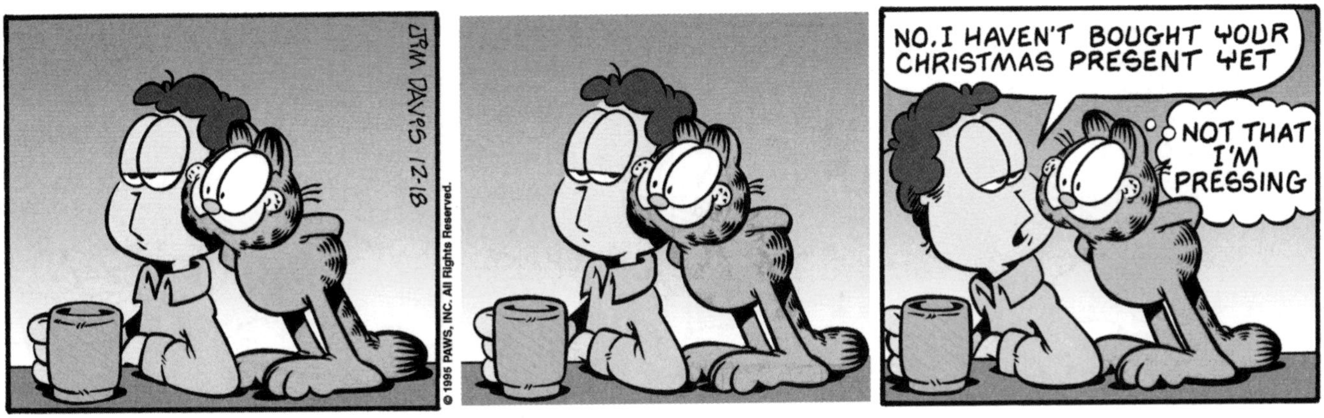
JIM DAVIS 12-18
© 1995 PAWS, INC. All Rights Reserved.
NO, I HAVEN'T BOUGHT YOUR CHRISTMAS PRESENT YET
NOT THAT I'M PRESSING

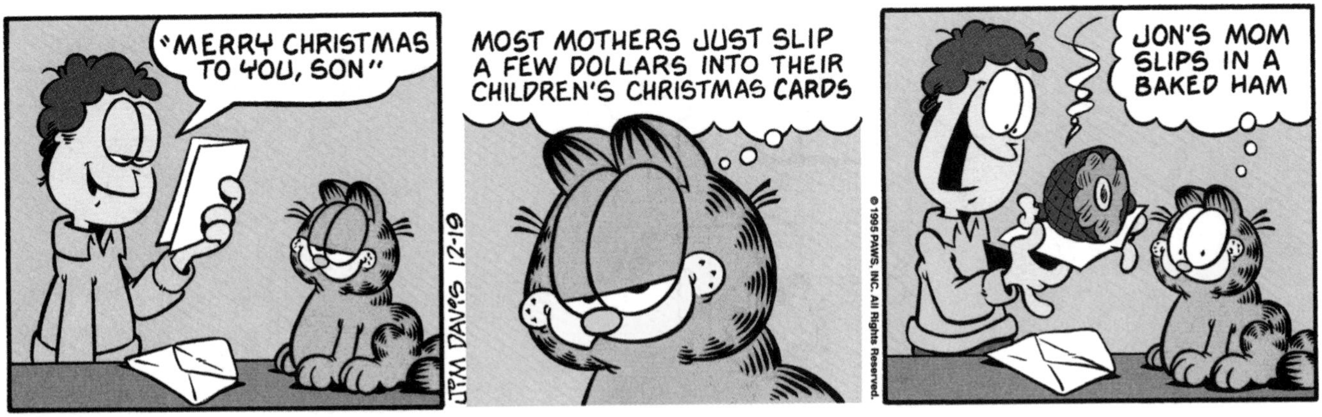
"MERRY CHRISTMAS TO YOU, SON"
JIM DAVIS 12-19
MOST MOTHERS JUST SLIP A FEW DOLLARS INTO THEIR CHILDREN'S CHRISTMAS CARDS
© 1995 PAWS, INC. All Rights Reserved.
JON'S MOM SLIPS IN A BAKED HAM

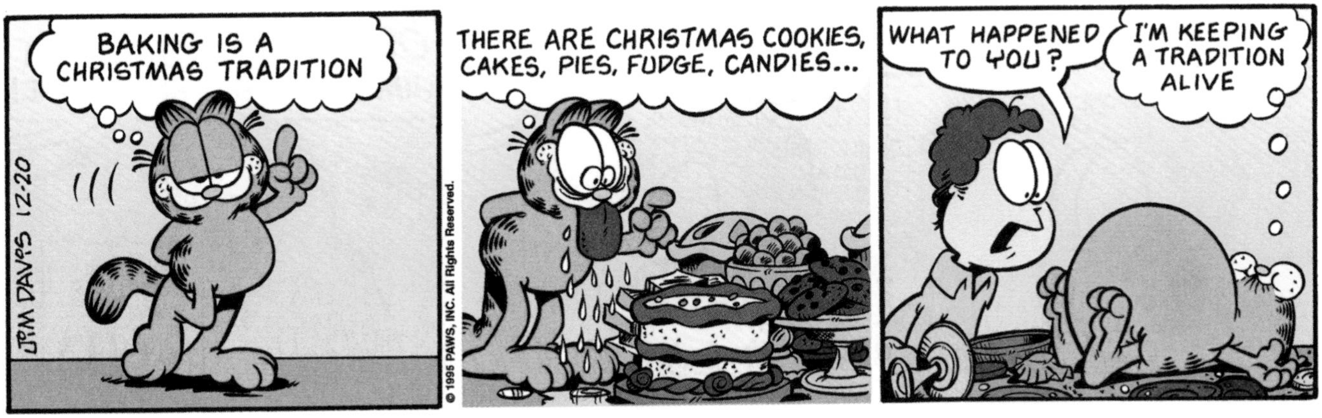
BAKING IS A CHRISTMAS TRADITION
JIM DAVIS 12-20
© 1995 PAWS, INC. All Rights Reserved.
THERE ARE CHRISTMAS COOKIES, CAKES, PIES, FUDGE, CANDIES...
WHAT HAPPENED TO YOU?
I'M KEEPING A TRADITION ALIVE

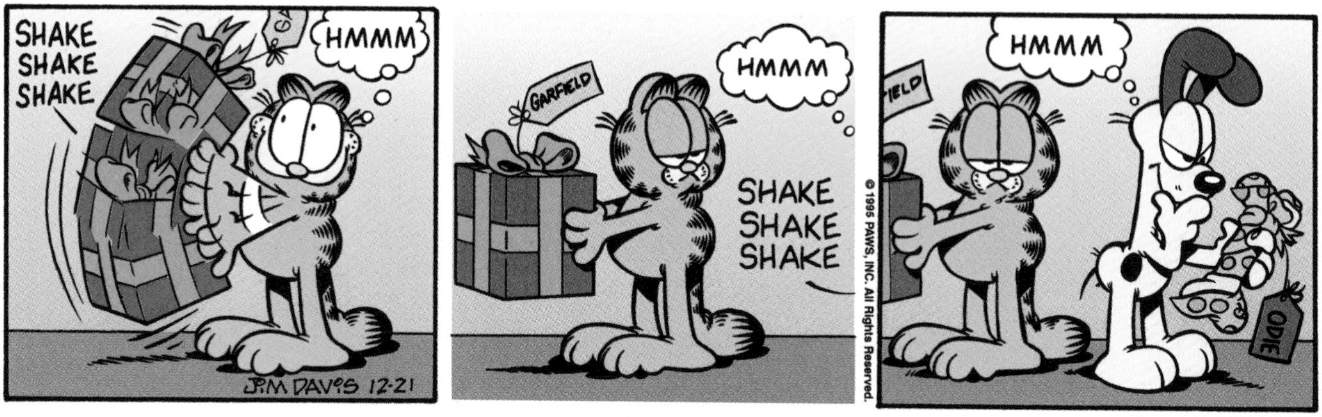

SHAKE
SHAKE
SHAKE
HMMM
JIM DAVIS 12-21
GARFIELD
HMMM
SHAKE
SHAKE
SHAKE
© 1995 PAWS, INC. All Rights Reserved.
HMMM
ODIE

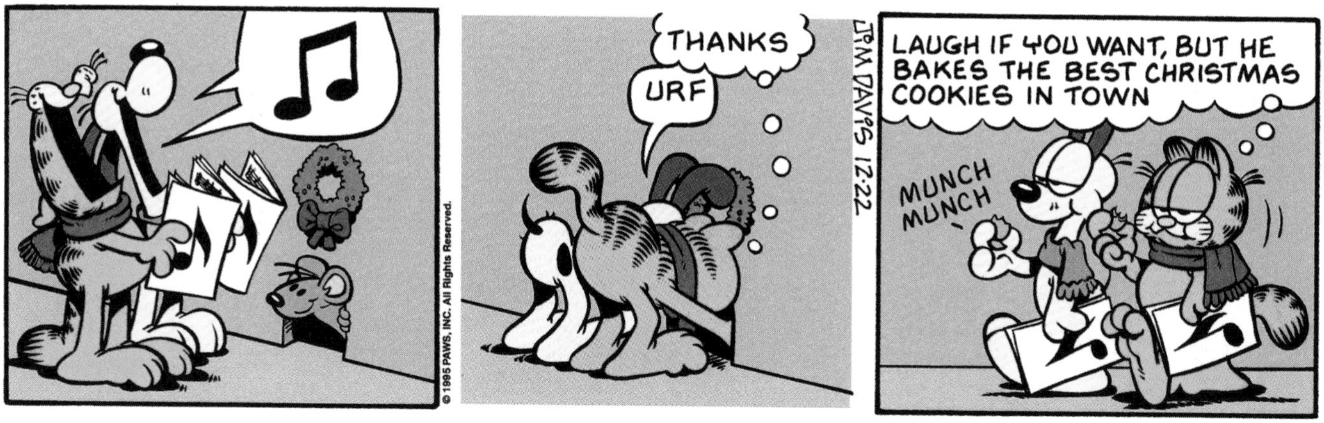

♫
© 1995 PAWS, INC. All Rights Reserved.
THANKS
URF
JIM DAVIS 12-22
LAUGH IF YOU WANT, BUT HE BAKES THE BEST CHRISTMAS COOKIES IN TOWN
MUNCH
MUNCH

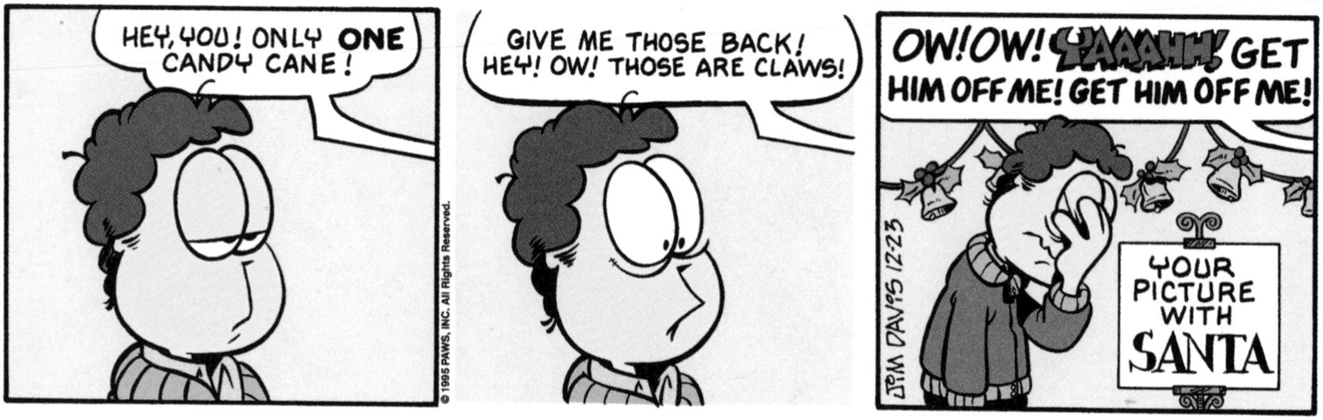

HEY, YOU! ONLY **ONE** CANDY CANE!
© 1995 PAWS, INC. All Rights Reserved.
GIVE ME THOSE BACK! HEY! OW! THOSE ARE CLAWS!
OW! OW! YAAAHH! GET HIM OFF ME! GET HIM OFF ME!
JIM DAVIS 12-23
YOUR PICTURE WITH SANTA

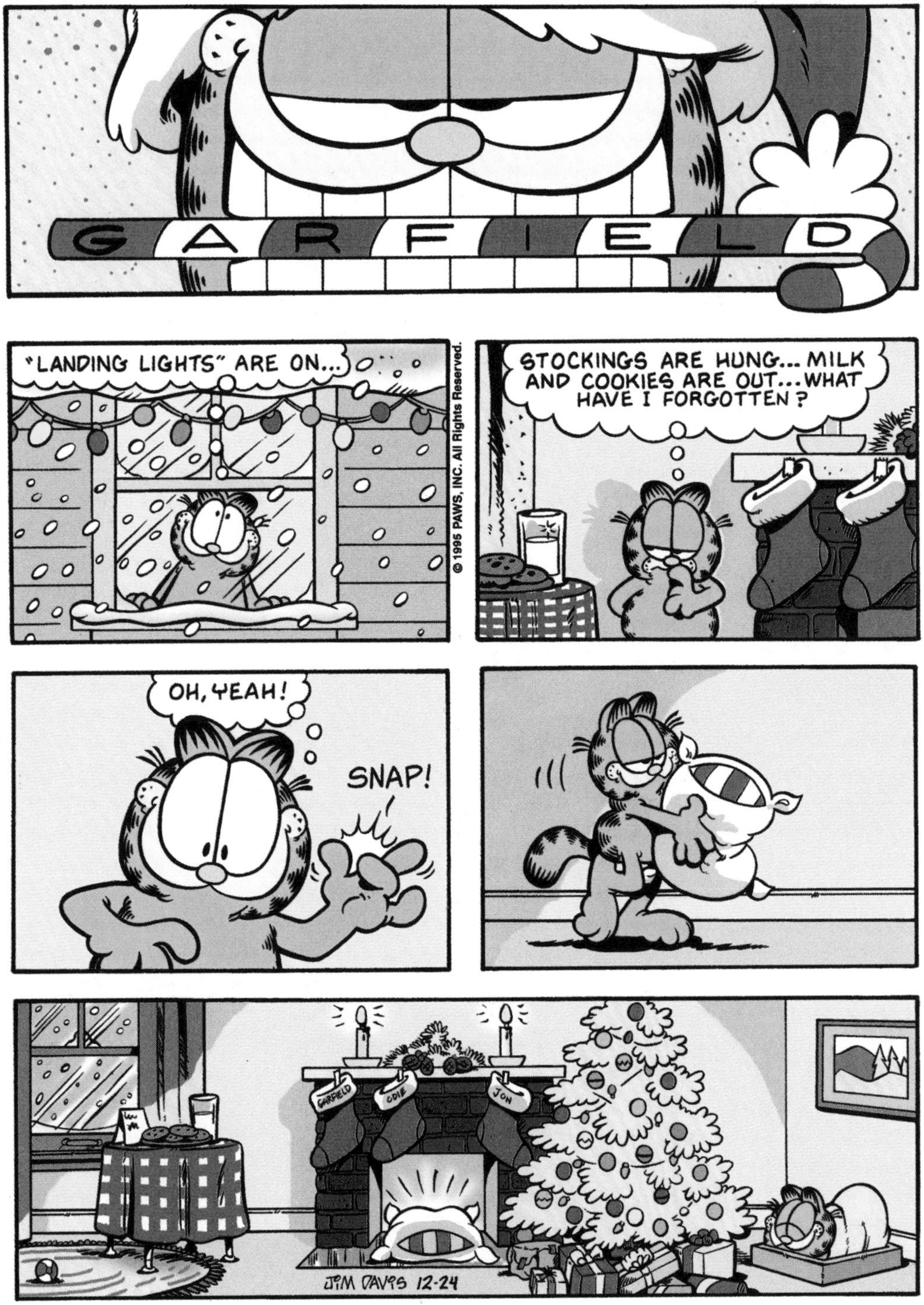
GARFIELD
"LANDING LIGHTS" ARE ON...
© 1995 PAWS, INC. All Rights Reserved.
STOCKINGS ARE HUNG... MILK AND COOKIES ARE OUT... WHAT HAVE I FORGOTTEN?
OH, YEAH!
SNAP!
GARFIELD
ODIE
JON
JIM DAVIS 12-24

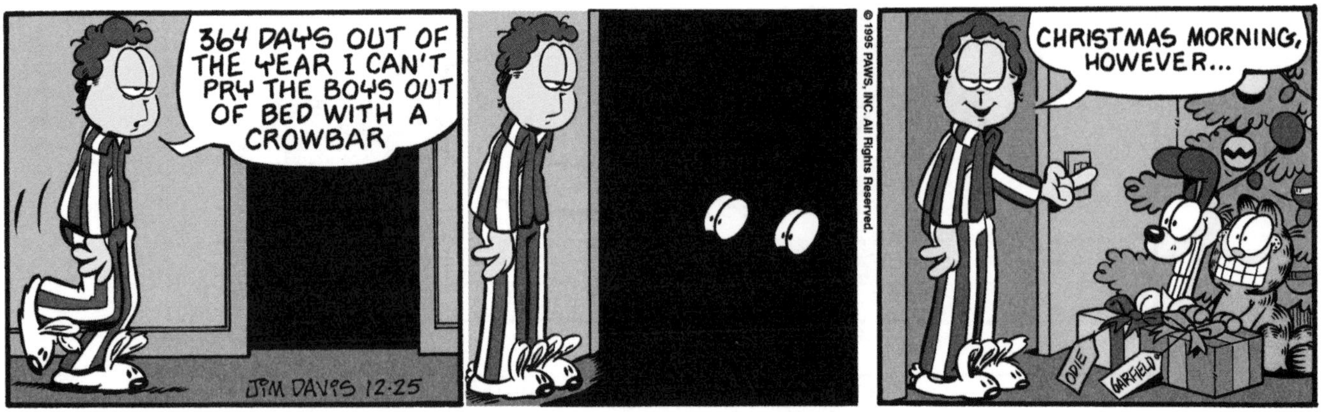
364 DAYS OUT OF THE YEAR I CAN'T PRY THE BOYS OUT OF BED WITH A CROWBAR
© 1995 PAWS, INC. All Rights Reserved.
CHRISTMAS MORNING, HOWEVER...
ODIE
GARFIELD
JIM DAVIS 12-25

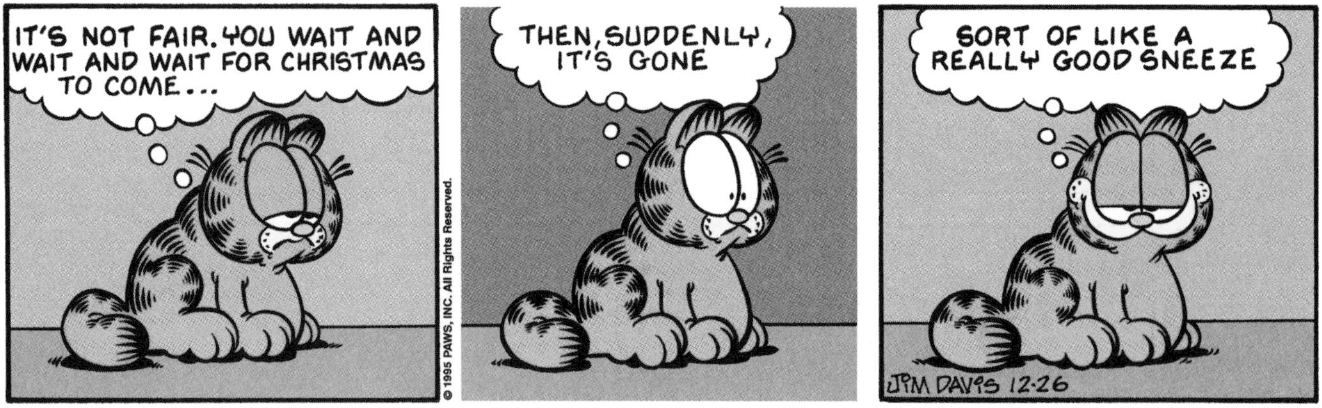
IT'S NOT FAIR. YOU WAIT AND WAIT AND WAIT FOR CHRISTMAS TO COME...
© 1995 PAWS, INC. All Rights Reserved.
THEN, SUDDENLY, IT'S GONE
SORT OF LIKE A REALLY GOOD SNEEZE
JIM DAVIS 12-26

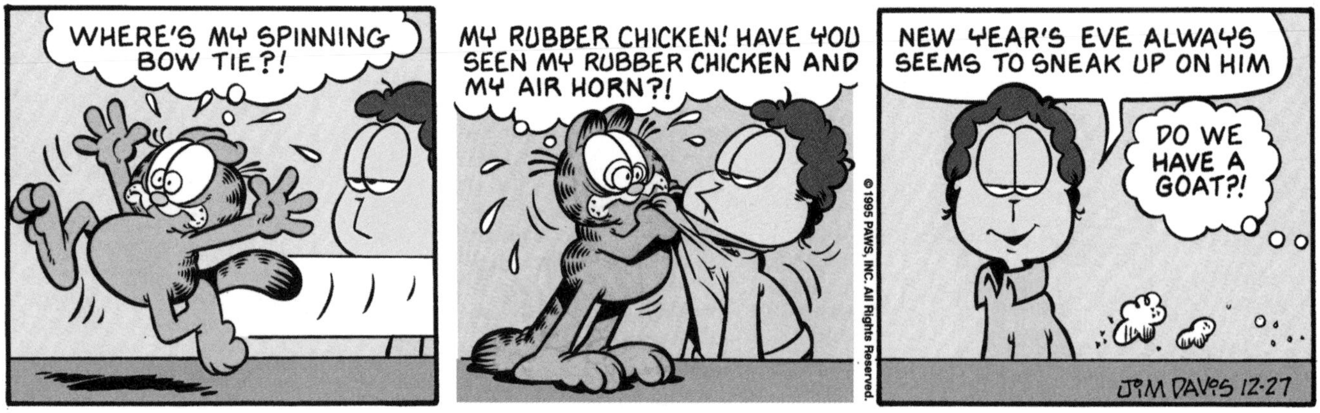
WHERE'S MY SPINNING BOW TIE?!
MY RUBBER CHICKEN! HAVE YOU SEEN MY RUBBER CHICKEN AND MY AIR HORN?!
© 1995 PAWS, INC. All Rights Reserved.
NEW YEAR'S EVE ALWAYS SEEMS TO SNEAK UP ON HIM
DO WE HAVE A GOAT?!
JIM DAVIS 12-27

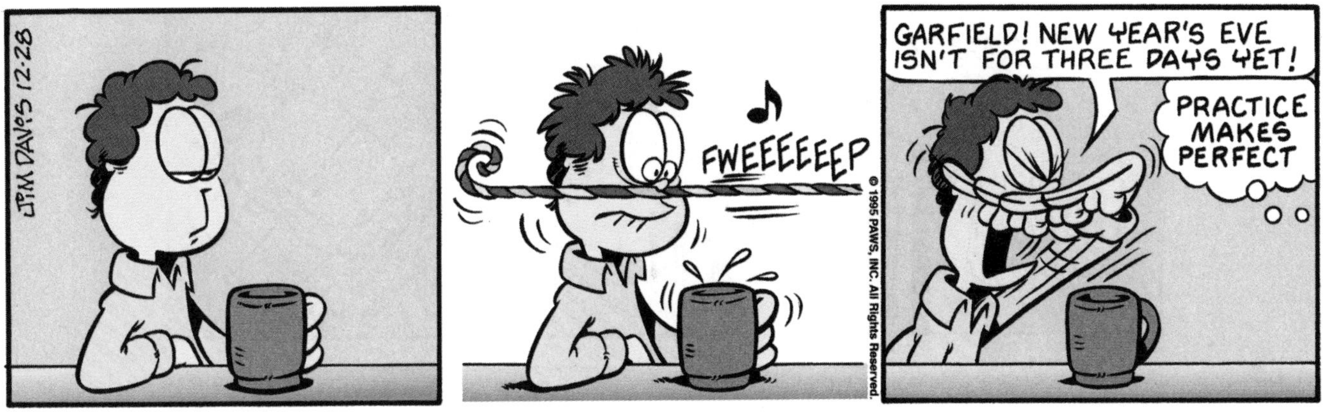
JIM DAVIS 12-28
FWEEEEEEEP
GARFIELD! NEW YEAR'S EVE ISN'T FOR THREE DAYS YET!
PRACTICE MAKES PERFECT
© 1995 PAWS, INC. All Rights Reserved.

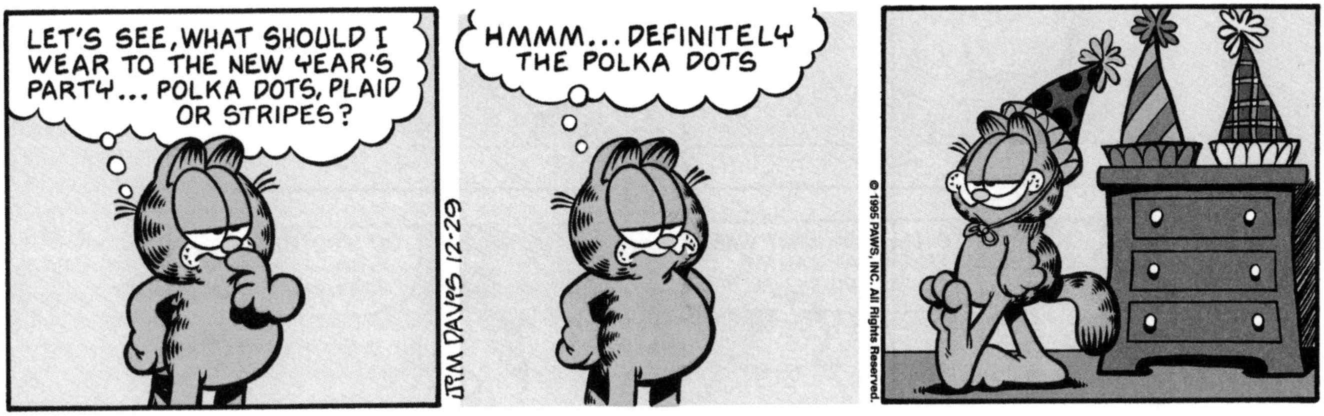
LET'S SEE, WHAT SHOULD I WEAR TO THE NEW YEAR'S PARTY... POLKA DOTS, PLAID OR STRIPES?
JIM DAVIS 12-29
HMMM... DEFINITELY THE POLKA DOTS
© 1995 PAWS, INC. All Rights Reserved.

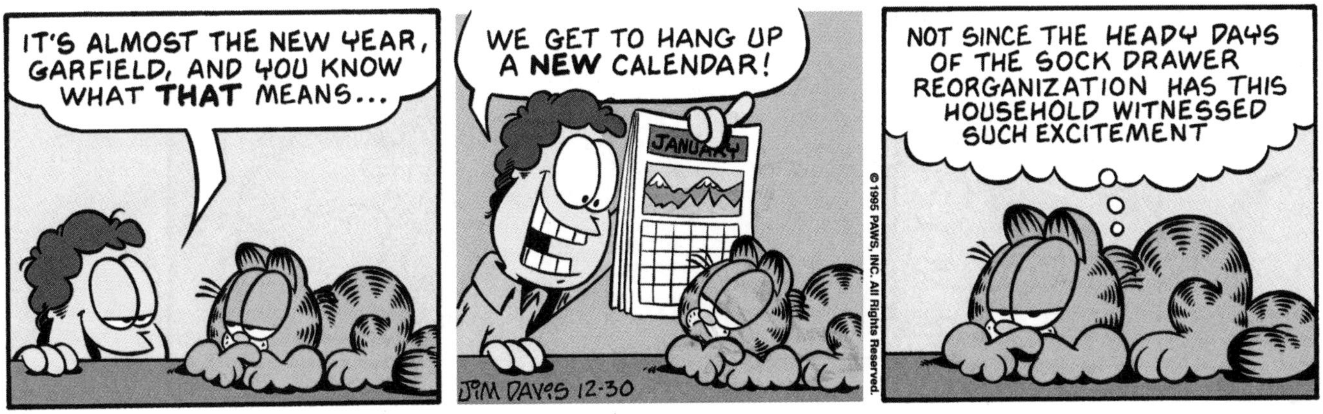
IT'S ALMOST THE NEW YEAR, GARFIELD, AND YOU KNOW WHAT **THAT** MEANS...
WE GET TO HANG UP A **NEW** CALENDAR!
JANUARY
JIM DAVIS 12-30
NOT SINCE THE HEADY DAYS OF THE SOCK DRAWER REORGANIZATION HAS THIS HOUSEHOLD WITNESSED SUCH EXCITEMENT
© 1995 PAWS, INC. All Rights Reserved.

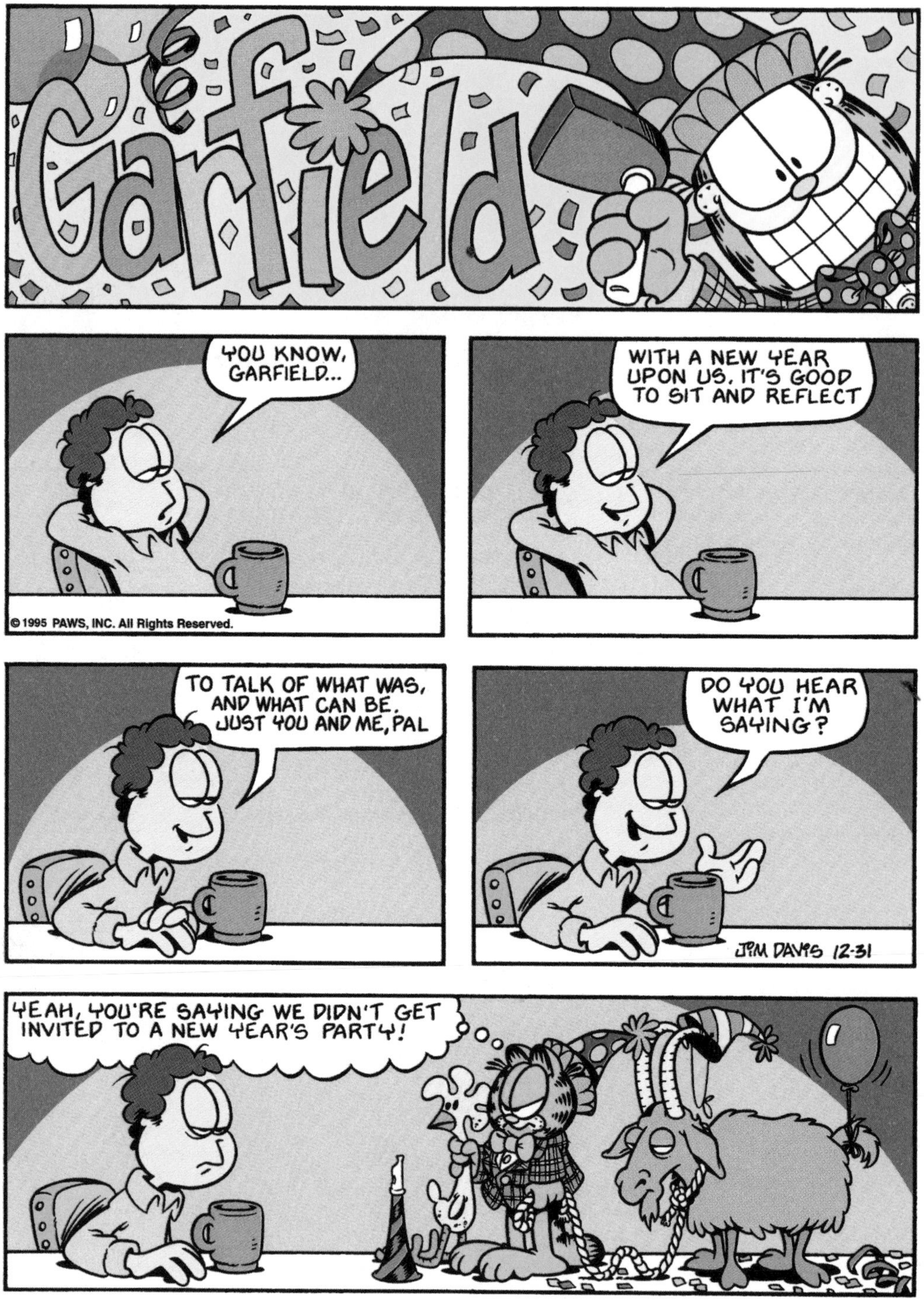
Garfield
YOU KNOW, GARFIELD...
WITH A NEW YEAR UPON US, IT'S GOOD TO SIT AND REFLECT
TO TALK OF WHAT WAS, AND WHAT CAN BE. JUST YOU AND ME, PAL
DO YOU HEAR WHAT I'M SAYING?
JIM DAVIS 12-31
YEAH, YOU'RE SAYING WE DIDN'T GET INVITED TO A NEW YEAR'S PARTY!
© 1995 PAWS, INC. All Rights Reserved.

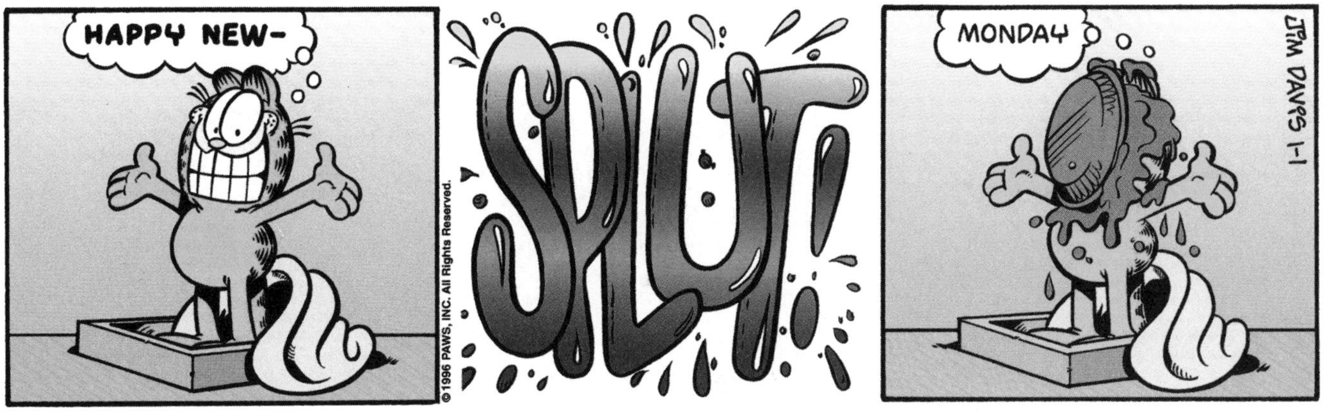
HAPPY NEW-
SPLUT!
MONDAY
JIM DAVIS 1-1
©1996 PAWS, INC. All Rights Reserved.

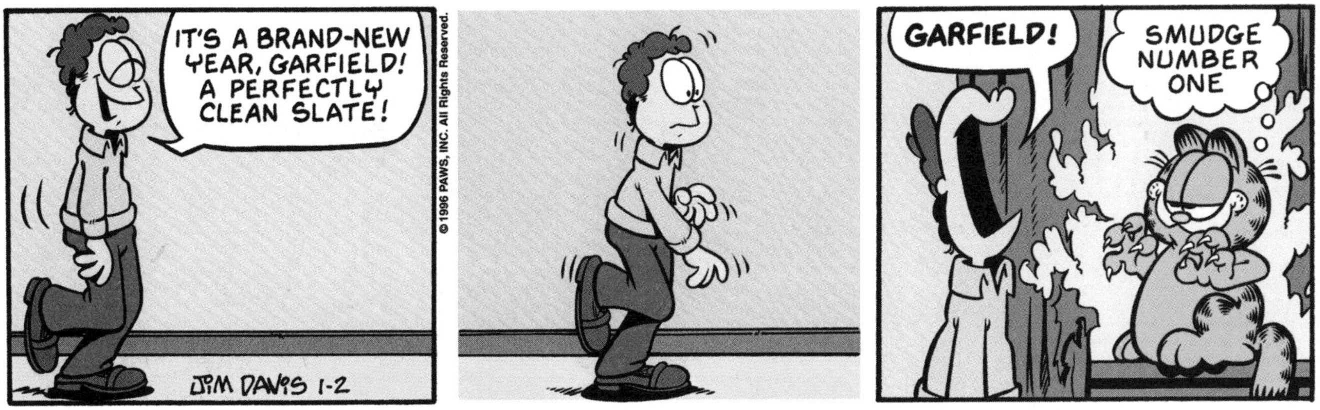
IT'S A BRAND-NEW YEAR, GARFIELD! A PERFECTLY CLEAN SLATE!
JIM DAVIS 1-2
©1996 PAWS, INC. All Rights Reserved.
GARFIELD!
SMUDGE NUMBER ONE

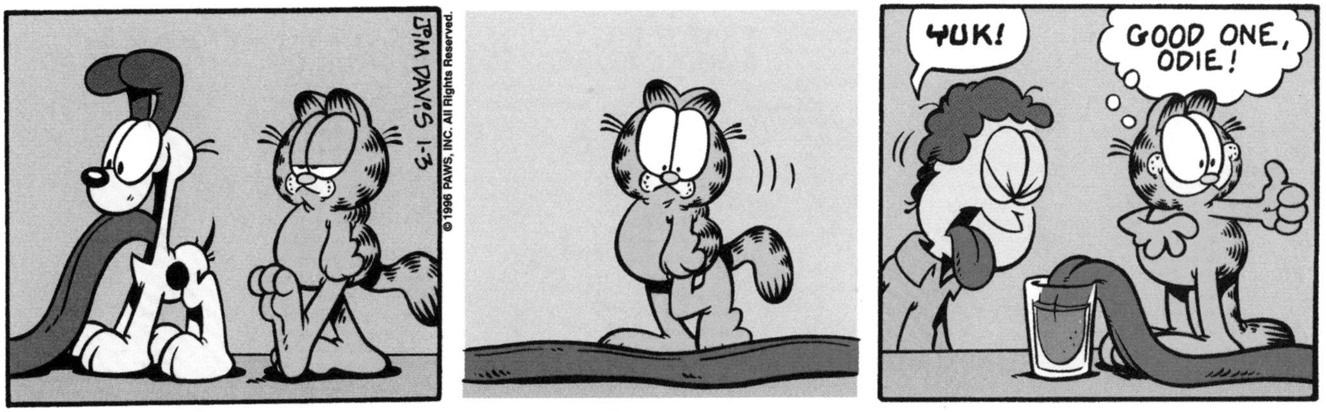
JIM DAVIS 1-3
©1996 PAWS, INC. All Rights Reserved.
YUK!
GOOD ONE, ODIE!

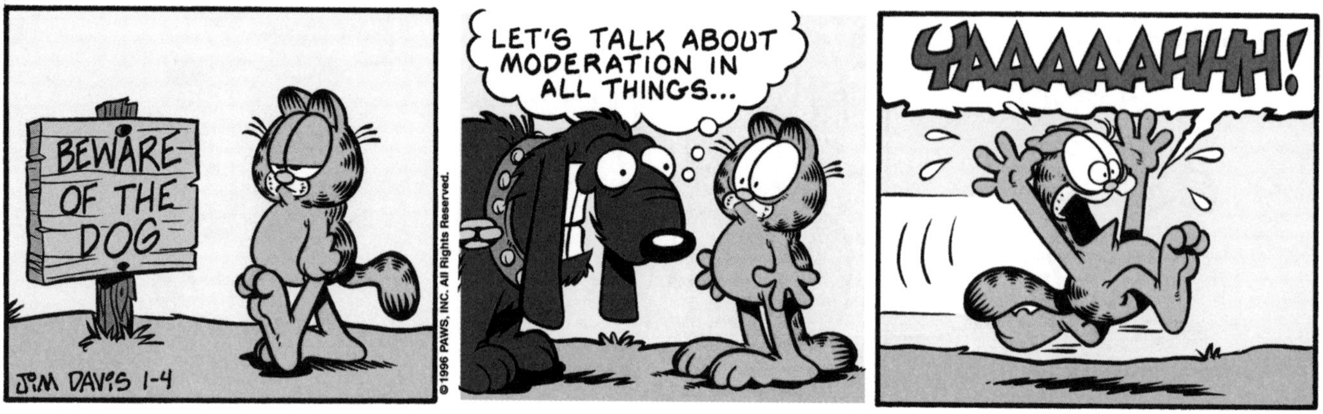
BEWARE OF THE DOG
JIM DAVIS 1-4
©1996 PAWS, INC. All Rights Reserved.
LET'S TALK ABOUT MODERATION IN ALL THINGS...
YAAAAAHHH!

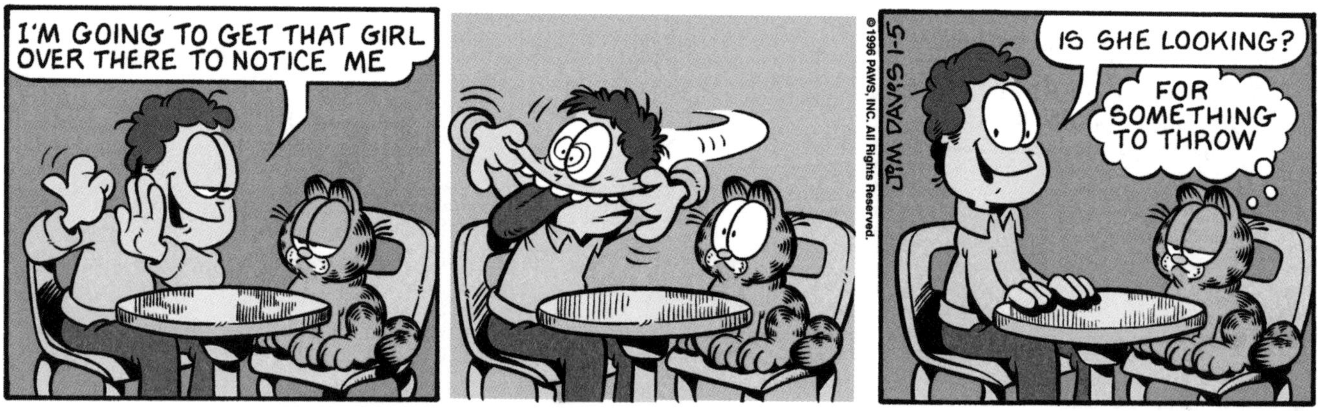
I'M GOING TO GET THAT GIRL OVER THERE TO NOTICE ME
©1996 PAWS, INC. All Rights Reserved.
JIM DAVIS 1-5
IS SHE LOOKING?
FOR SOMETHING TO THROW

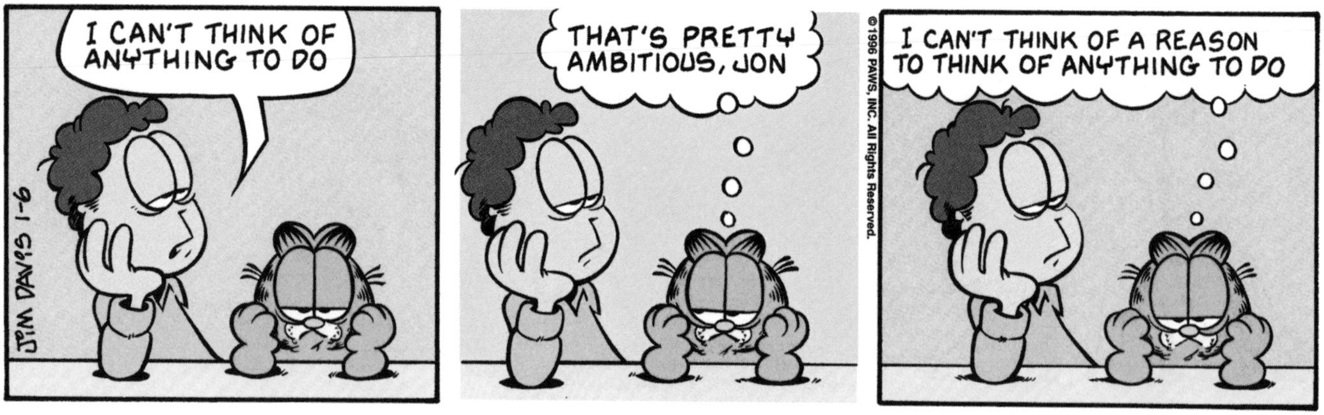
JIM DAVIS 1-6
I CAN'T THINK OF ANYTHING TO DO
THAT'S PRETTY AMBITIOUS, JON
©1996 PAWS, INC. All Rights Reserved.
I CAN'T THINK OF A REASON TO THINK OF ANYTHING TO DO

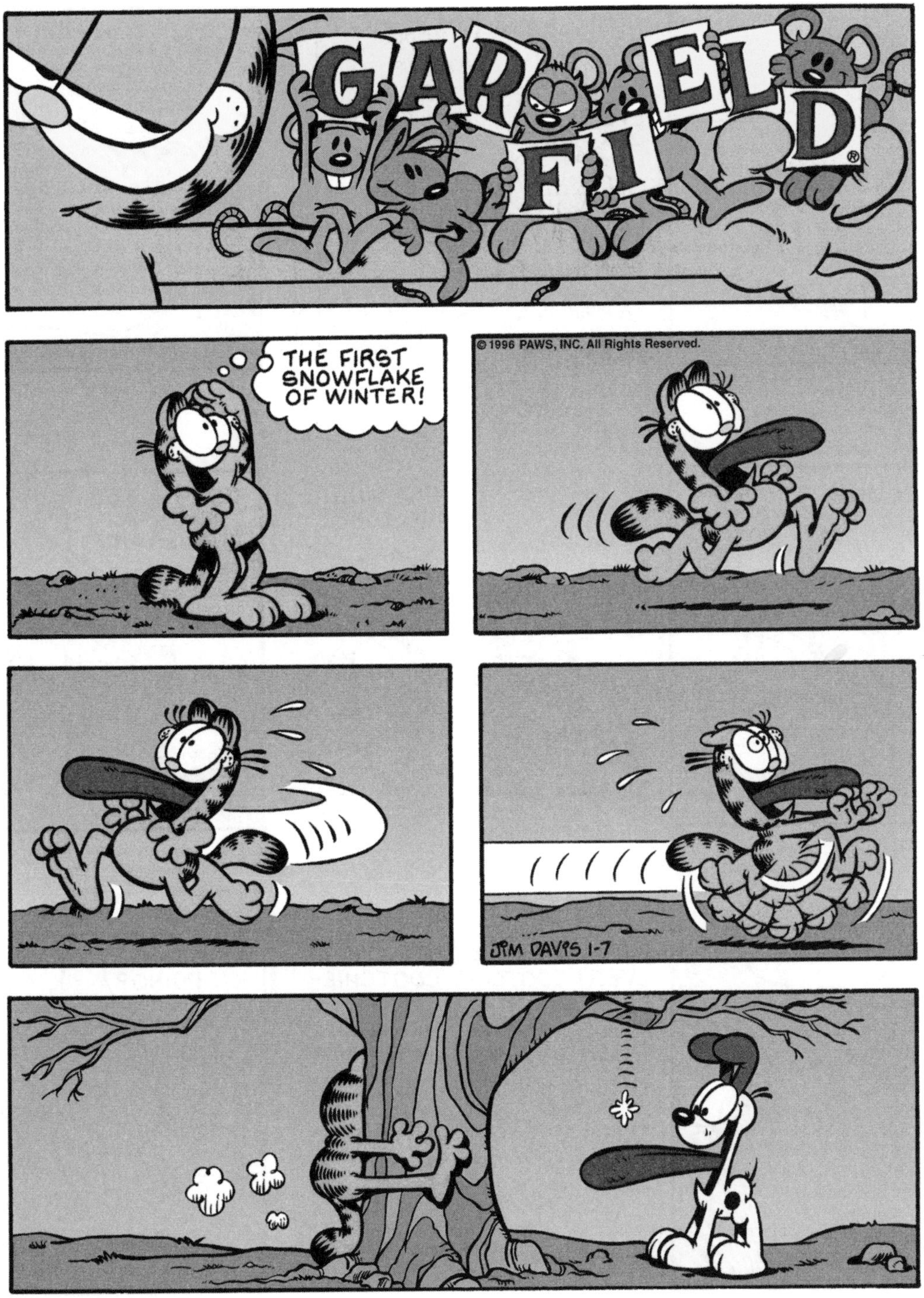
GARFIELD®
THE FIRST SNOWFLAKE OF WINTER!
© 1996 PAWS, INC. All Rights Reserved.
JIM DAVIS 1-7

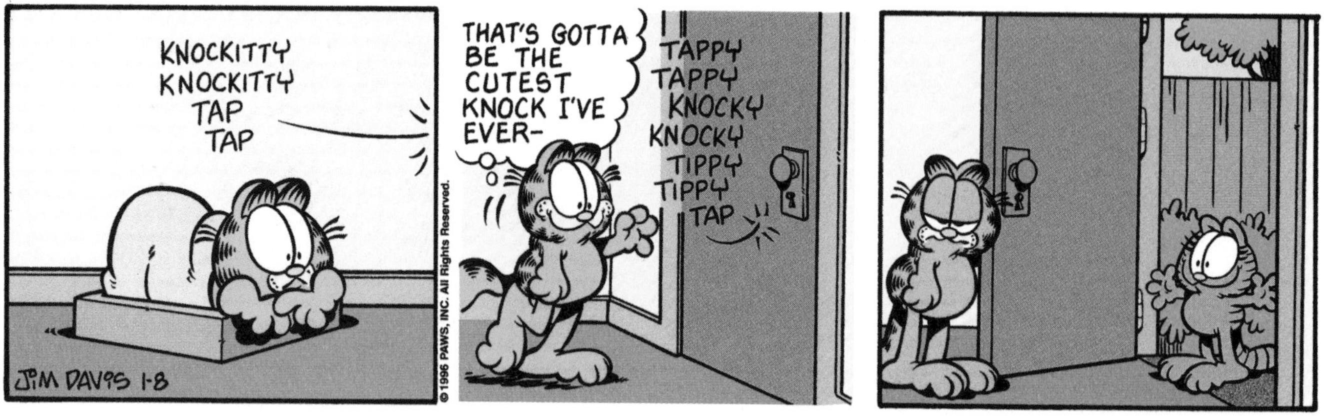
KNOCKITTY
KNOCKITTY
TAP
TAP
JIM DAVIS 1-8
© 1996 PAWS, INC. All Rights Reserved.
THAT'S GOTTA BE THE CUTEST KNOCK I'VE EVER-
TAPPY
TAPPY
KNOCKY
KNOCKY
TIPPY
TIPPY
TAP

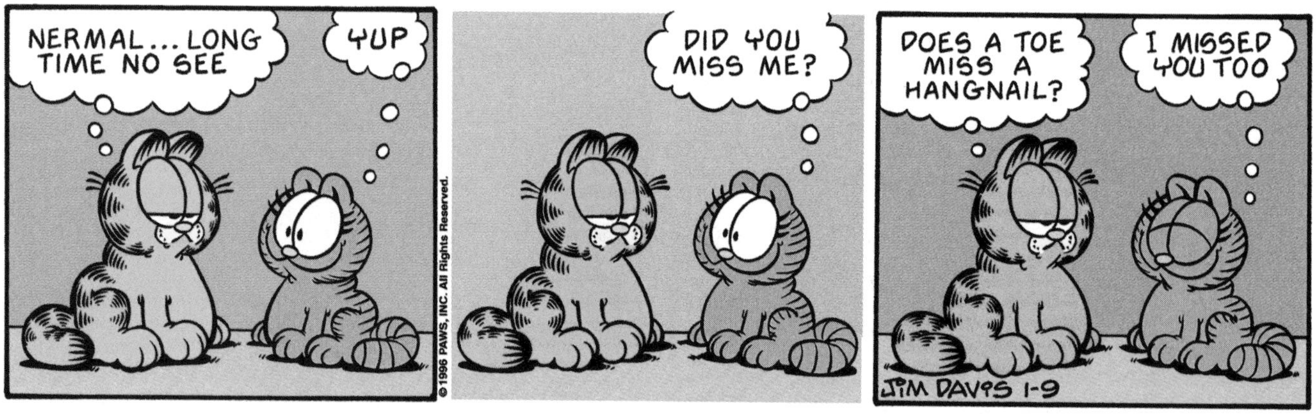
NERMAL... LONG TIME NO SEE
YUP
© 1996 PAWS, INC. All Rights Reserved.
DID YOU MISS ME?
DOES A TOE MISS A HANGNAIL?
I MISSED YOU TOO
JIM DAVIS 1-9

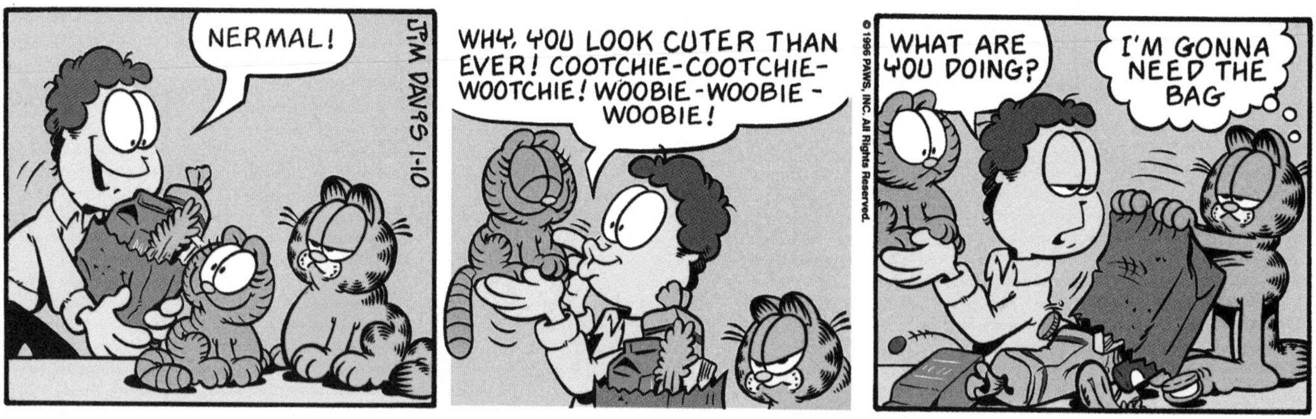
NERMAL!
JIM DAVIS 1-10
WHY, YOU LOOK CUTER THAN EVER! COOTCHIE-COOTCHIE-WOOTCHIE! WOOBIE-WOOBIE-WOOBIE!
© 1996 PAWS, INC. All Rights Reserved.
WHAT ARE YOU DOING?
I'M GONNA NEED THE BAG

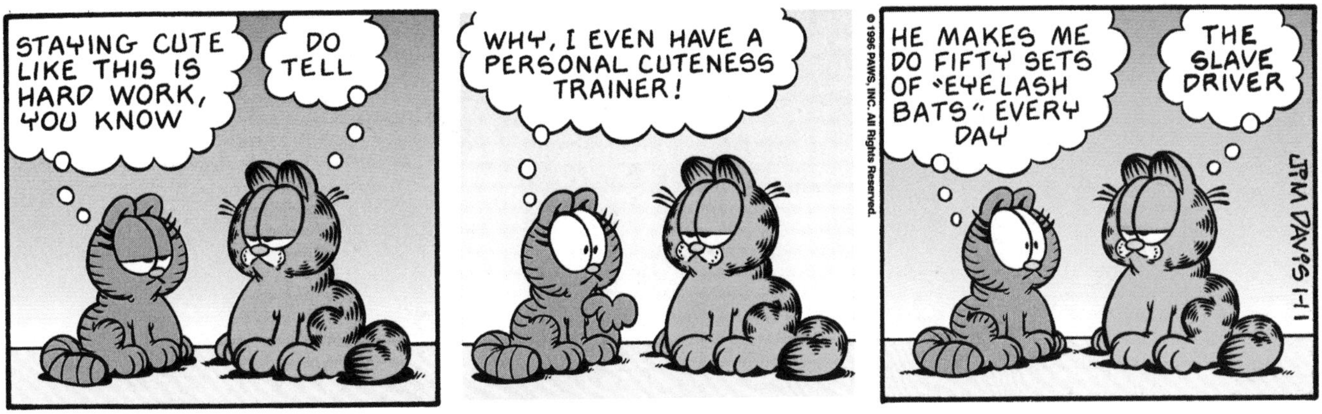
STAYING CUTE LIKE THIS IS HARD WORK, YOU KNOW
DO TELL
WHY, I EVEN HAVE A PERSONAL CUTENESS TRAINER!
© 1996 PAWS, INC. All Rights Reserved.
HE MAKES ME DO FIFTY SETS OF "EYELASH BATS" EVERY DAY
THE SLAVE DRIVER
JIM DAVIS 1-11

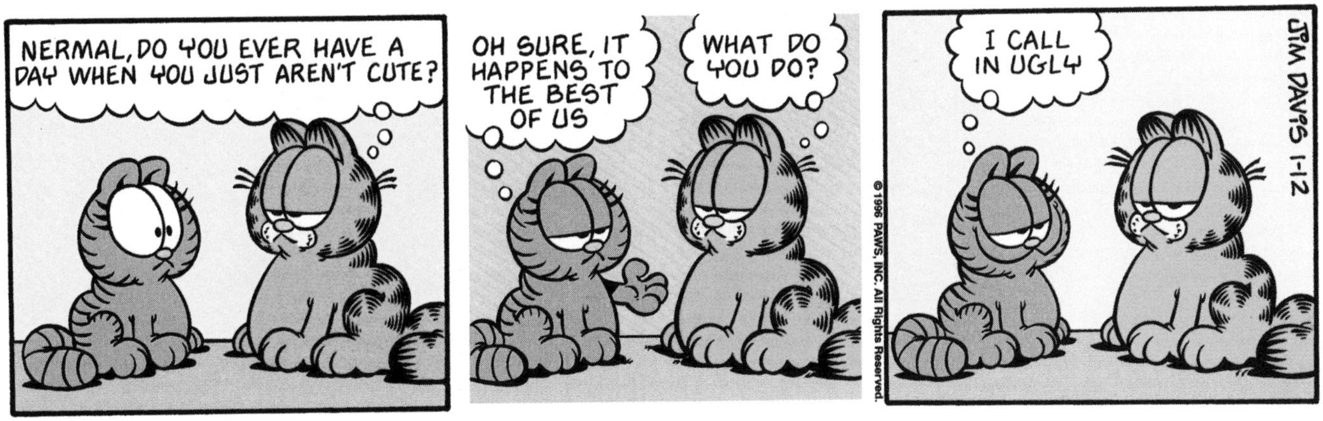
NERMAL, DO YOU EVER HAVE A DAY WHEN YOU JUST AREN'T CUTE?
OH SURE, IT HAPPENS TO THE BEST OF US
WHAT DO YOU DO?
© 1996 PAWS, INC. All Rights Reserved.
I CALL IN UGLY
JIM DAVIS 1-12

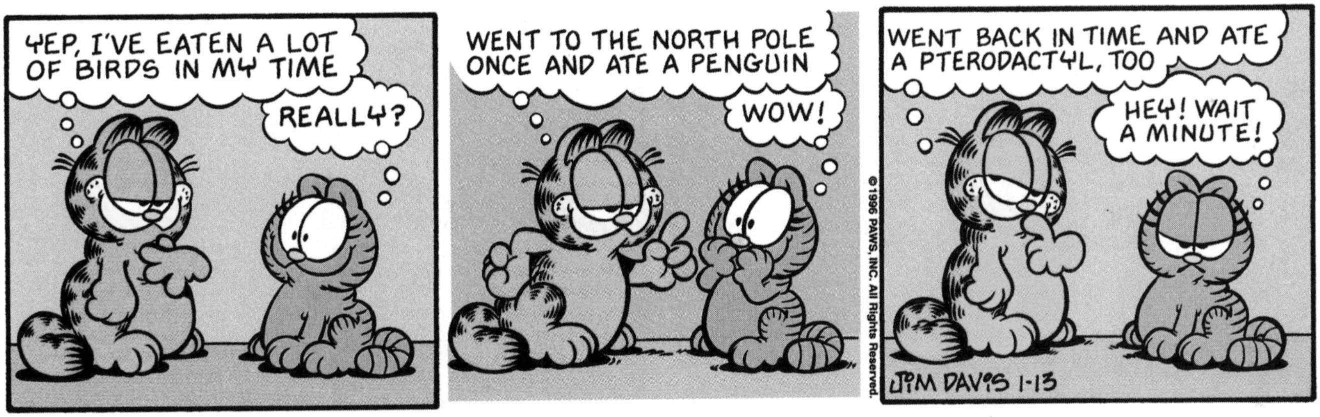
YEP, I'VE EATEN A LOT OF BIRDS IN MY TIME
REALLY?
WENT TO THE NORTH POLE ONCE AND ATE A PENGUIN
WOW!
© 1996 PAWS, INC. All Rights Reserved.
WENT BACK IN TIME AND ATE A PTERODACTYL, TOO
HEY! WAIT A MINUTE!
JIM DAVIS 1-13

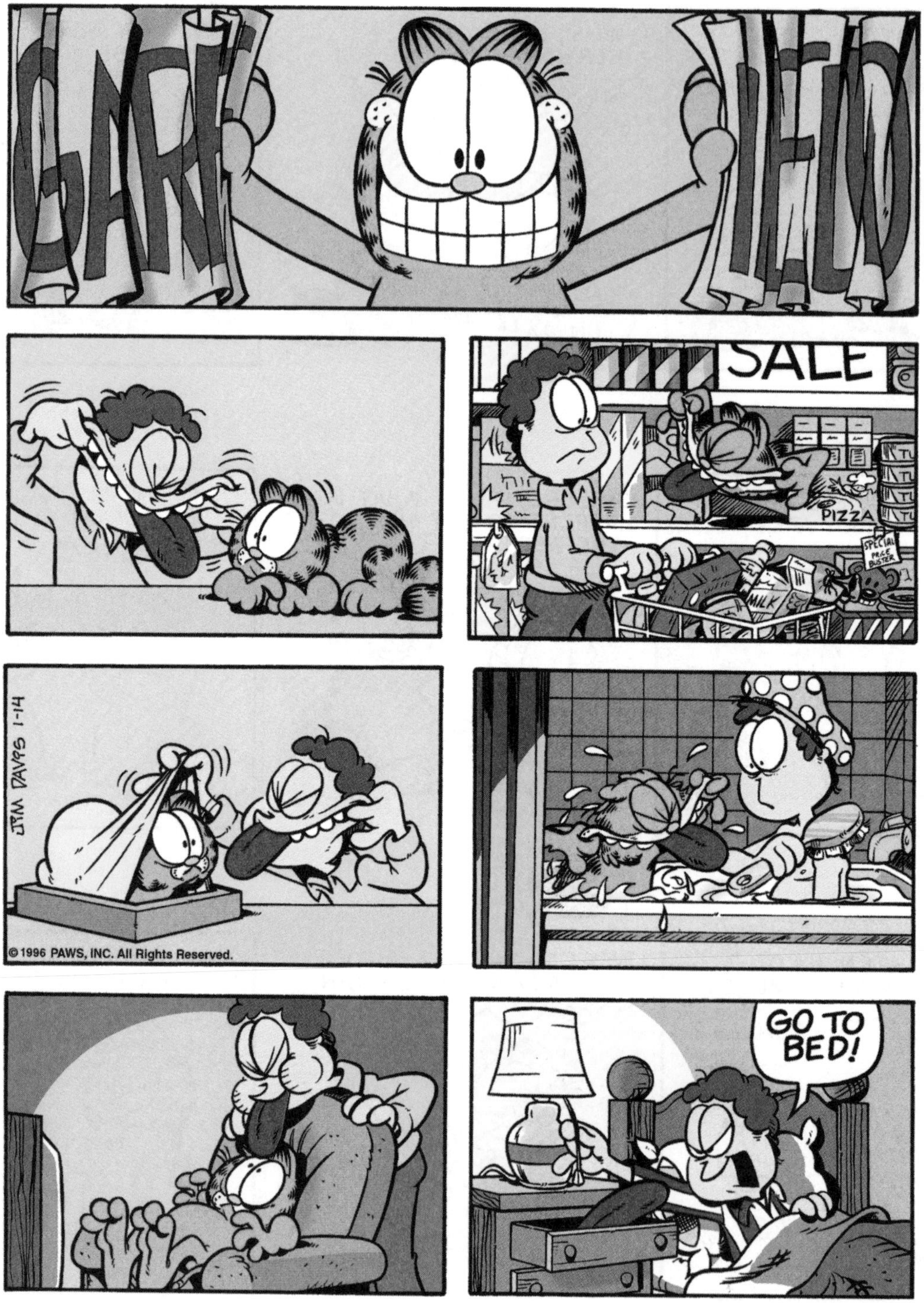
SALE
PIZZA
SPECIAL PRICE BUSTER
MILK
JIM DAVIS 1-14
GO TO BED!

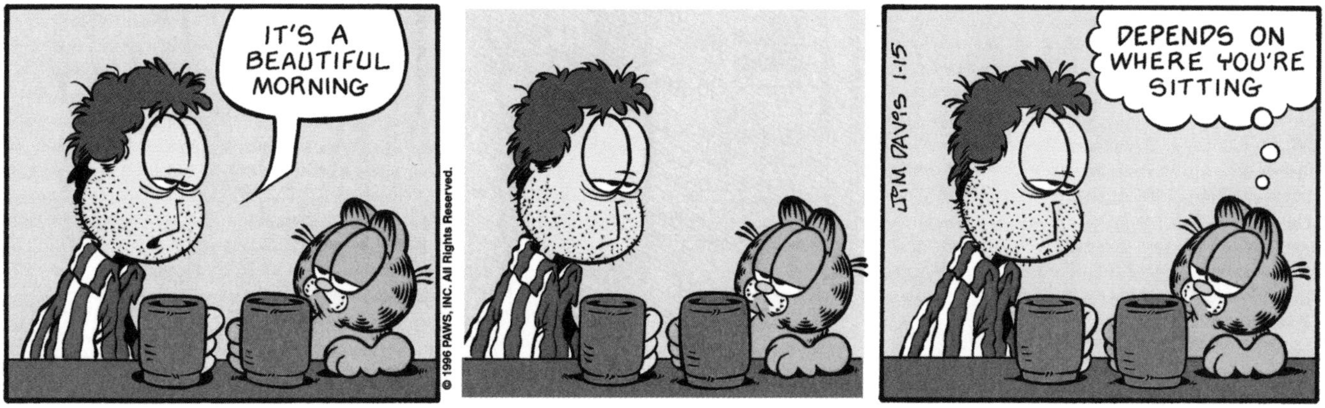
IT'S A BEAUTIFUL MORNING
© 1996 PAWS, INC. All Rights Reserved.
JIM DAVIS 1-15
DEPENDS ON WHERE YOU'RE SITTING

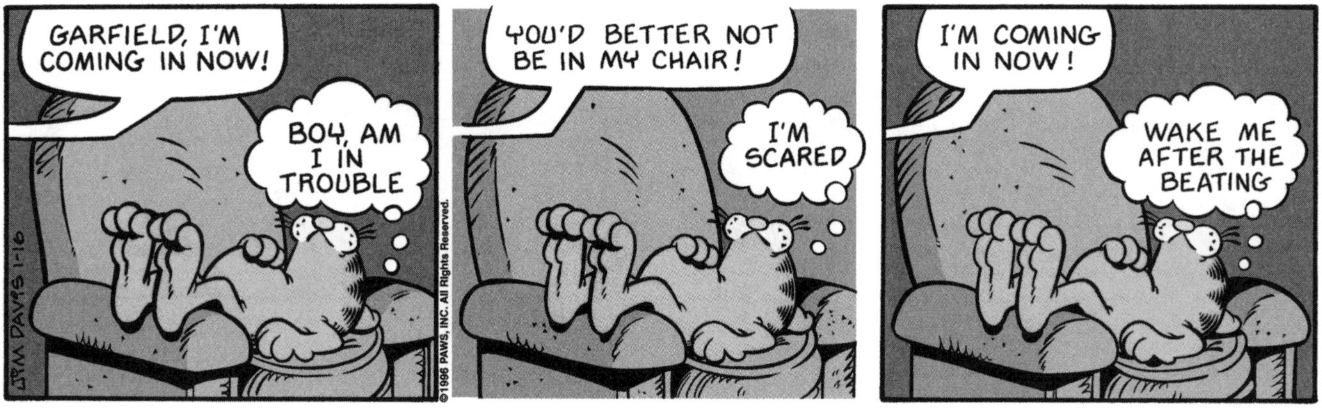
GARFIELD, I'M COMING IN NOW!
BOY, AM I IN TROUBLE
JIM DAVIS 1-16
© 1996 PAWS, INC. All Rights Reserved.
YOU'D BETTER NOT BE IN MY CHAIR!
I'M SCARED
I'M COMING IN NOW!
WAKE ME AFTER THE BEATING

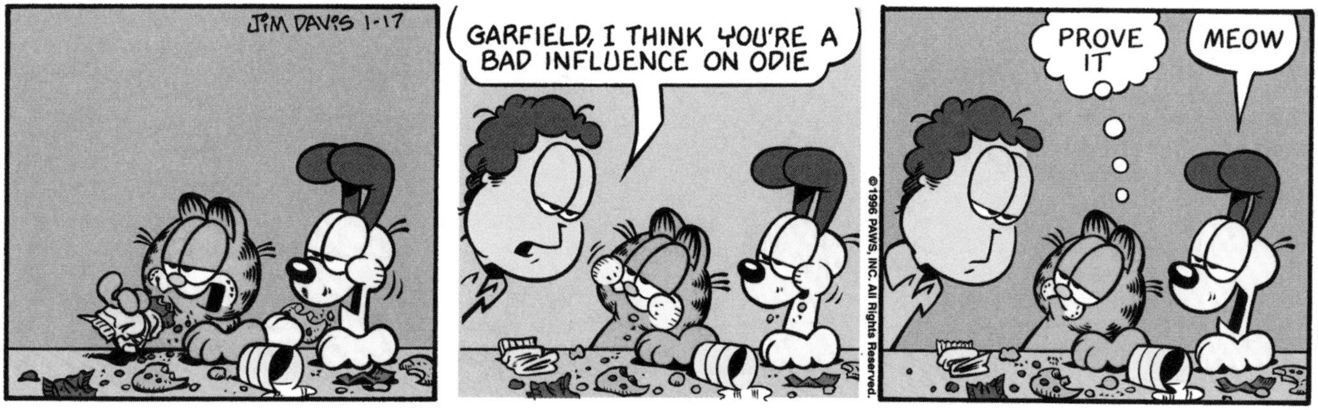
JIM DAVIS 1-17
GARFIELD, I THINK YOU'RE A BAD INFLUENCE ON ODIE
© 1996 PAWS, INC. All Rights Reserved.
PROVE IT
MEOW

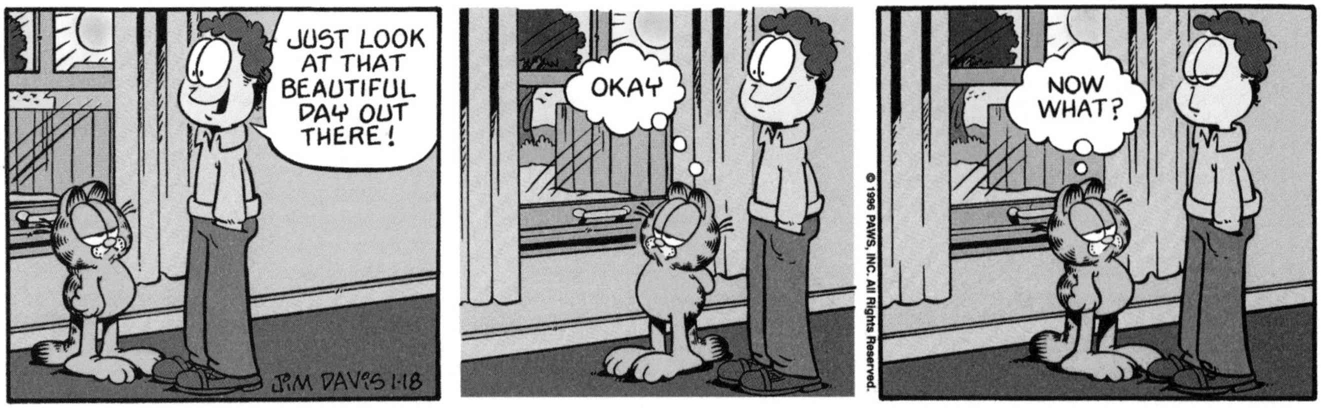
JUST LOOK AT THAT BEAUTIFUL DAY OUT THERE!
JIM DAVIS 1-18
OKAY
NOW WHAT?
© 1996 PAWS, INC. All Rights Reserved.

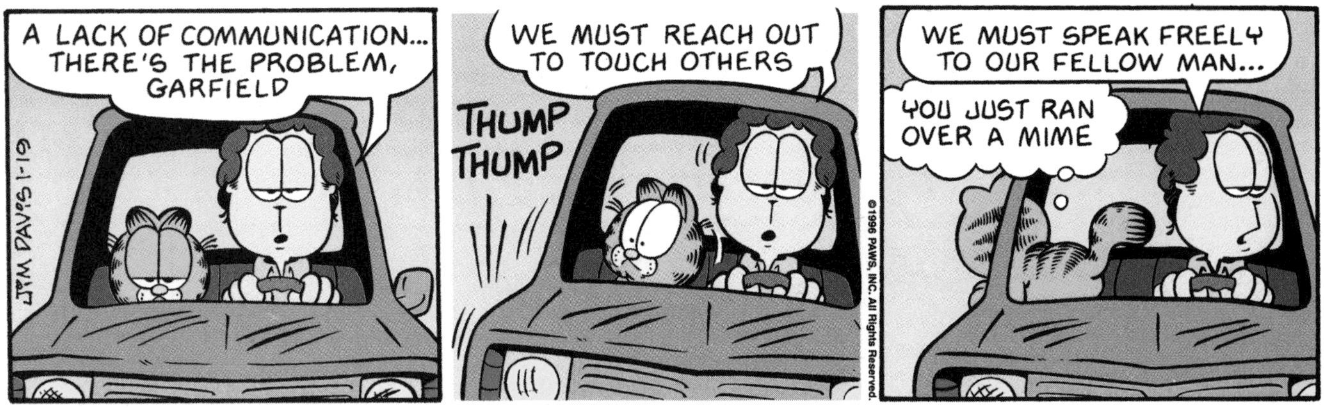
A LACK OF COMMUNICATION... THERE'S THE PROBLEM, GARFIELD
JIM DAVIS 1-19
WE MUST REACH OUT TO TOUCH OTHERS
THUMP THUMP
© 1996 PAWS, INC. All Rights Reserved.
WE MUST SPEAK FREELY TO OUR FELLOW MAN...
YOU JUST RAN OVER A MIME

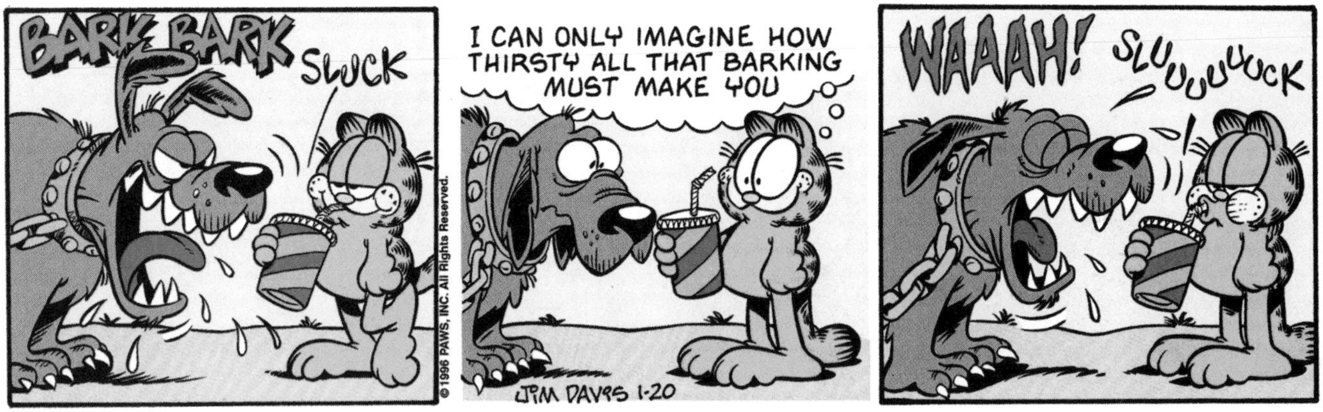
BARK BARK
SLUCK
© 1996 PAWS, INC. All Rights Reserved.
I CAN ONLY IMAGINE HOW THIRSTY ALL THAT BARKING MUST MAKE YOU
JIM DAVIS 1-20
WAAAH!
SLUUUUUUCK

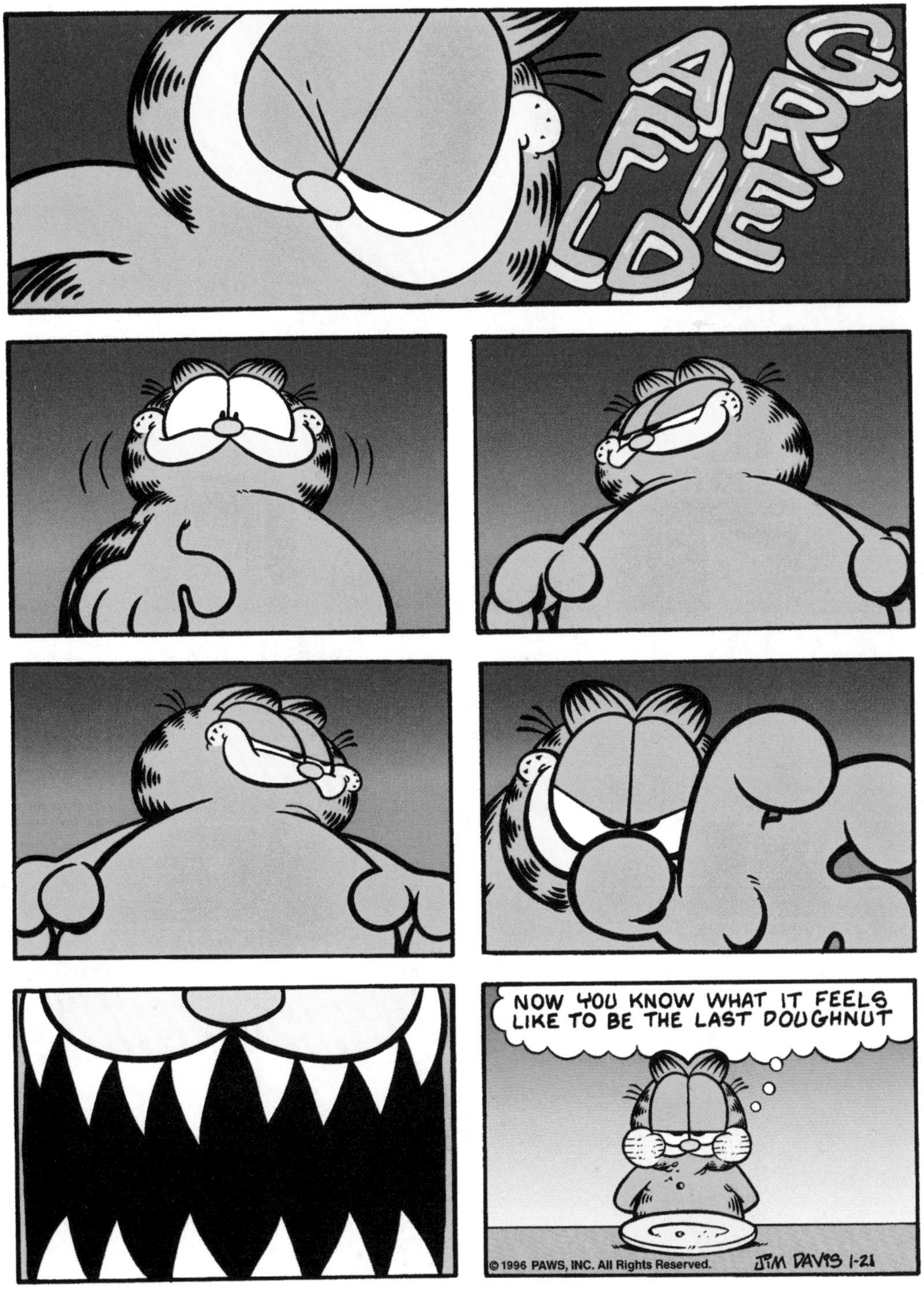
GARFIELD
NOW YOU KNOW WHAT IT FEELS LIKE TO BE THE LAST DOUGHNUT
© 1996 PAWS, INC. All Rights Reserved.
JIM DAVIS 1-21

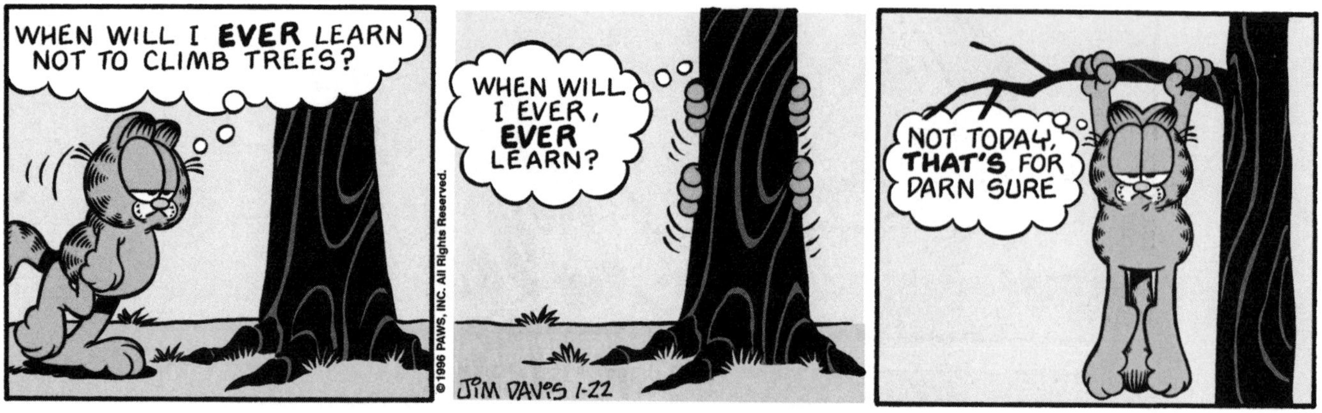
WHEN WILL I **EVER** LEARN NOT TO CLIMB TREES?
WHEN WILL I EVER, **EVER** LEARN?
© 1996 PAWS, INC. All Rights Reserved.
JIM DAVIS 1-22
NOT TODAY, **THAT'S** FOR DARN SURE

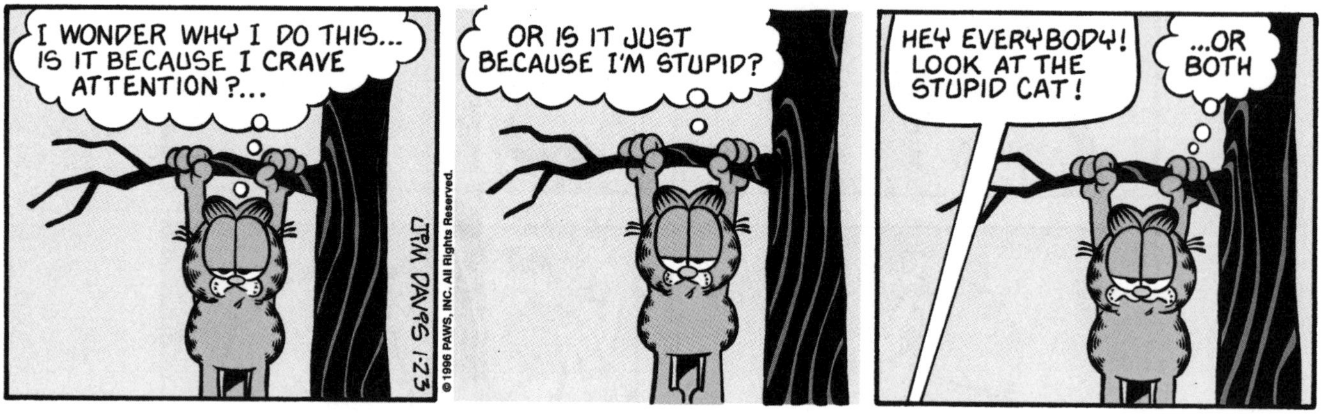
I WONDER WHY I DO THIS... IS IT BECAUSE I CRAVE ATTENTION?...
JIM DAVIS 1-23
© 1996 PAWS, INC. All Rights Reserved.
OR IS IT JUST BECAUSE I'M STUPID?
HEY EVERYBODY! LOOK AT THE STUPID CAT!
...OR BOTH

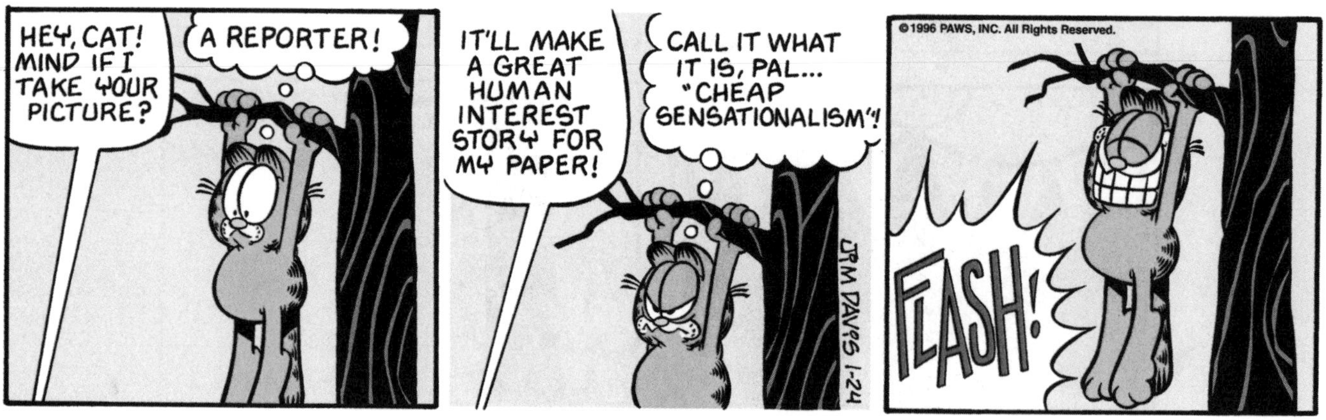
HEY, CAT! MIND IF I TAKE YOUR PICTURE?
A REPORTER!
IT'LL MAKE A GREAT HUMAN INTEREST STORY FOR MY PAPER!
CALL IT WHAT IT IS, PAL... "CHEAP SENSATIONALISM"!
JIM DAVIS 1-24
© 1996 PAWS, INC. All Rights Reserved.
FLASH!

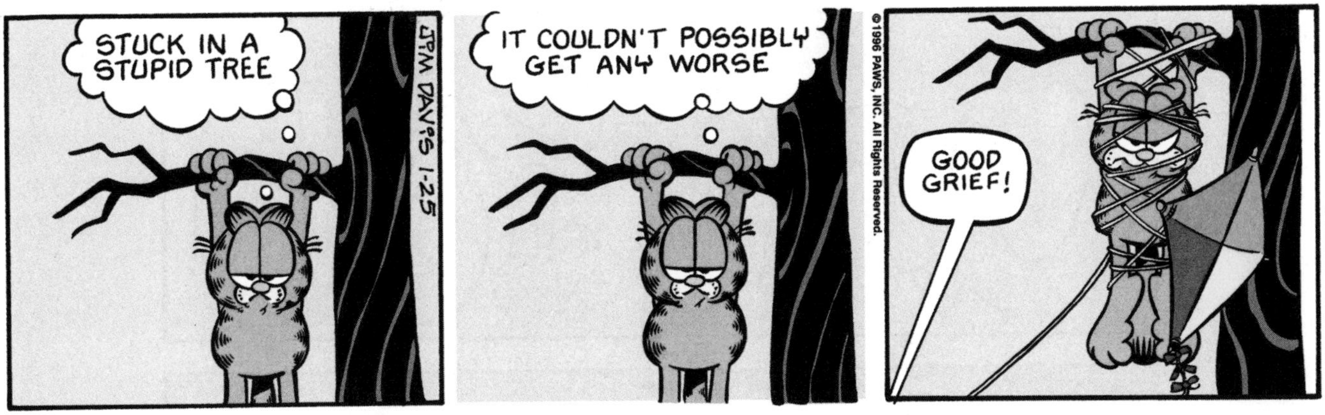
STUCK IN A STUPID TREE
JPM DAVPS 1-25
IT COULDN'T POSSIBLY GET ANY WORSE
© 1996 PAWS, INC. All Rights Reserved.
GOOD GRIEF!

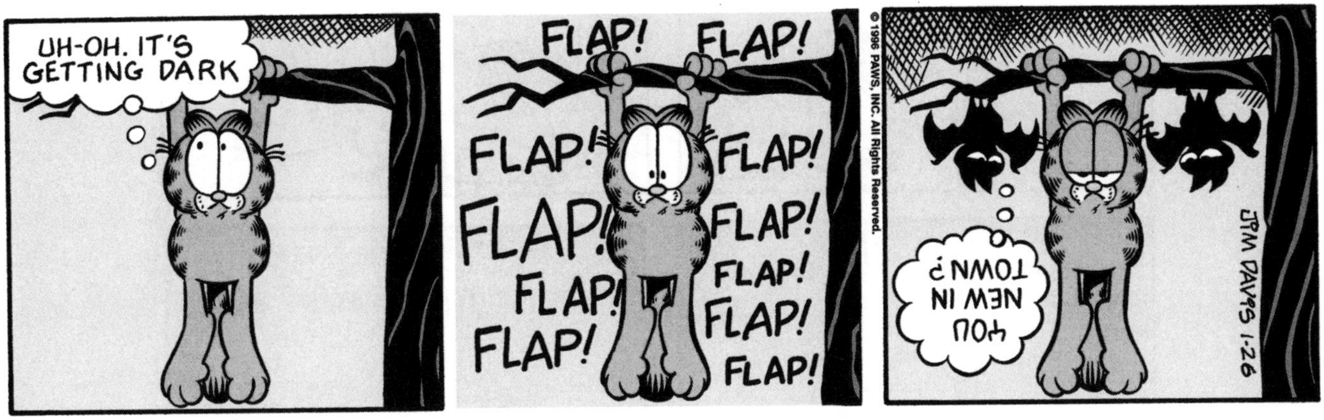
UH-OH. IT'S GETTING DARK
FLAP! FLAP!
FLAP! FLAP!
FLAP! FLAP!
FLAP! FLAP!
FLAP! FLAP!
FLAP!
© 1996 PAWS, INC. All Rights Reserved.
YOU NEW IN TOWN?
JPM DAVPS 1-26

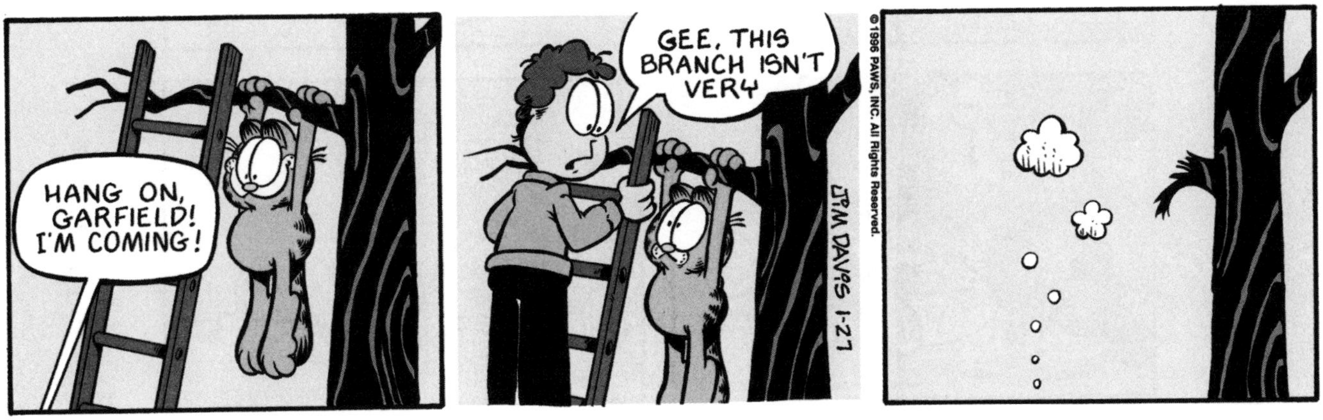
HANG ON, GARFIELD! I'M COMING!
GEE, THIS BRANCH ISN'T VERY
JPM DAVPS 1-27
© 1996 PAWS, INC. All Rights Reserved.

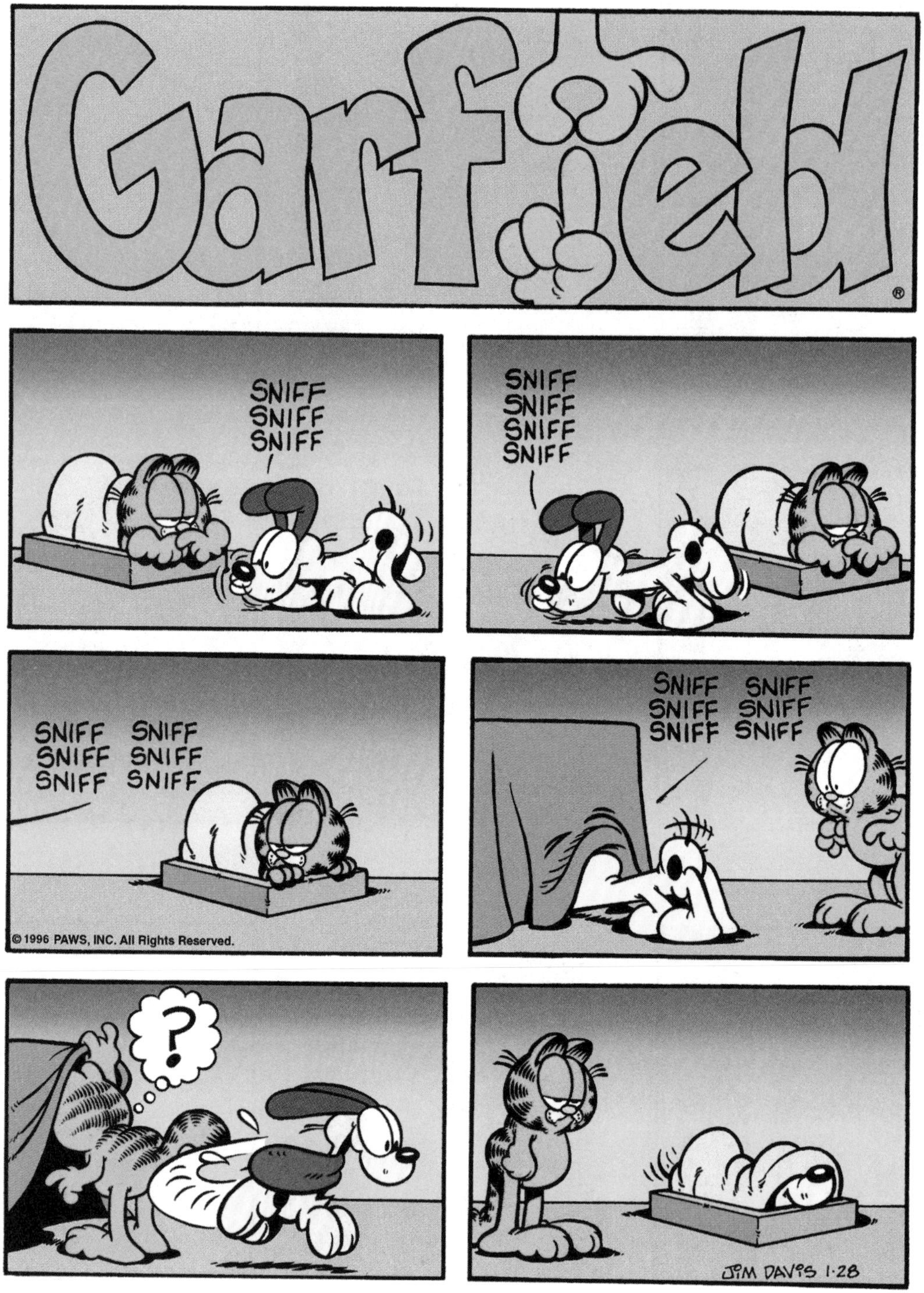
Garfield
SNIFF SNIFF SNIFF
SNIFF SNIFF SNIFF SNIFF
SNIFF SNIFF SNIFF SNIFF SNIFF SNIFF
© 1996 PAWS, INC. All Rights Reserved.
SNIFF SNIFF SNIFF SNIFF SNIFF SNIFF
?
JIM DAVIS 1-28

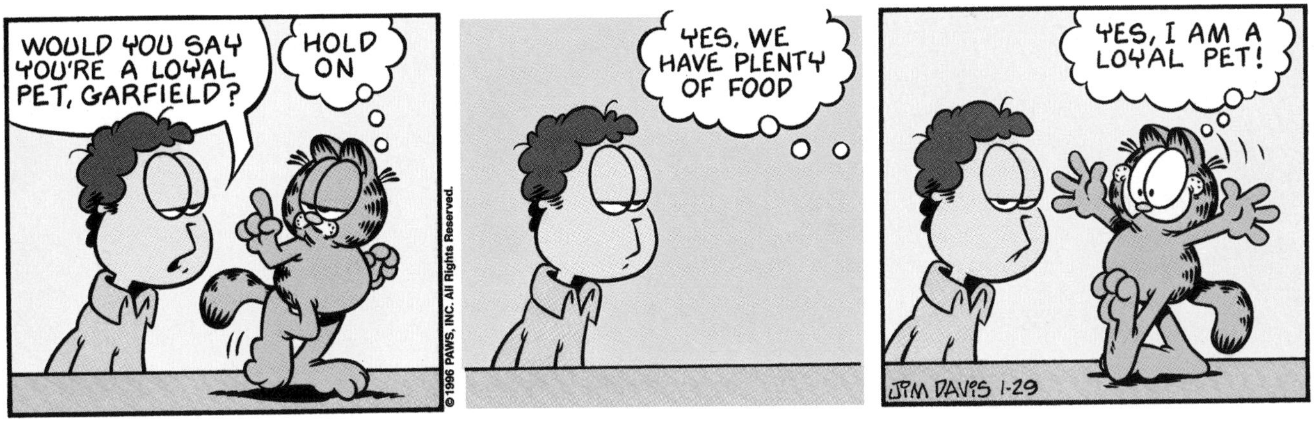
WOULD YOU SAY YOU'RE A LOYAL PET, GARFIELD?
HOLD ON
YES, WE HAVE PLENTY OF FOOD
YES, I AM A LOYAL PET!
JIM DAVIS 1-29
© 1996 PAWS, INC. All Rights Reserved.

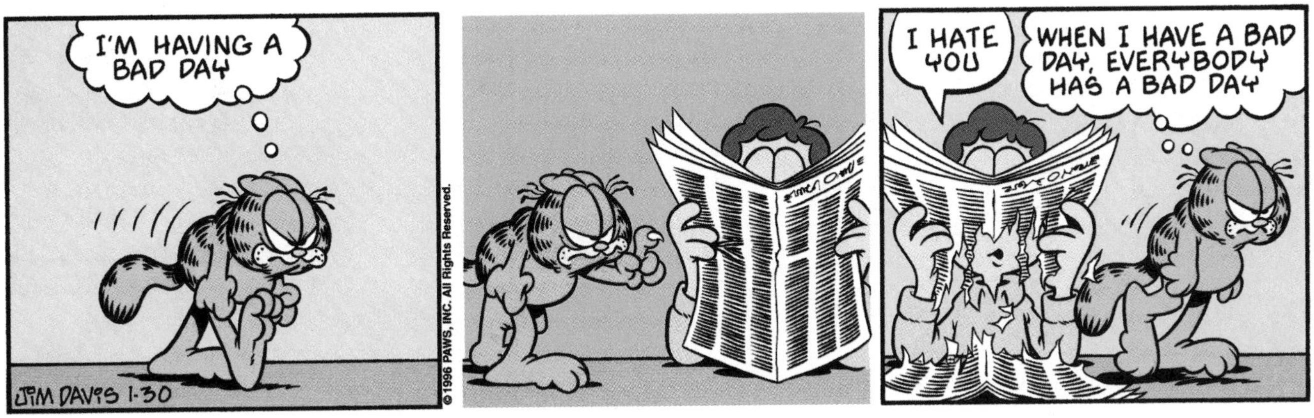
I'M HAVING A BAD DAY
I HATE YOU
WHEN I HAVE A BAD DAY, EVERYBODY HAS A BAD DAY
JIM DAVIS 1-30
© 1996 PAWS, INC. All Rights Reserved.

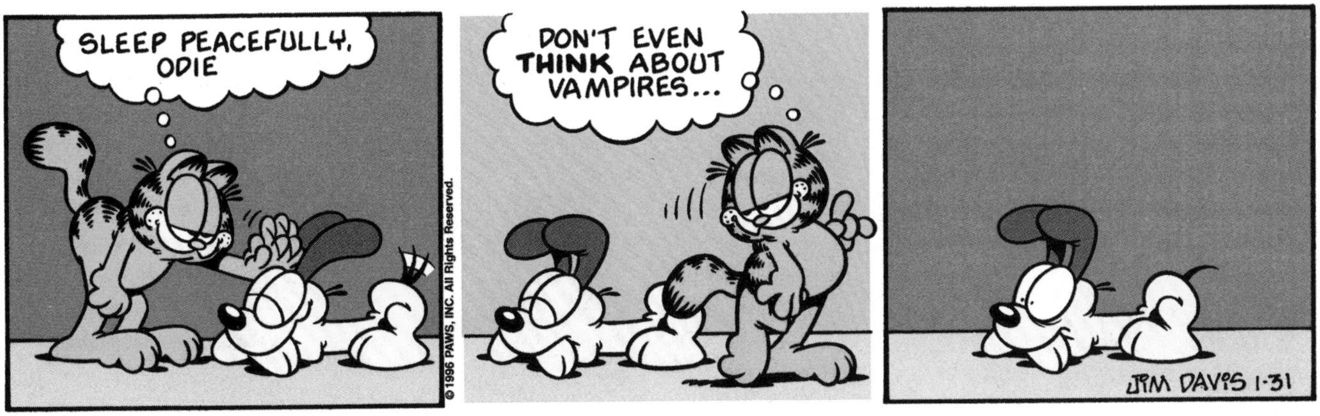
SLEEP PEACEFULLY, ODIE
DON'T EVEN **THINK** ABOUT VAMPIRES...
JIM DAVIS 1-31
© 1996 PAWS, INC. All Rights Reserved.

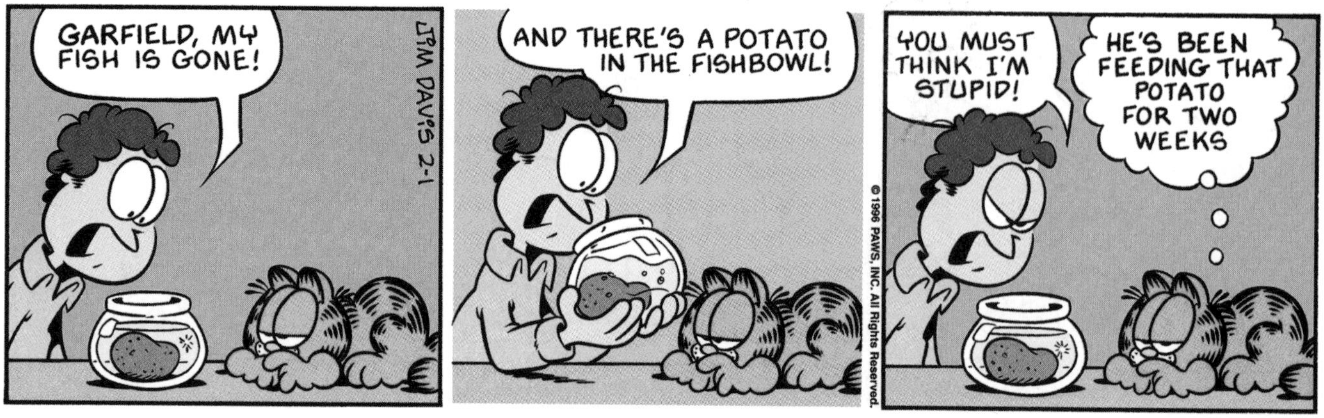
GARFIELD, MY FISH IS GONE!
JIM DAVIS 2-1
AND THERE'S A POTATO IN THE FISHBOWL!
© 1996 PAWS, INC. All Rights Reserved.
YOU MUST THINK I'M STUPID!
HE'S BEEN FEEDING THAT POTATO FOR TWO WEEKS

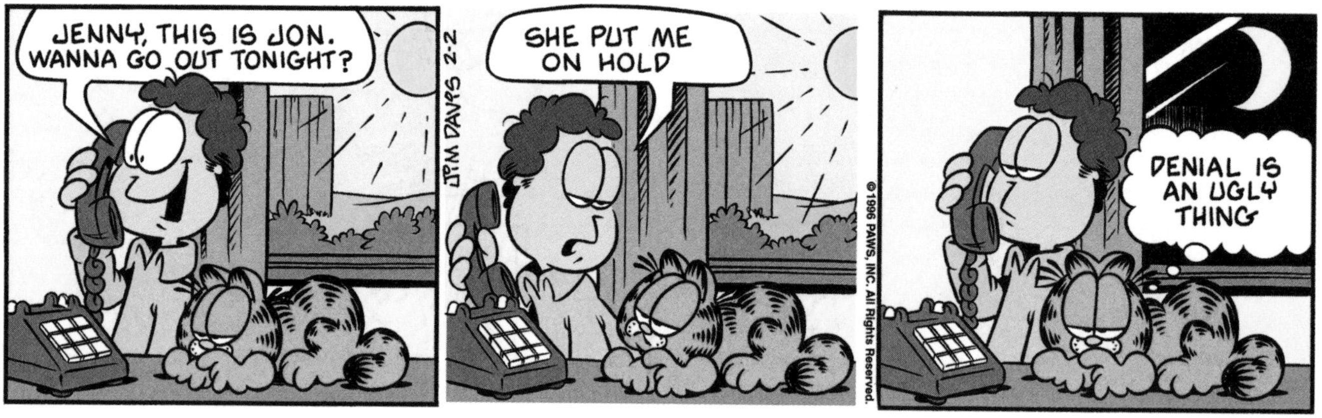
JENNY, THIS IS JON. WANNA GO OUT TONIGHT?
JIM DAVIS 2-2
SHE PUT ME ON HOLD
© 1996 PAWS, INC. All Rights Reserved.
DENIAL IS AN UGLY THING

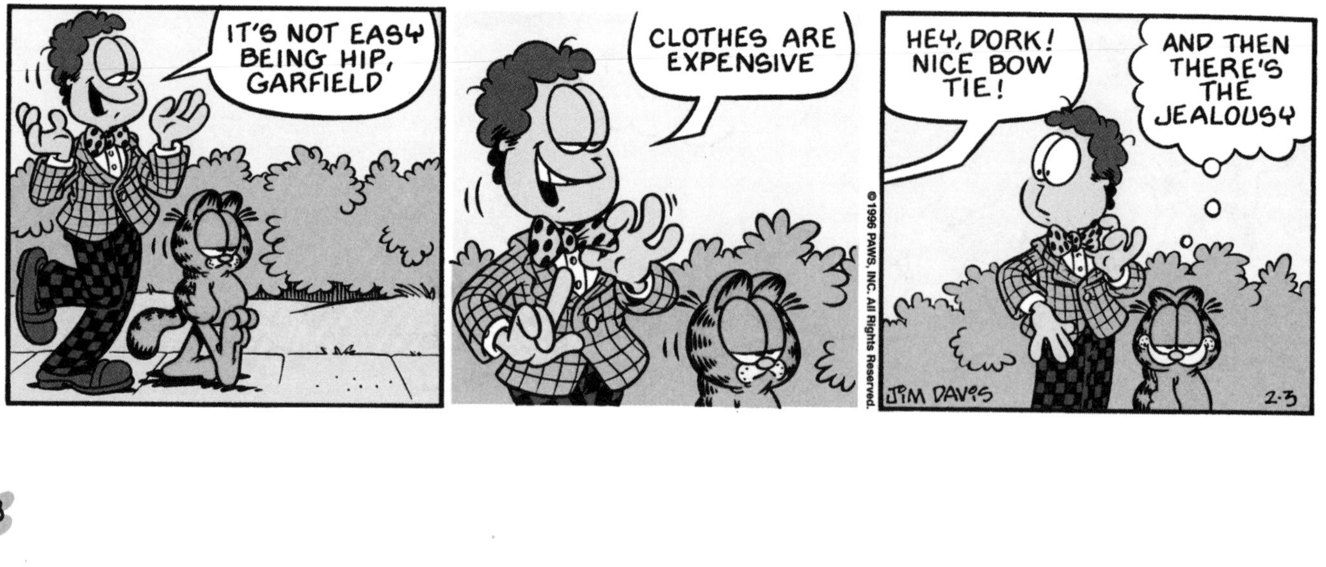
IT'S NOT EASY BEING HIP, GARFIELD
CLOTHES ARE EXPENSIVE
© 1996 PAWS, INC. All Rights Reserved.
HEY, DORK! NICE BOW TIE!
AND THEN THERE'S THE JEALOUSY
JIM DAVIS
2-3

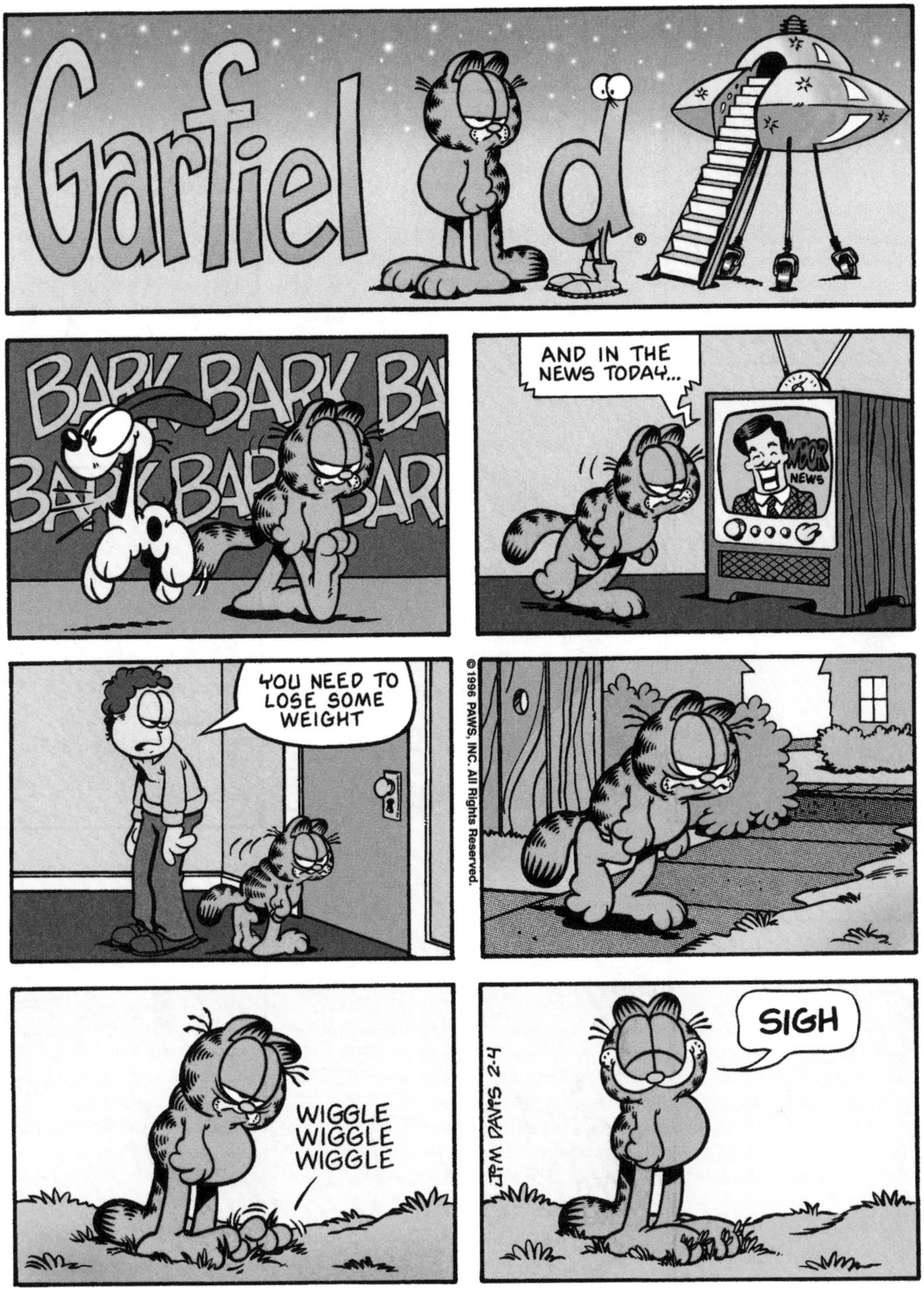
Garfield
BARK BARK BARK BARK BARK
AND IN THE NEWS TODAY...
WGOR NEWS
YOU NEED TO LOSE SOME WEIGHT
WIGGLE WIGGLE WIGGLE
SIGH
JPM DAVPS 2-4

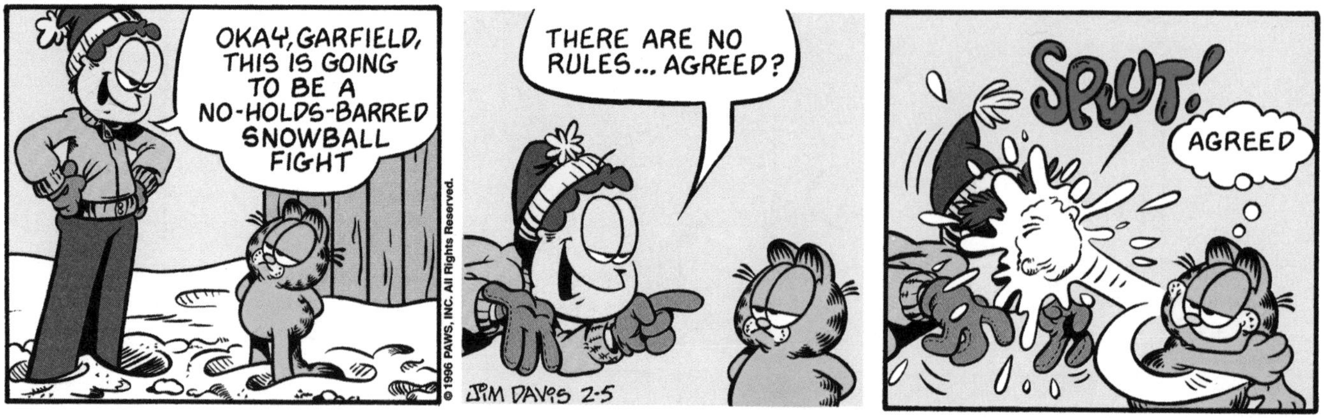
OKAY, GARFIELD, THIS IS GOING TO BE A NO-HOLDS-BARRED SNOWBALL FIGHT
THERE ARE NO RULES... AGREED?
© 1996 PAWS, INC. All Rights Reserved.
JIM DAVIS 2-5
SPLUT!
AGREED

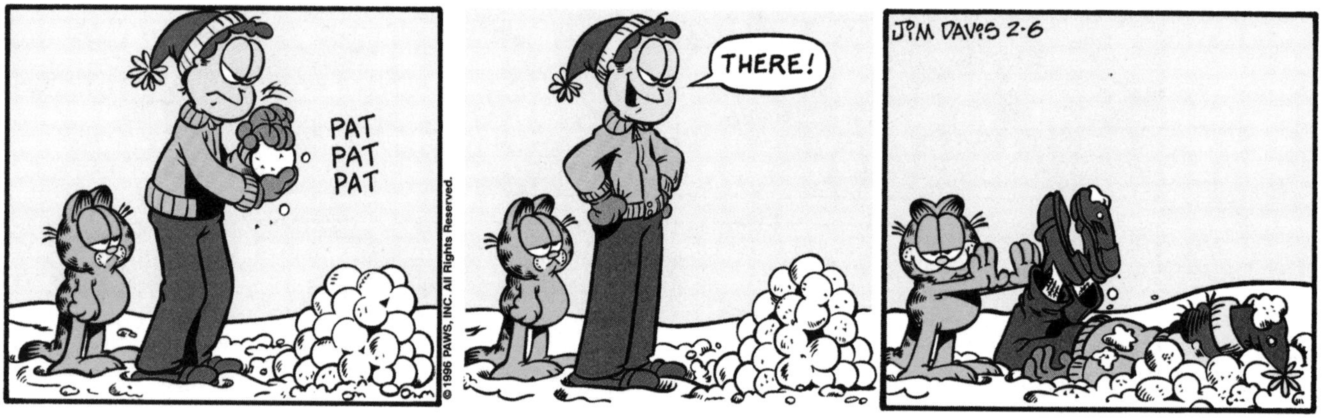
PAT PAT PAT
© 1996 PAWS, INC. All Rights Reserved.
THERE!
JIM DAVIS 2-6

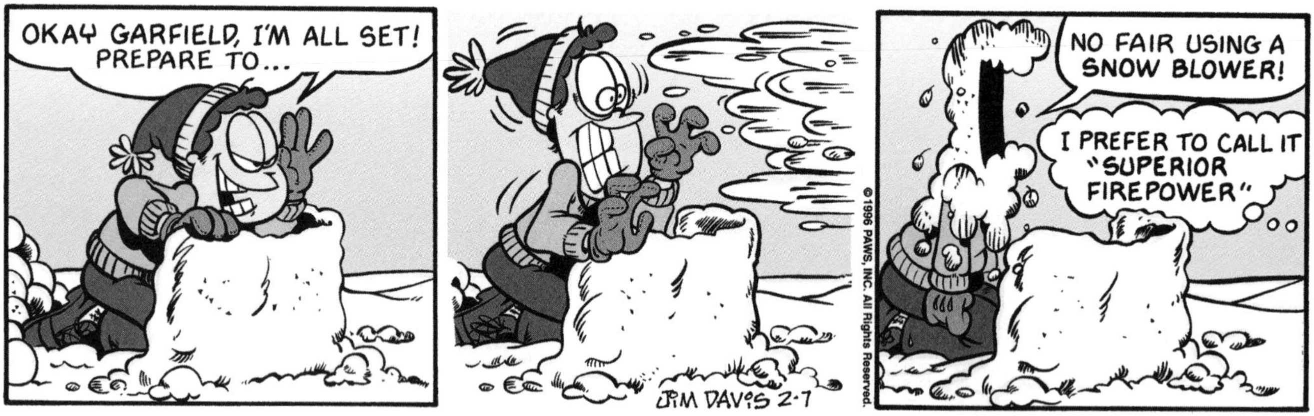
OKAY GARFIELD, I'M ALL SET! PREPARE TO...
JIM DAVIS 2-7
© 1996 PAWS, INC. All Rights Reserved.
NO FAIR USING A SNOW BLOWER!
I PREFER TO CALL IT "SUPERIOR FIREPOWER"

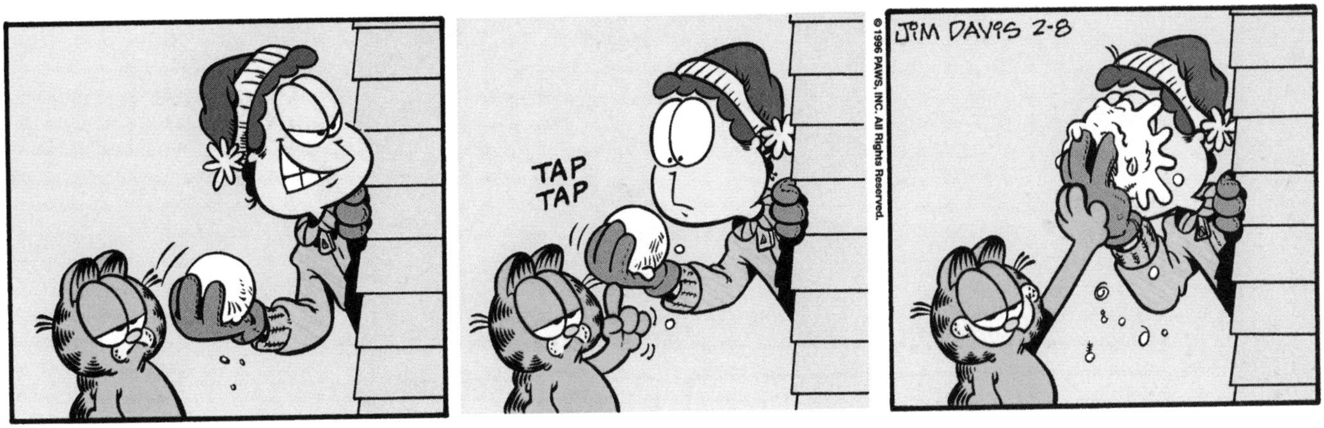
TAP TAP
© 1996 PAWS, INC. All Rights Reserved.
JIM DAVIS 2-8

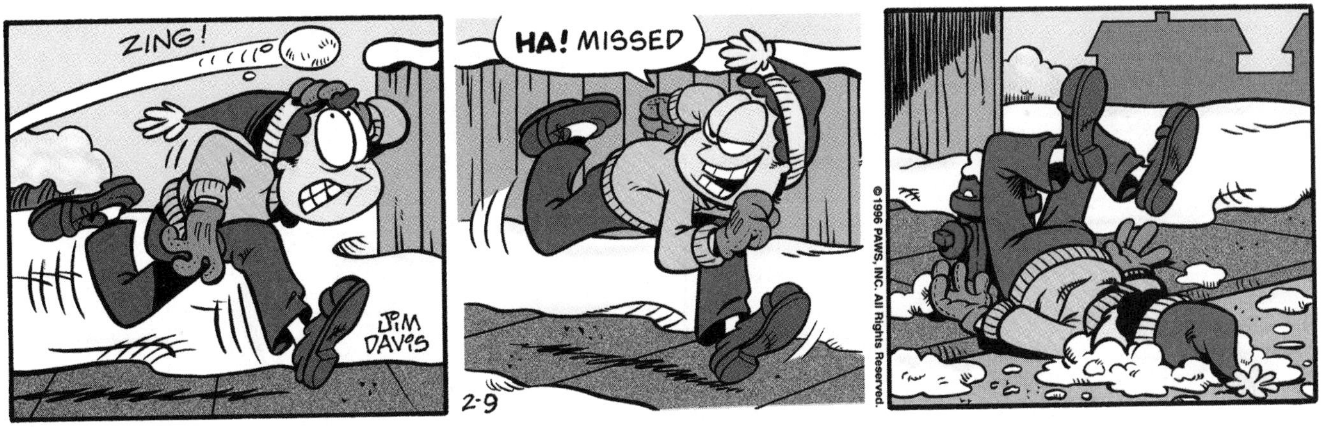
ZING!
JIM DAVIS
HA! MISSED
2-9
© 1996 PAWS, INC. All Rights Reserved.

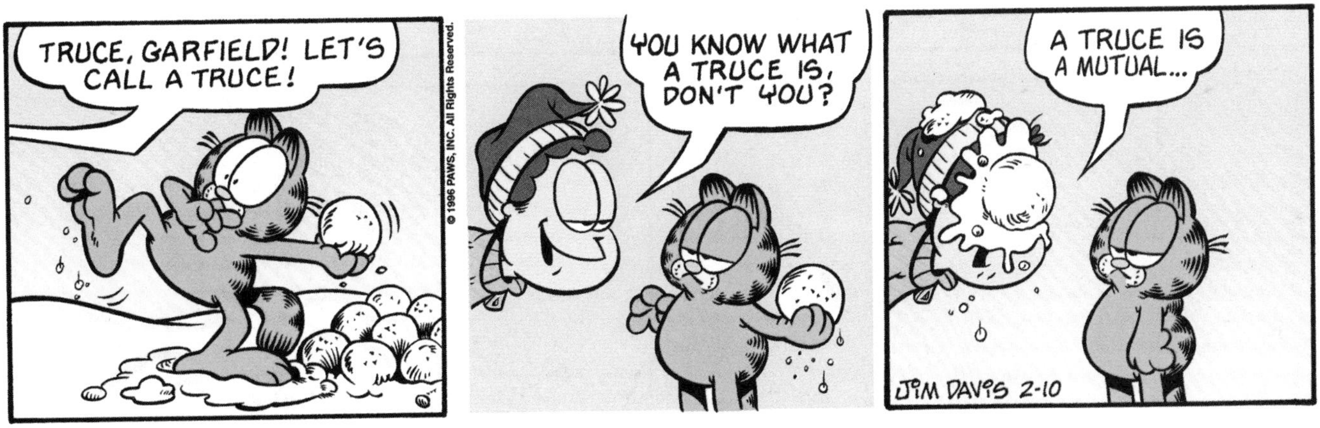
TRUCE, GARFIELD! LET'S CALL A TRUCE!
© 1996 PAWS, INC. All Rights Reserved.
YOU KNOW WHAT A TRUCE IS, DON'T YOU?
A TRUCE IS A MUTUAL...
JIM DAVIS 2-10

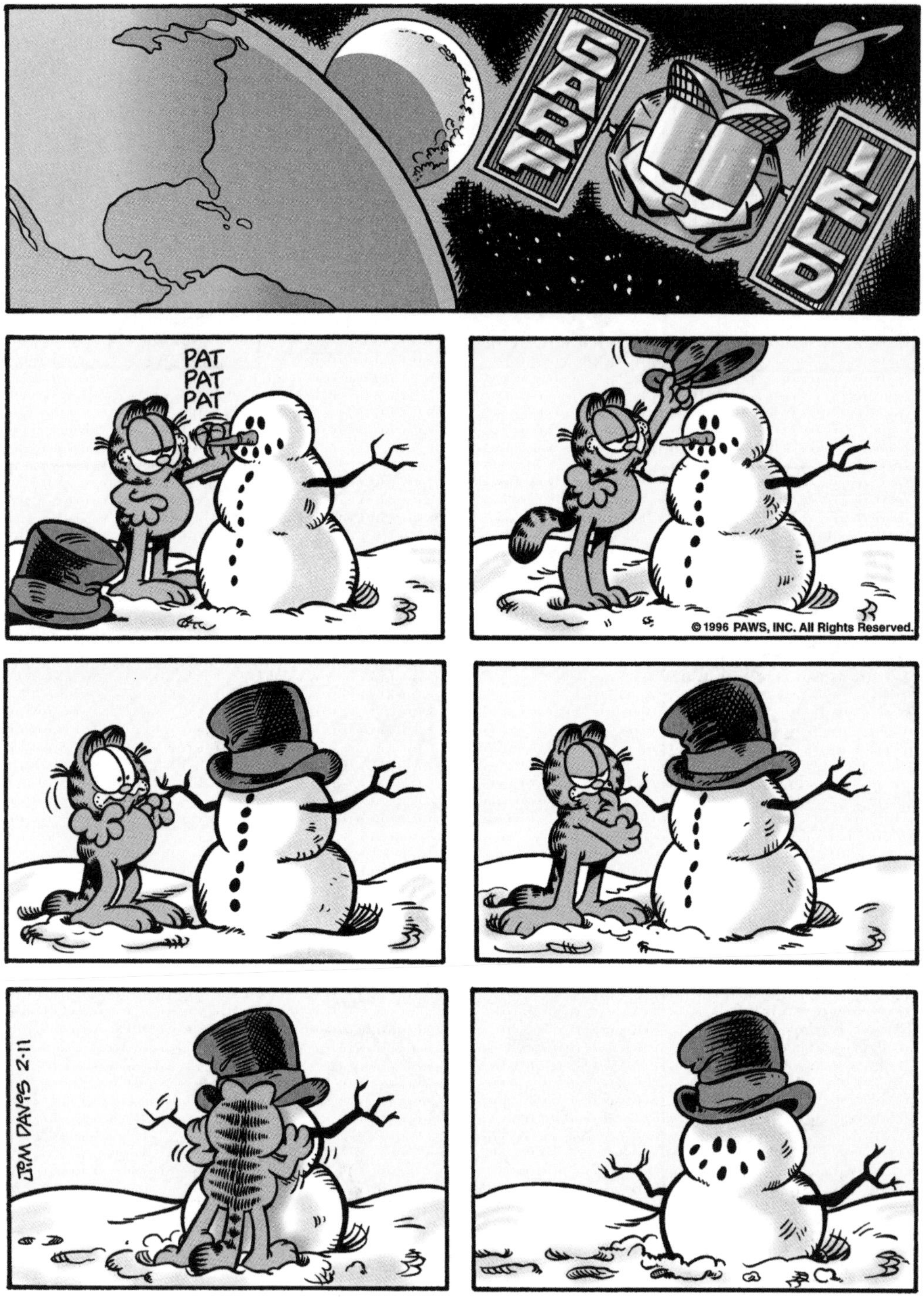
GARFIELD
PAT
PAT
PAT
© 1996 PAWS, INC. All Rights Reserved.
JIM DAVIS 2-11

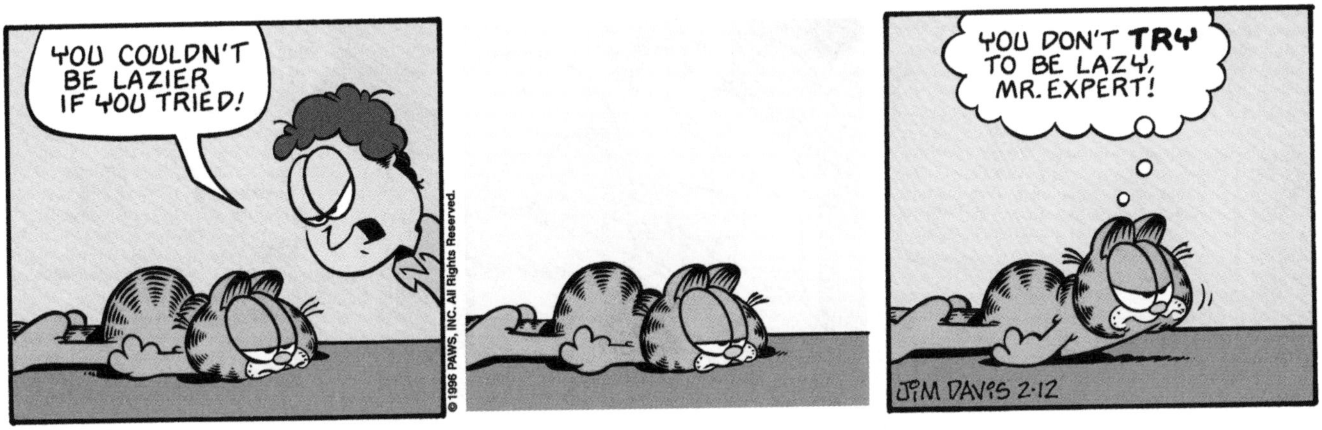
YOU COULDN'T BE LAZIER IF YOU TRIED!
© 1996 PAWS, INC. All Rights Reserved.
YOU DON'T **TRY** TO BE LAZY, MR. EXPERT!
JIM DAVIS 2-12

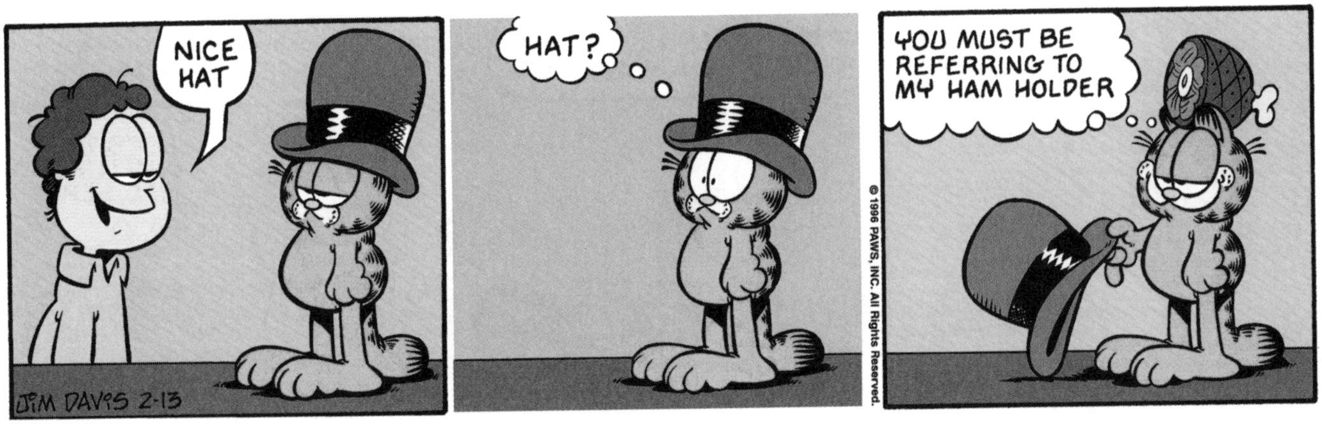
NICE HAT
JIM DAVIS 2-13
HAT?
© 1996 PAWS, INC. All Rights Reserved.
YOU MUST BE REFERRING TO MY HAM HOLDER

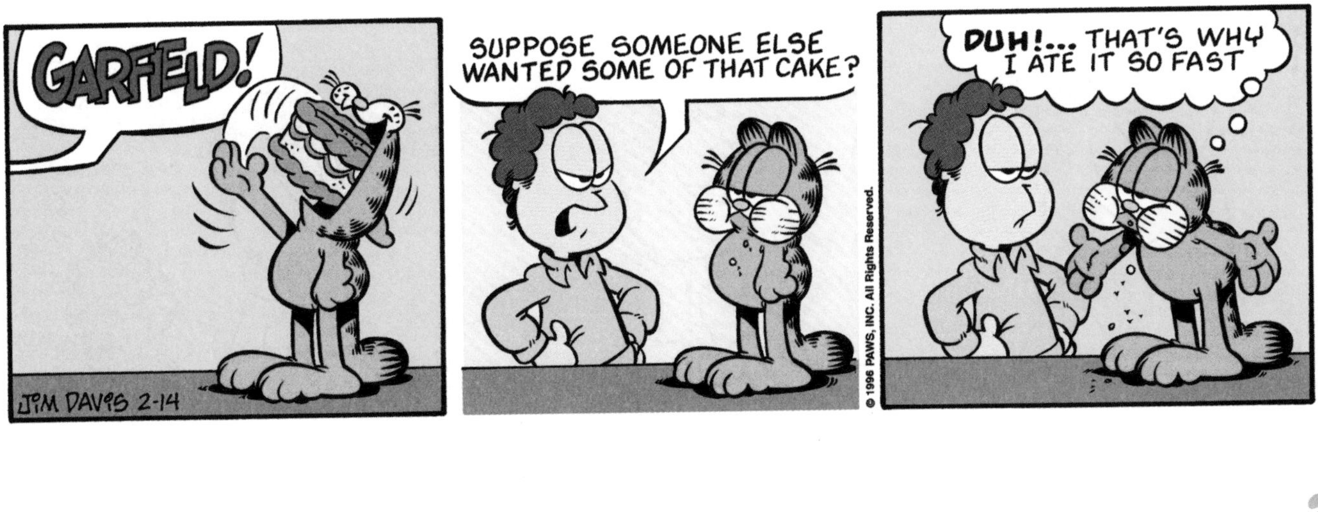
GARFIELD!
JIM DAVIS 2-14
SUPPOSE SOMEONE ELSE WANTED SOME OF THAT CAKE?
© 1996 PAWS, INC. All Rights Reserved.
DUH!... THAT'S WHY I ATE IT SO FAST

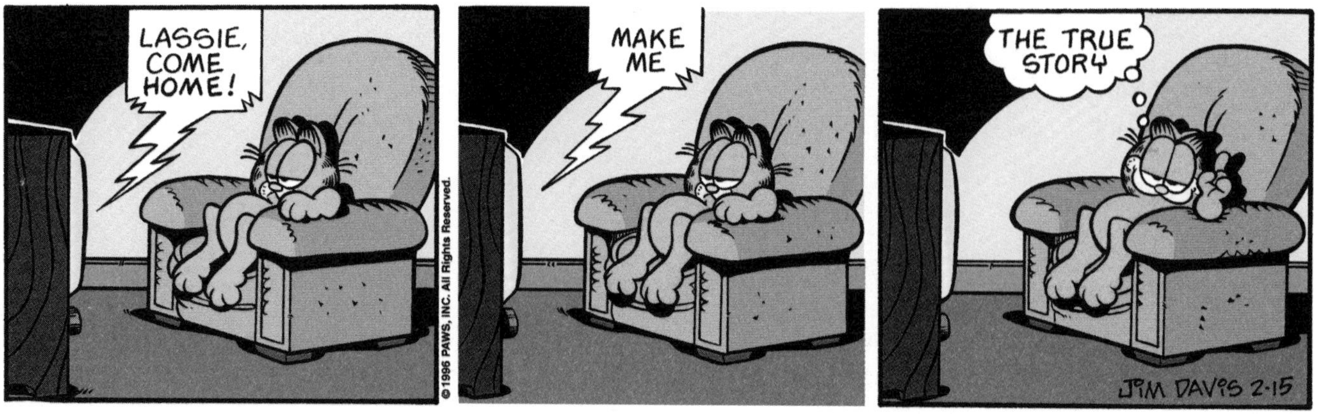
LASSIE, COME HOME!
MAKE ME
THE TRUE STORY
©1996 PAWS, INC. All Rights Reserved.
JIM DAVIS 2-15

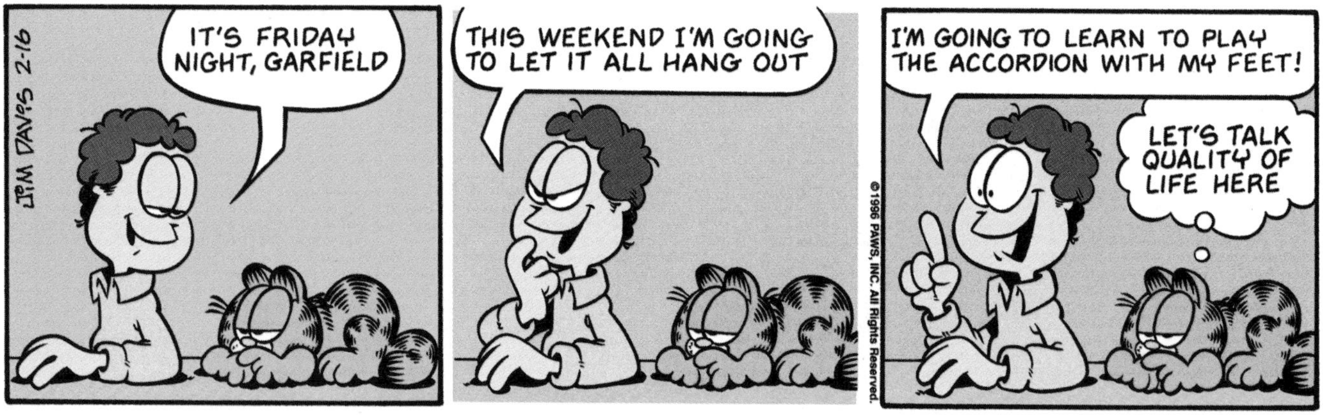
JIM DAVIS 2-16
IT'S FRIDAY NIGHT, GARFIELD
THIS WEEKEND I'M GOING TO LET IT ALL HANG OUT
©1996 PAWS, INC. All Rights Reserved.
I'M GOING TO LEARN TO PLAY THE ACCORDION WITH MY FEET!
LET'S TALK QUALITY OF LIFE HERE

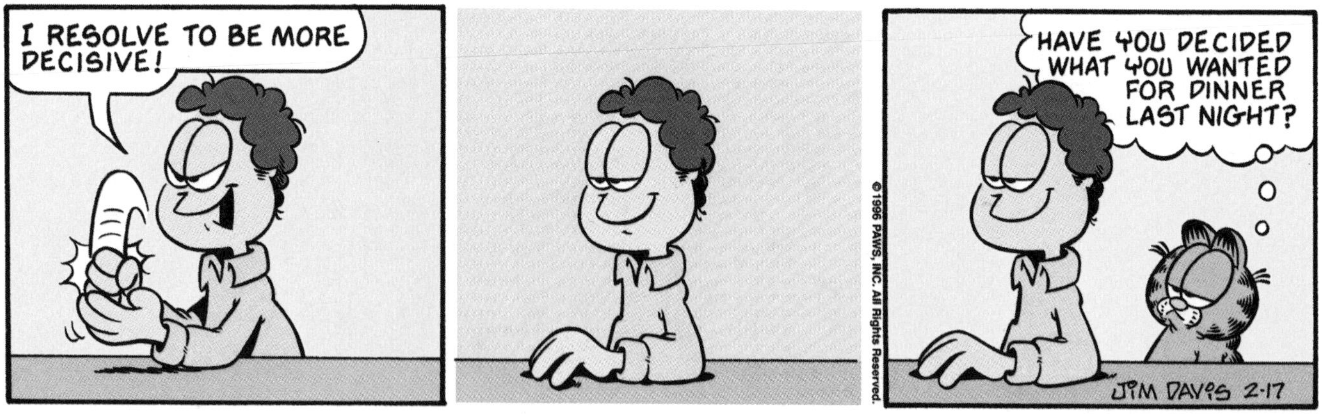
I RESOLVE TO BE MORE DECISIVE!
©1996 PAWS, INC. All Rights Reserved.
HAVE YOU DECIDED WHAT YOU WANTED FOR DINNER LAST NIGHT?
JIM DAVIS 2-17

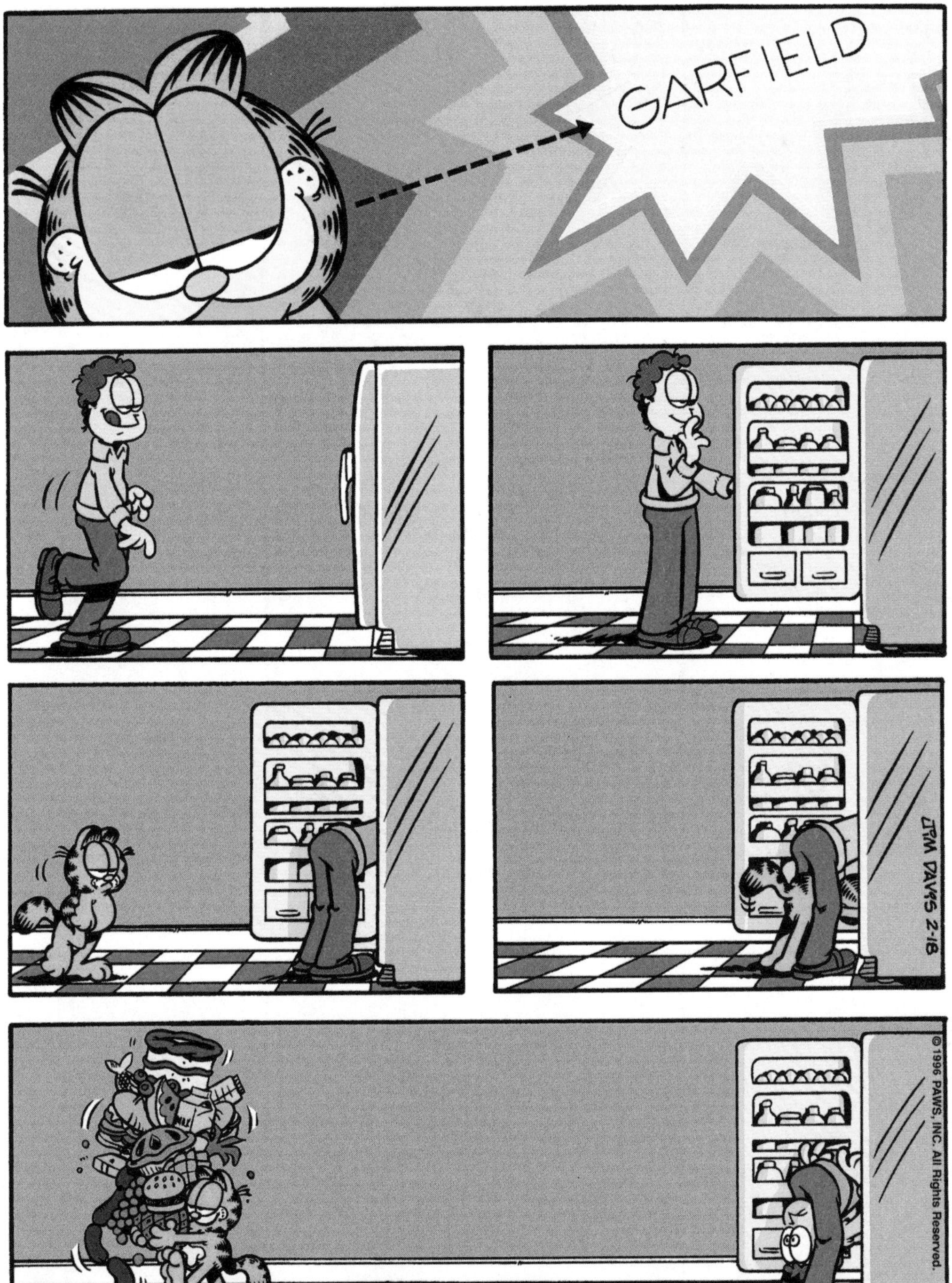
GARFIELD
JIM DAVIS 2-18
© 1996 PAWS, INC. All Rights Reserved.

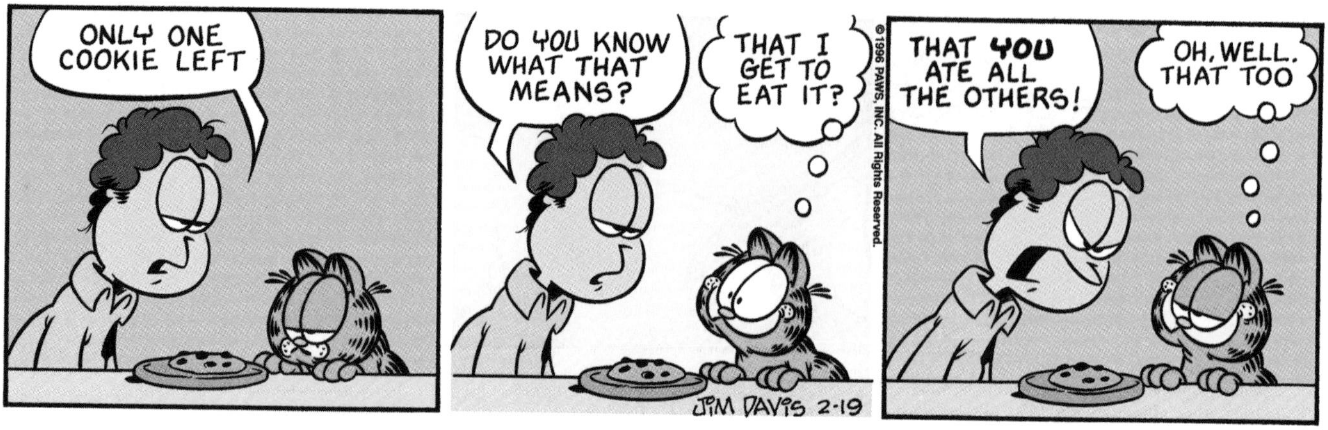
ONLY ONE COOKIE LEFT
DO YOU KNOW WHAT THAT MEANS?
THAT I GET TO EAT IT?
THAT YOU ATE ALL THE OTHERS!
OH, WELL. THAT TOO
JIM DAVIS 2-19
© 1996 PAWS, INC. All Rights Reserved.

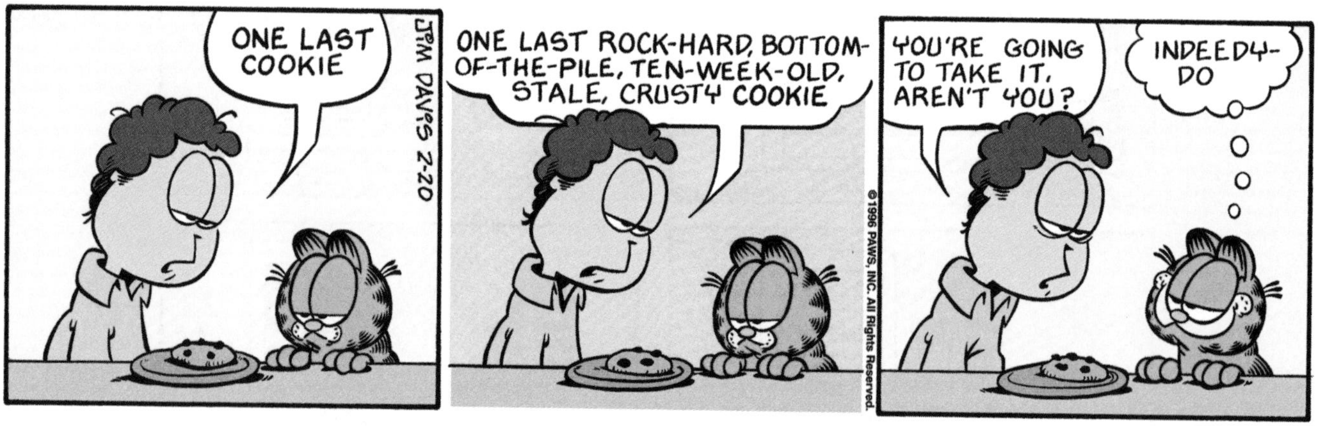
ONE LAST COOKIE
ONE LAST ROCK-HARD, BOTTOM-OF-THE-PILE, TEN-WEEK-OLD, STALE, CRUSTY COOKIE
YOU'RE GOING TO TAKE IT, AREN'T YOU?
INDEEDY-DO
JIM DAVIS 2-20
© 1996 PAWS, INC. All Rights Reserved.

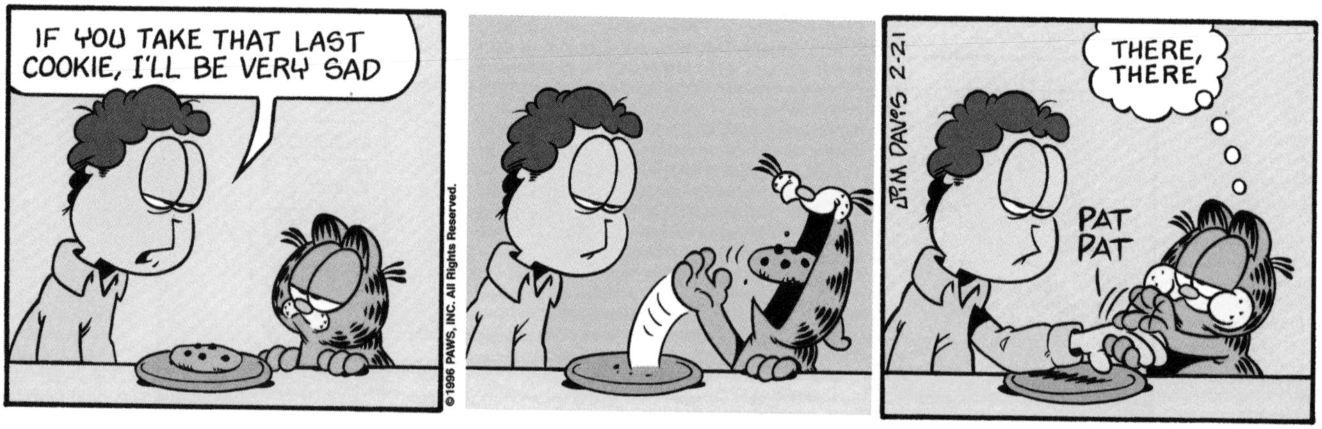
IF YOU TAKE THAT LAST COOKIE, I'LL BE VERY SAD
THERE, THERE
PAT PAT
JIM DAVIS 2-21
© 1996 PAWS, INC. All Rights Reserved.

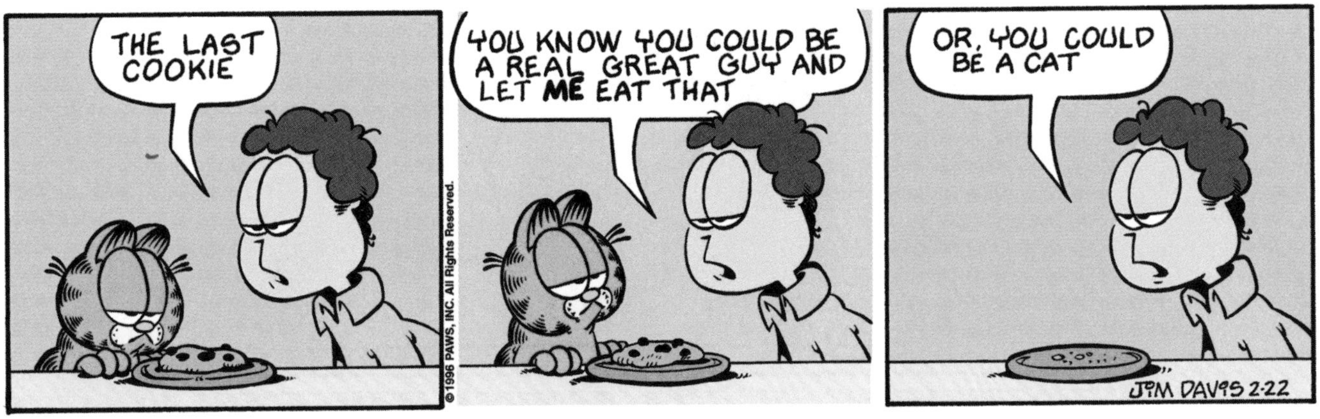
THE LAST COOKIE
YOU KNOW YOU COULD BE A REAL GREAT GUY AND LET **ME** EAT THAT
OR, YOU COULD BE A CAT
JIM DAVIS 2-22
© 1996 PAWS, INC. All Rights Reserved.

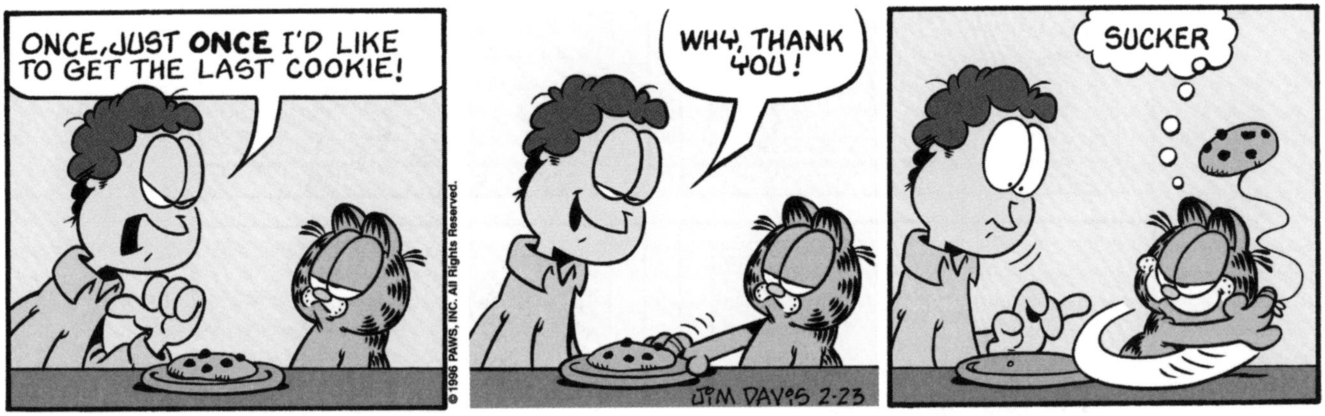
ONCE, JUST **ONCE** I'D LIKE TO GET THE LAST COOKIE!
WHY, THANK YOU!
SUCKER
JIM DAVIS 2-23
© 1996 PAWS, INC. All Rights Reserved.

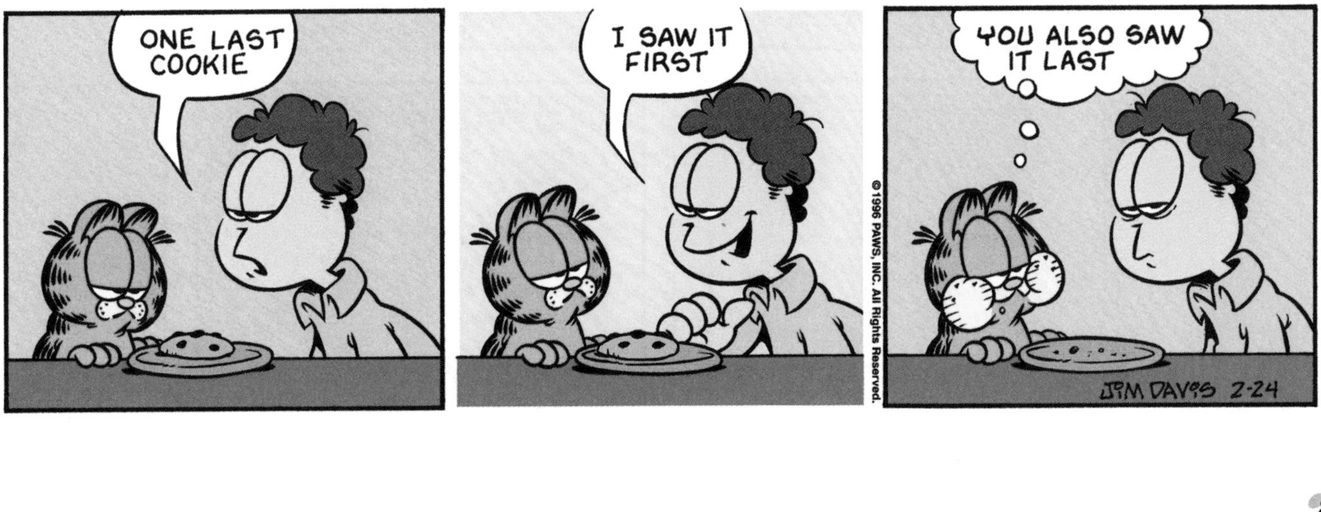
ONE LAST COOKIE
I SAW IT FIRST
YOU ALSO SAW IT LAST
JIM DAVIS 2-24
© 1996 PAWS, INC. All Rights Reserved.

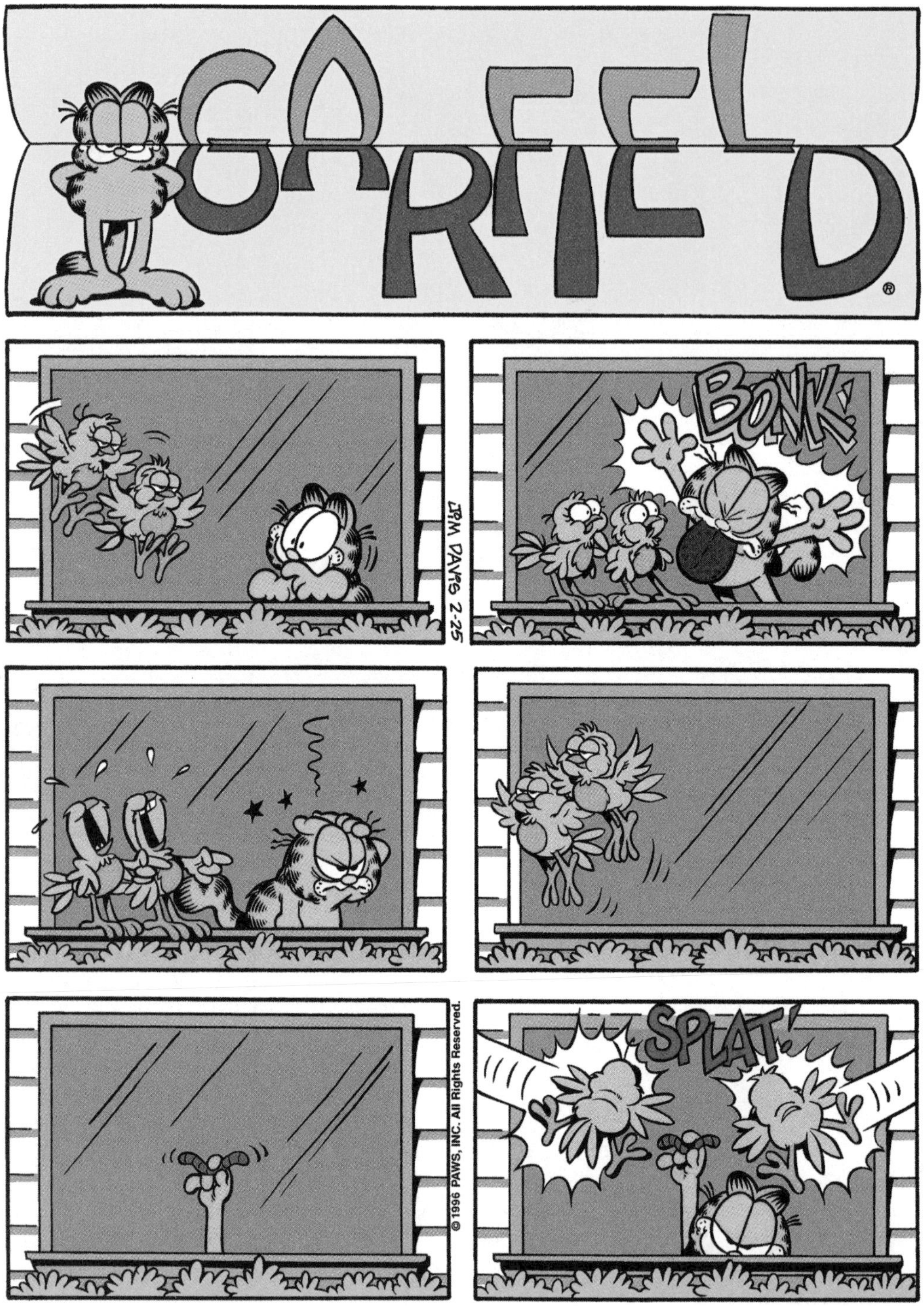
GARFIELD®
JIM DAVIS 2-25
BONK!
SPLAT!
© 1996 PAWS, INC. All Rights Reserved.

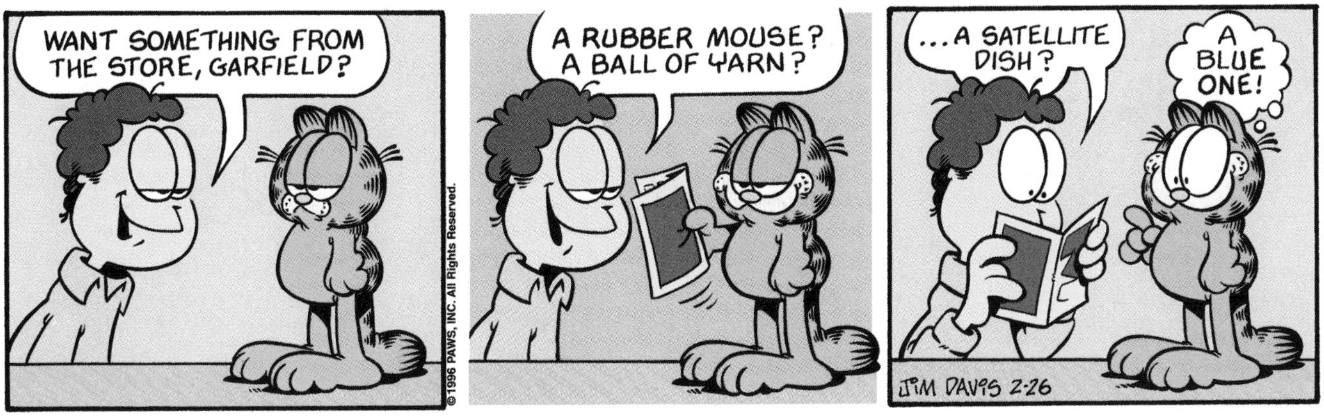
WANT SOMETHING FROM THE STORE, GARFIELD?
© 1996 PAWS, INC. All Rights Reserved.
A RUBBER MOUSE? A BALL OF YARN?
...A SATELLITE DISH?
A BLUE ONE!
JIM DAVIS 2-26

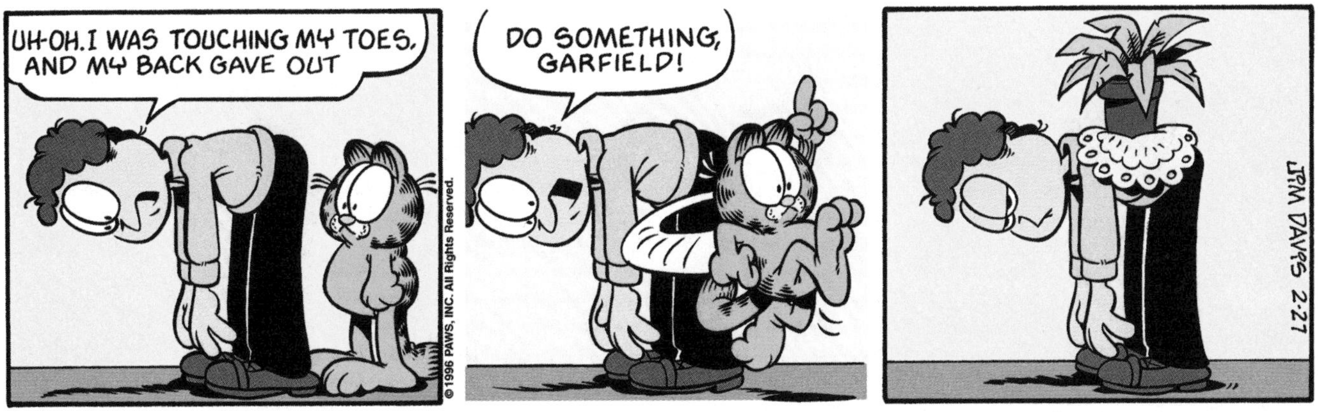
UH-OH. I WAS TOUCHING MY TOES, AND MY BACK GAVE OUT
© 1996 PAWS, INC. All Rights Reserved.
DO SOMETHING, GARFIELD!
JIM DAVIS 2-27

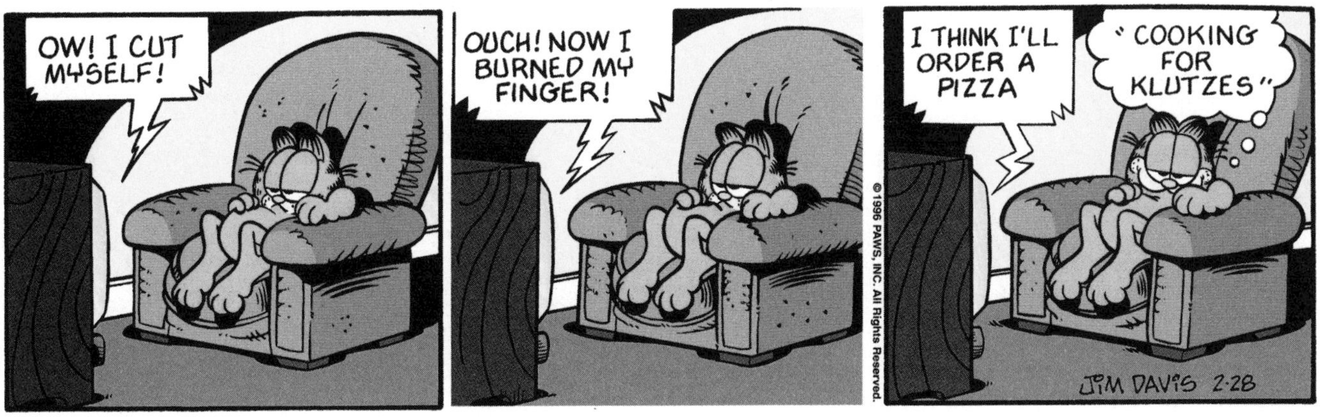
OW! I CUT MYSELF!
OUCH! NOW I BURNED MY FINGER!
© 1996 PAWS, INC. All Rights Reserved.
I THINK I'LL ORDER A PIZZA
"COOKING FOR KLUTZES"
JIM DAVIS 2-28

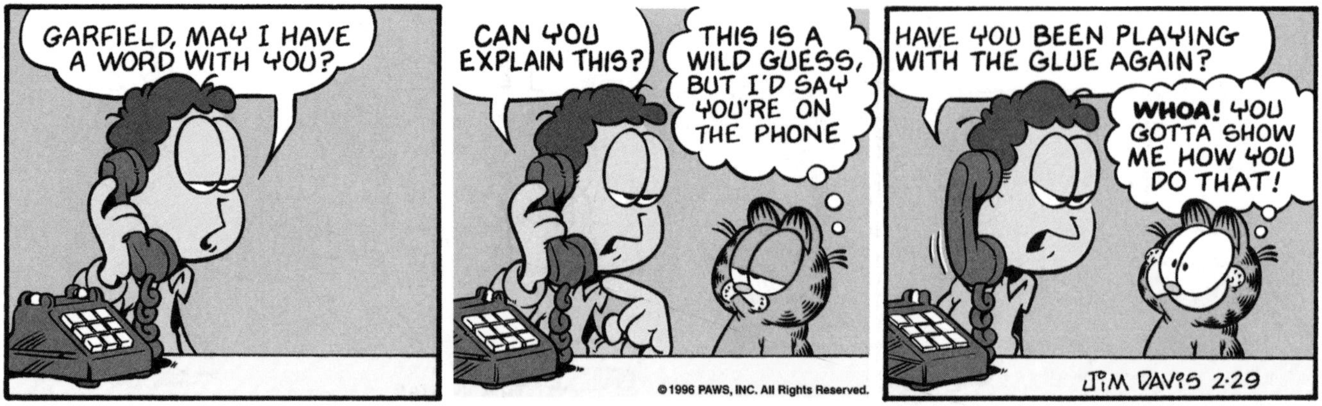
GARFIELD, MAY I HAVE A WORD WITH YOU?
CAN YOU EXPLAIN THIS?
THIS IS A WILD GUESS, BUT I'D SAY YOU'RE ON THE PHONE
HAVE YOU BEEN PLAYING WITH THE GLUE AGAIN?
WHOA! YOU GOTTA SHOW ME HOW YOU DO THAT!
© 1996 PAWS, INC. All Rights Reserved.
JIM DAVIS 2-29

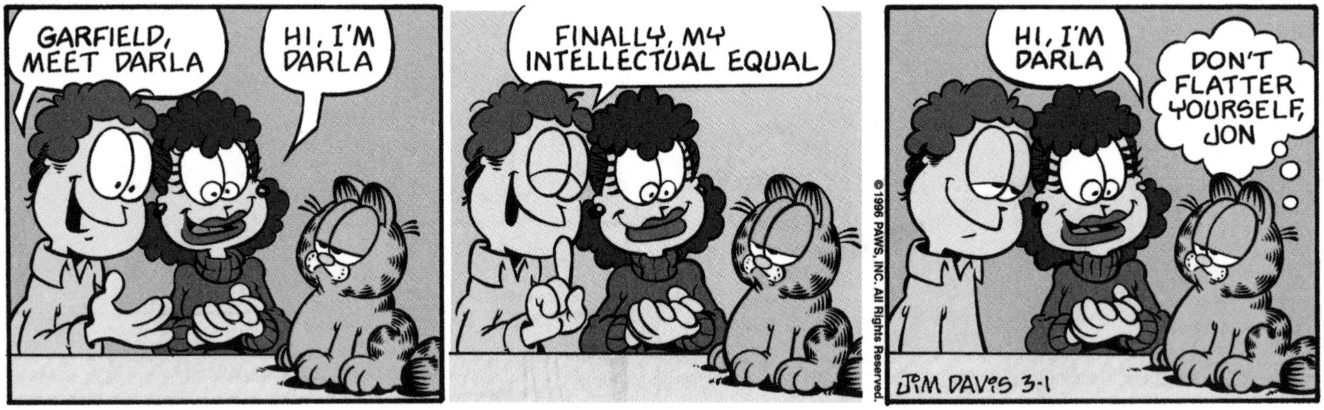
GARFIELD, MEET DARLA
HI, I'M DARLA
FINALLY, MY INTELLECTUAL EQUAL
© 1996 PAWS, INC. All Rights Reserved.
HI, I'M DARLA
DON'T FLATTER YOURSELF, JON
JIM DAVIS 3-1

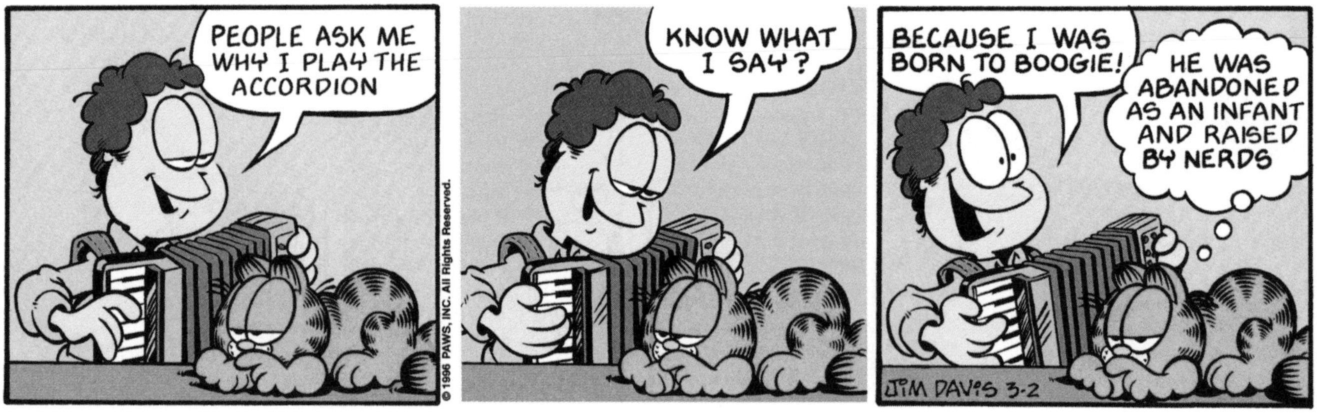
PEOPLE ASK ME WHY I PLAY THE ACCORDION
© 1996 PAWS, INC. All Rights Reserved.
KNOW WHAT I SAY?
BECAUSE I WAS BORN TO BOOGIE!
HE WAS ABANDONED AS AN INFANT AND RAISED BY NERDS
JIM DAVIS 3-2

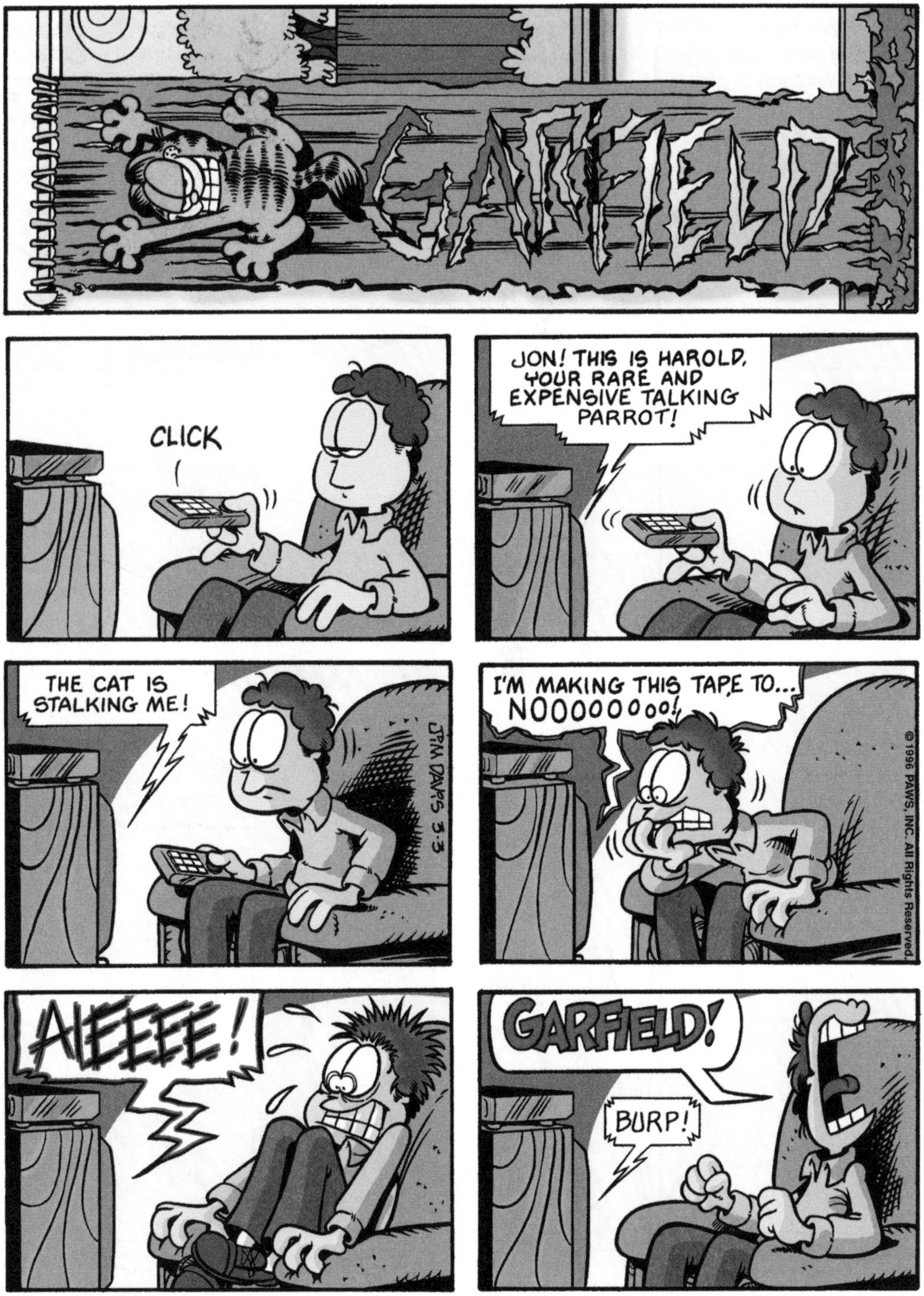
GARFIELD
CLICK
JON! THIS IS HAROLD, YOUR RARE AND EXPENSIVE TALKING PARROT!
THE CAT IS STALKING ME!
JIM DAVIS 3-3
I'M MAKING THIS TAPE TO... NOOOOOooo!
© 1996 PAWS, INC. All Rights Reserved.
AIEEEE!
GARFIELD!
BURP!

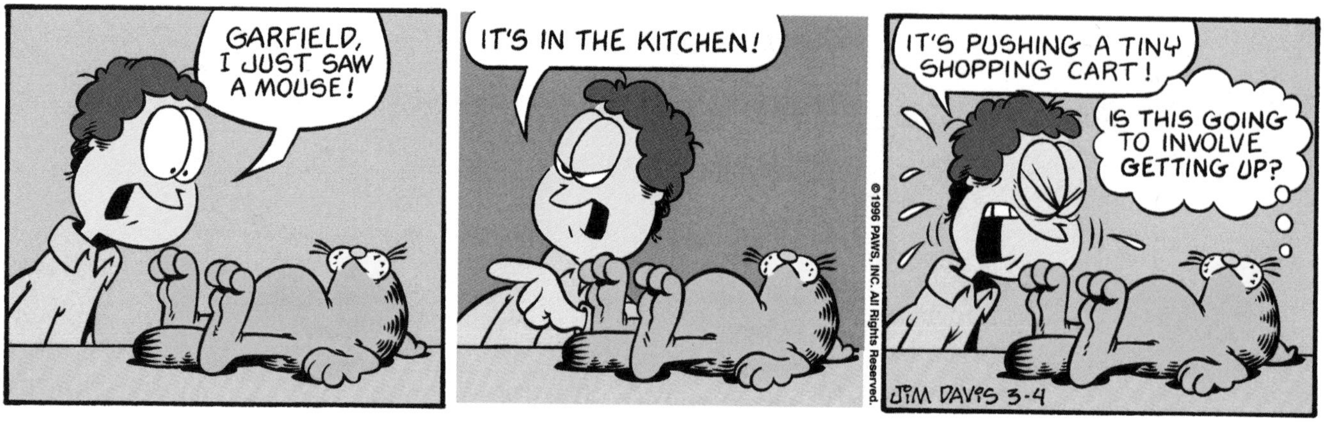
GARFIELD, I JUST SAW A MOUSE!
IT'S IN THE KITCHEN!
IT'S PUSHING A TINY SHOPPING CART!
IS THIS GOING TO INVOLVE GETTING UP?
© 1996 PAWS, INC. All Rights Reserved.
JIM DAVIS 3-4

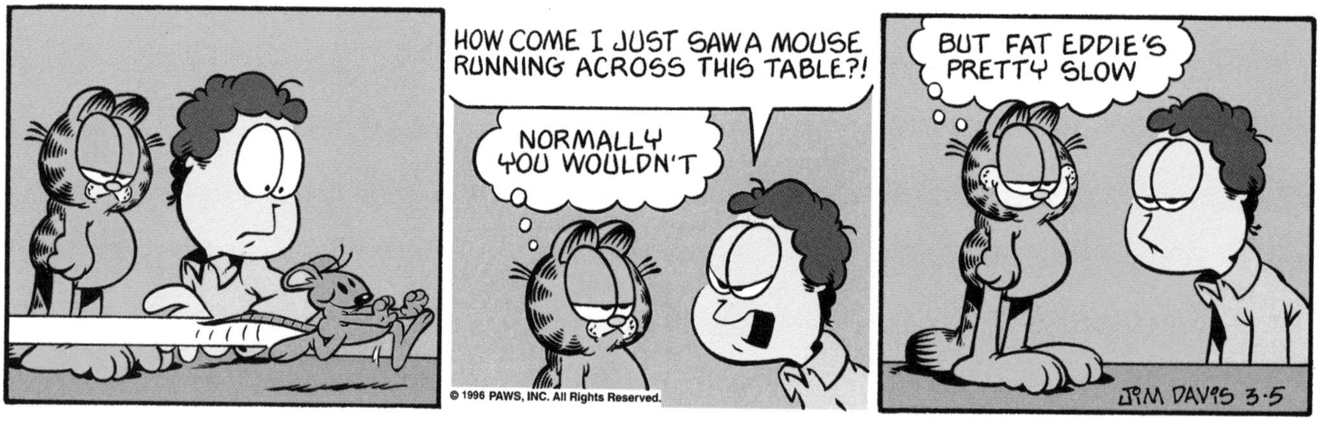
HOW COME I JUST SAW A MOUSE RUNNING ACROSS THIS TABLE?!
NORMALLY YOU WOULDN'T
© 1996 PAWS, INC. All Rights Reserved.
BUT FAT EDDIE'S PRETTY SLOW
JIM DAVIS 3-5

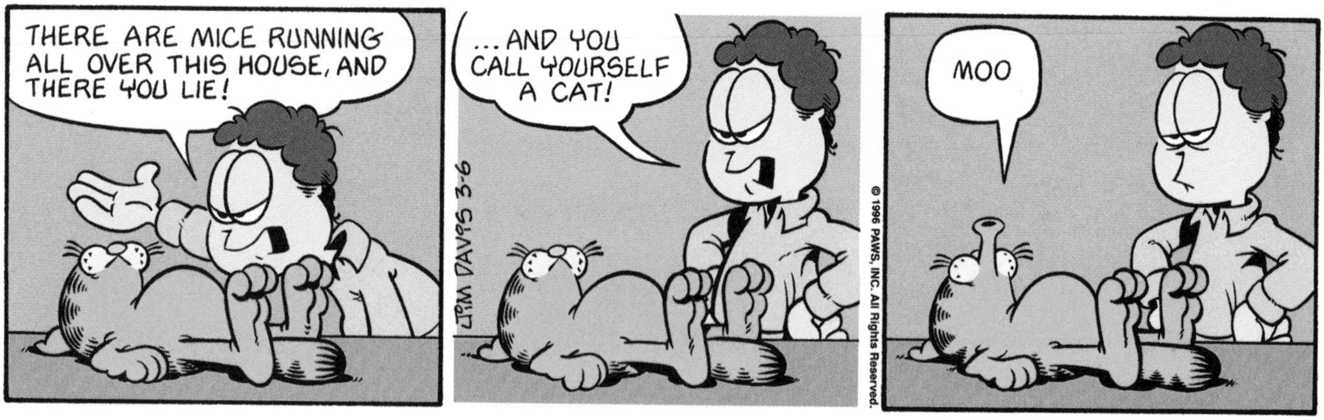
THERE ARE MICE RUNNING ALL OVER THIS HOUSE, AND THERE YOU LIE!
JIM DAVIS 3-6
...AND YOU CALL YOURSELF A CAT!
© 1996 PAWS, INC. All Rights Reserved.
MOO

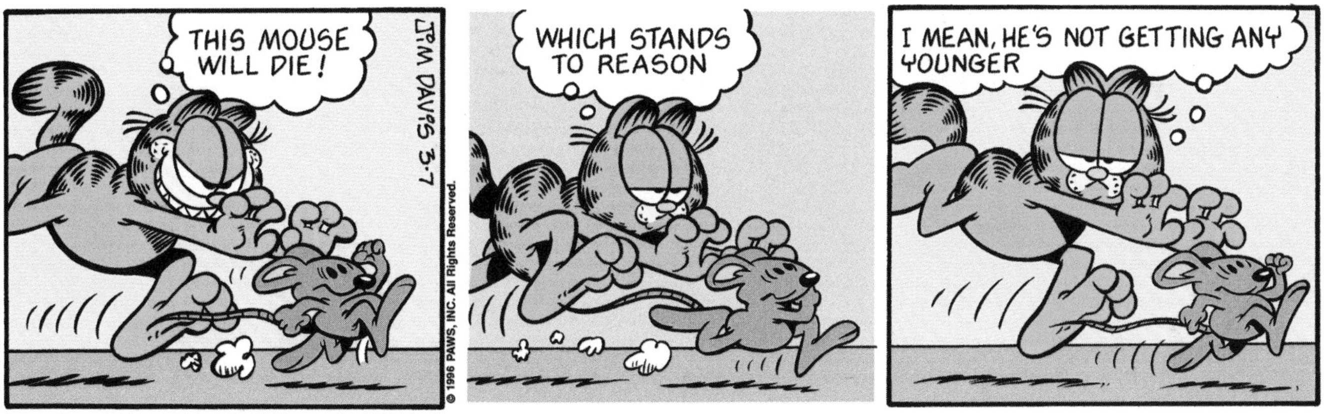
THIS MOUSE WILL DIE!
JIM DAVIS 3-7
© 1996 PAWS, INC. All Rights Reserved.
WHICH STANDS TO REASON
I MEAN, HE'S NOT GETTING ANY YOUNGER

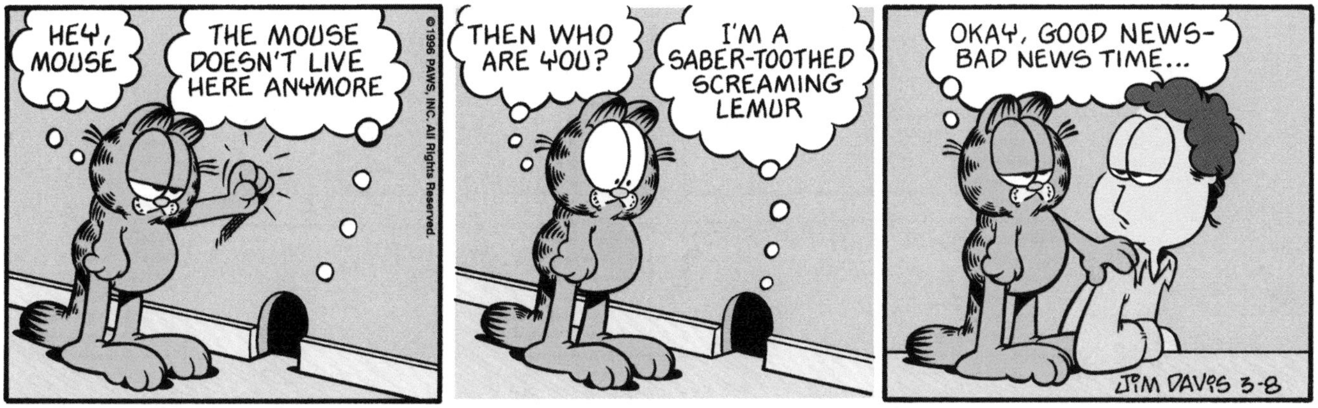
HEY, MOUSE
THE MOUSE DOESN'T LIVE HERE ANYMORE
© 1996 PAWS, INC. All Rights Reserved.
THEN WHO ARE YOU?
I'M A SABER-TOOTHED SCREAMING LEMUR
OKAY, GOOD NEWS-BAD NEWS TIME...
JIM DAVIS 3-8

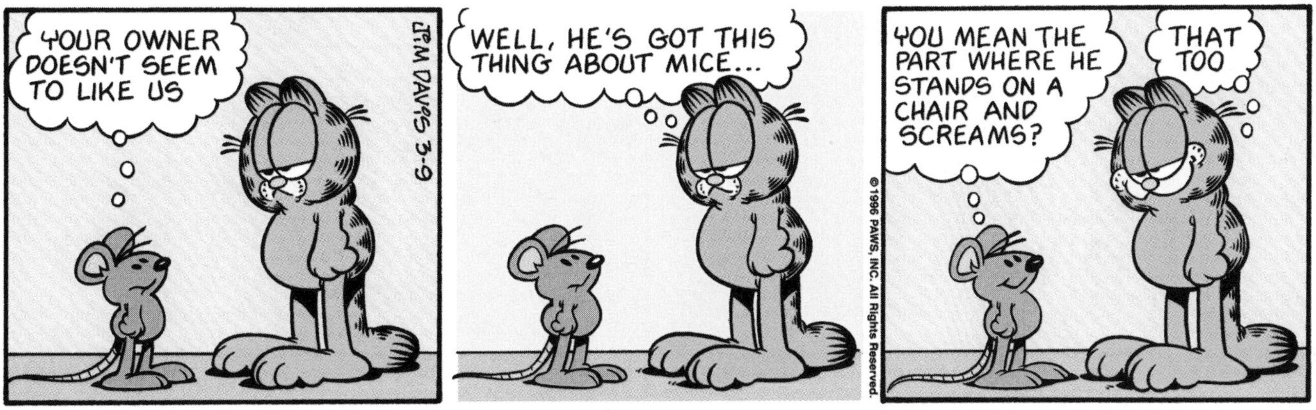
YOUR OWNER DOESN'T SEEM TO LIKE US
JIM DAVIS 3-9
WELL, HE'S GOT THIS THING ABOUT MICE...
© 1996 PAWS, INC. All Rights Reserved.
YOU MEAN THE PART WHERE HE STANDS ON A CHAIR AND SCREAMS?
THAT TOO

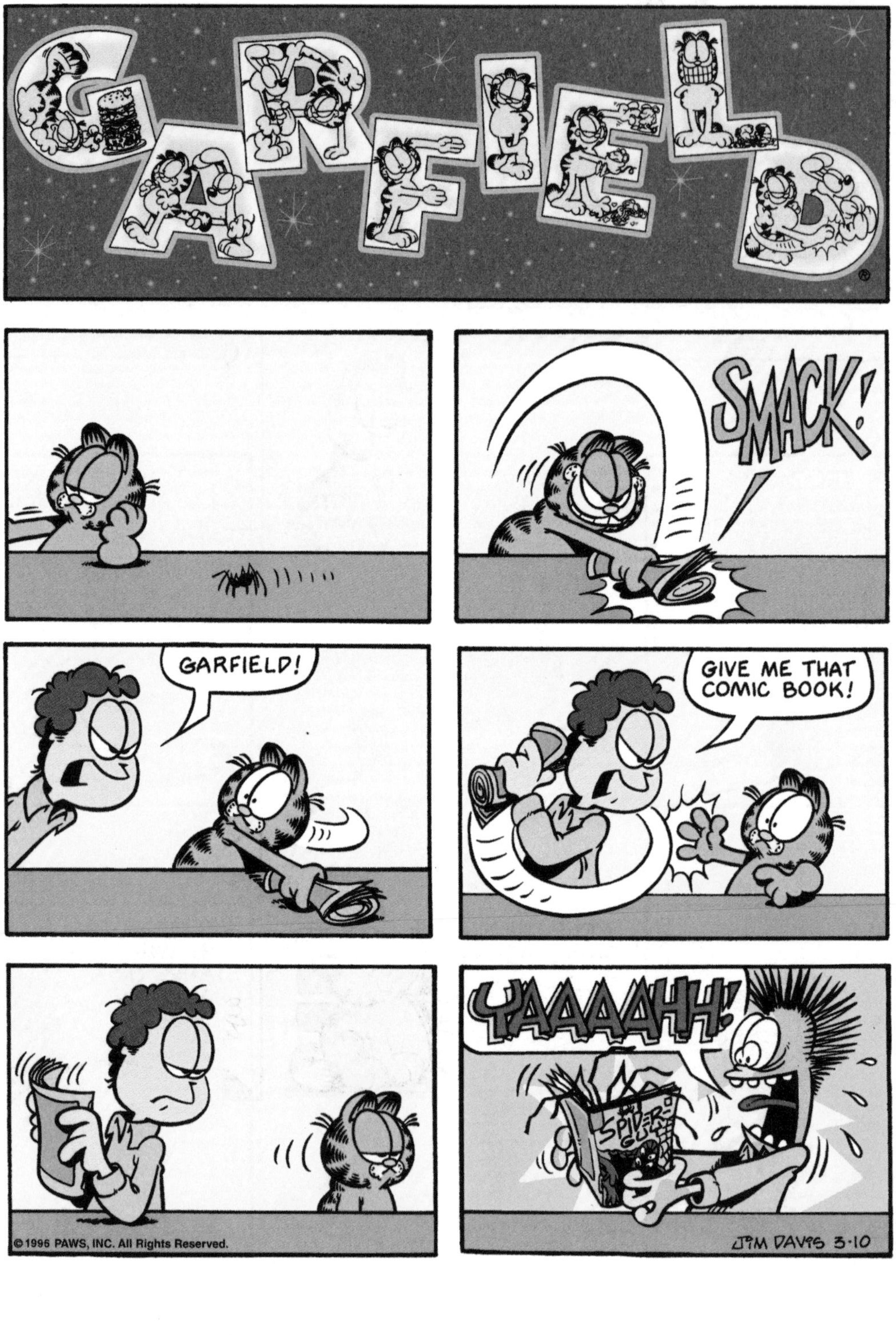
GARFIELD
SMACK!
GARFIELD!
GIVE ME THAT COMIC BOOK!
YAAAAHH!
SPIDER-GUY
©1996 PAWS, INC. All Rights Reserved.
JIM DAVIS 3-10

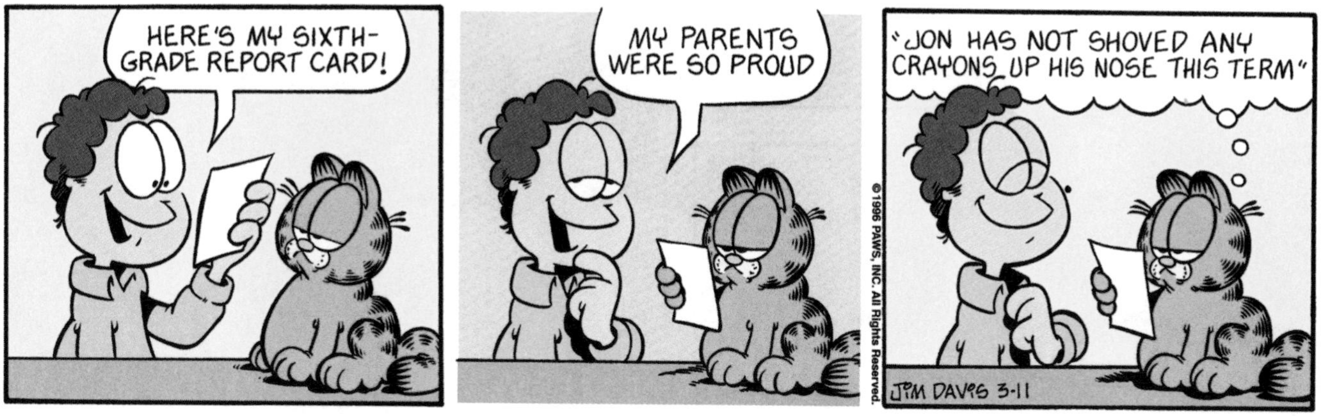
HERE'S MY SIXTH-GRADE REPORT CARD!
MY PARENTS WERE SO PROUD
"JON HAS NOT SHOVED ANY CRAYONS UP HIS NOSE THIS TERM"
©1996 PAWS, INC. All Rights Reserved.
JIM DAVIS 3-11

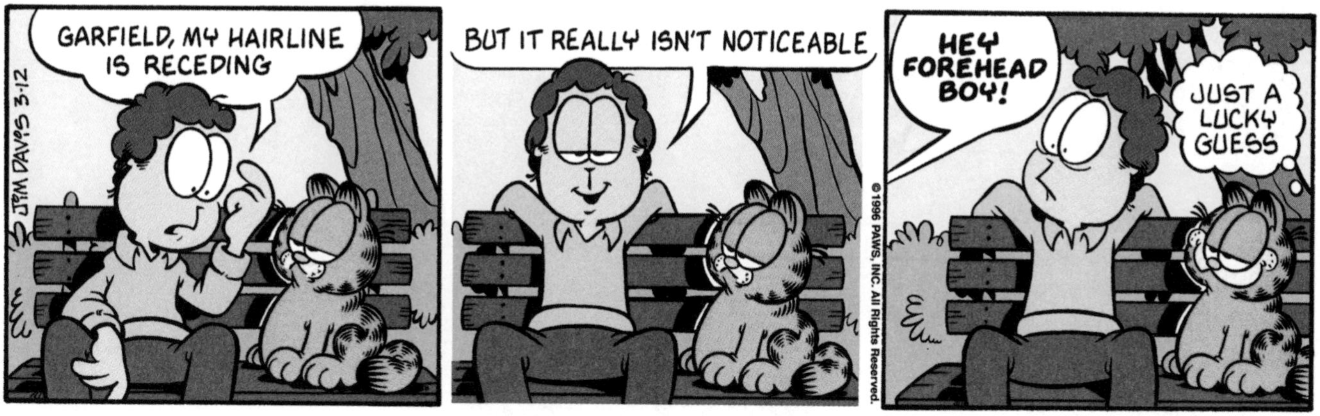
JIM DAVIS 3-12
GARFIELD, MY HAIRLINE IS RECEDING
BUT IT REALLY ISN'T NOTICEABLE
©1996 PAWS, INC. All Rights Reserved.
HEY FOREHEAD BOY!
JUST A LUCKY GUESS

"Don't make me beg!"

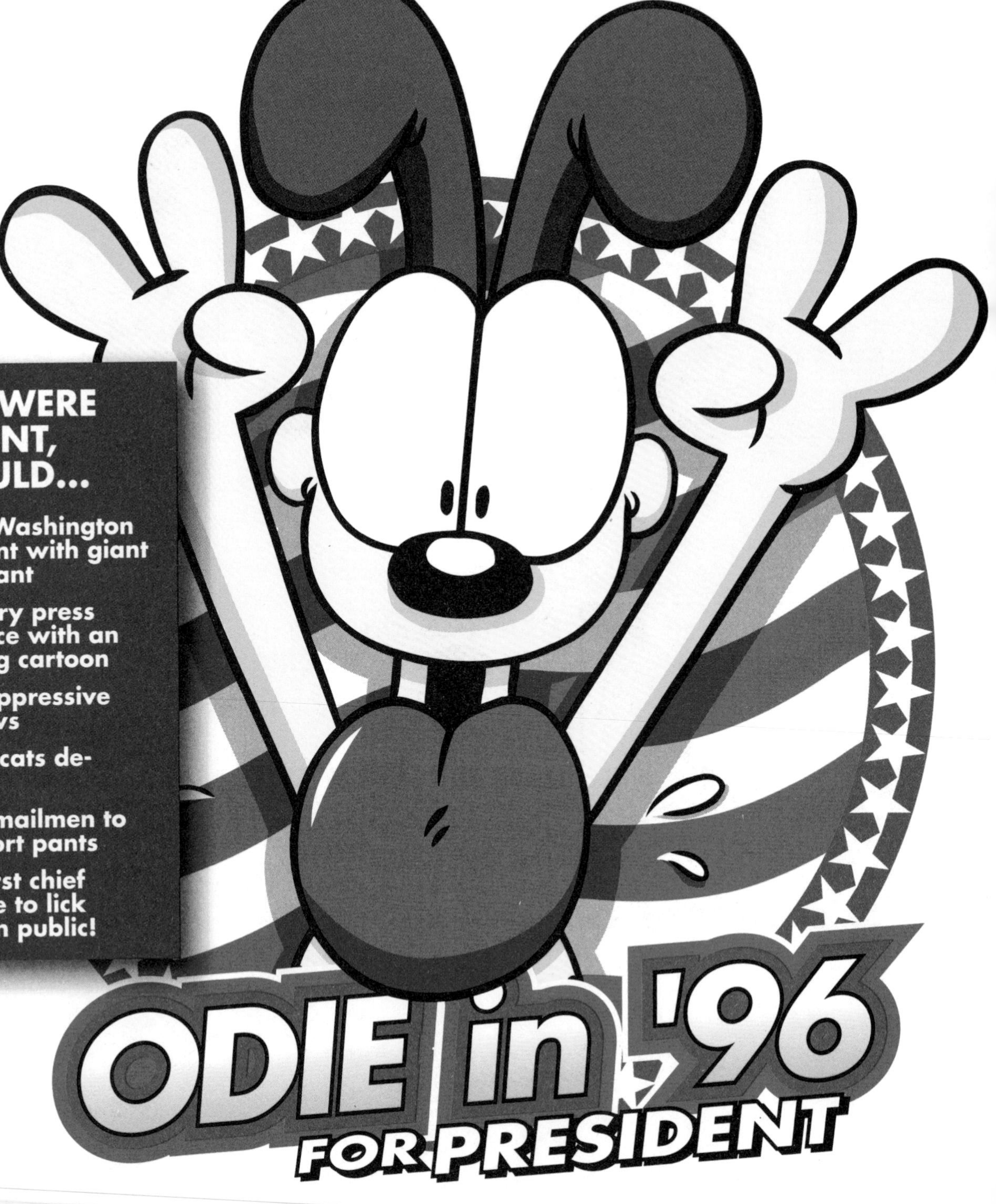
ODIE in '96
FOR PRESIDENT

IF ODIE WERE PRESIDENT, HE WOULD...

- Replace Washington Monument with giant fire hydrant
- Start every press conference with an Underdog cartoon
- Repeal oppressive leash laws
- Have all cats de-clawed
- Require mailmen to wear short pants
- Be the first chief executive to lick himself in public!